LONGRIDER

A Million Miles on Motorcycles
And The Story That Goes With Them

********** A tale of just passin' through ***********

LONGRIDER

By

Mark "Tiger" Edmonds

Livingston Press
at
The University of West Alabama

ISBN 0-942979-52-4, cloth
ISBN 0-942979-51-6, paper

Library of Congress Catalog # 98-73130

Manufactured in the United States of America.
Printed by: Patterson Printing
Printed on acid-free paper

First Edition, second printing

Typsetting and layout: Joe Taylor
Cover Photo: Justin Chief Godfrey
Cover Design: Joe Taylor & Jill Wallace
Proofreading: Jill Wallace, Lee Holland-Moore, Stephanie Parnell

"Specializing in offbeat & Southern literature"
Livingston Press
Station 22
The University of West Alabama
Livingston, AL 35470

Chapters

CHAPTER ONE

Once Upon a Time

The first motorcycle I ever got on was back in 1950 or '51. I was four or five. A woman my mom worked with rode a huge Monsterglide Harley, all tricked out with fringe and chrome and lights. And she threw me up behind her and took off for about a hundred miles one night. Even for a little kid, I didn't know very much. But I knew then that I was going to get a bike when I was old enough. Took me another ten years or so to get old enough to get my own cycle. Took me another thirty years to figure out why.

The first bike I ever rode by myself was an old Matchless 500. Matchlesses were English bikes, like BSAs and Triumphs and a few others that will get mentioned in here. And, like most English motorcycles, they are no longer in production. The 500 means it had a 500 cc engine. That's sort of a mid-sized bike. Little bitty bikes run from about fifty cc to around 200 cc engines. Mid-sized machines go up to around five or six hundred CCs. Anything over that is a big bike. That Harley I mentioned that belonged to my mom's friend was a 1200 cc machine.

The Matchless 500 belonged to a neighborhood character named Screwy Louie. Louie and a bunch of old boys turned me loose on his Matchless in a huge, open field. I hit the only tree in the whole expanse like it was a damn magnet.

A few years later, several of us were involved in breaking old Louie out of the hospital, and lifting him, body cast and all, onto his bike out in the parking lot so he could escape. It's a wonder any of us escaped.

The first motorcycle I ever owned was a 1961, 175 Bultaco. I think the model was called a Matralla. They were Spanish scooters. That model came in kind of a blue and silver color. Later, I had a couple of Bultaco 250s. That one was called a Matador. They were black and silver. They weren't very big, but they were fast and cheap and durable and real easy to work on. Then I had a Yamaha 250, a Catalina I believe it was, which was none of those things. Was a nasty two-stroke with a bad oil injection system was what it was.

There are basically two kinds of motorcycle engines, two and four stroke engines. The basic difference is that you have to mix the gas and oil together in the gas tank in a two stroke, like you do in some lawn mowers. Four stroke machines have a separate oil system. Bike engines also come with various combinations of cylinders, like automobile engines. Most cycles are either two or four cylinder machines, twins or fours. But there are, or have been, singles, and triples, and even a couple V-6 designs. But none of that technical stuff has much to do with any of these stories.

Around owning those I rode a whole bunch of other bikes. I had a 1966 Harley Sportster at my disposal one whole summer while the guy who owned it was out of the country not getting drafted. Harleys are the only remaining American made motorcycles. The Sportster is a classic 900cc model. The other classic American bike you'll read about here is an Indian. One other summer I had an 850 BSA Lightning for about a month until I found out it was stolen and that the Flyin' Wheels, the Road Rats, the local police, the Chicago police, and the insurance company were all looking for it. But that's another story.

I was part owner of a 450 Honda (basic rice burning Jap bike) briefly, and I had a Suzuki 500 (another Chinese chainsaw) long enough to know it wasn't a good idea.

I've rode Ducatis (Italian cycles), and Nortons (another, no longer produced English machine), and Moto Guzzis (big Italian road bikes), and Triumphs, and a BSA Victor (two more extinct English motorcycles) for about two hundred yards one time. I spent a little time on Zundaps and Greeveses and Whites and Husquvarnas (all unpopular, but finely crafted northern European motorcycles). I've ridden Suzukis and Hondas and Kawasakis and Riversides, and a 1937 Indian Chief with a suicide clutch. Contemporary machines have the clutch on the left handlebar, and the gears are shifted with the left foot. The Indian Chief had the clutch on a pedal operated with the left foot and the gears were shifted by a lever on the tank. So you had to take one hand off the handlebars to shift them, hence the term suicide clutch. I could just barely start it. Now there was a ride. It was painted DuBonet Iridescent (look that up in your 1957 stock Lincoln color book) and had a velvetexed frame.

I rode a couple of Jawas (look that up in your Hungarian motorcycle directory) along the way. In fact I got a hell of a Jawa story to tell. I got to sit on a 1938 Harley just like the one Lee Marvin rode in *The Wild One*. And I got to ride an old Aerial square four (another classic English model) one time, and one night in the moonlight down in the Florida Keys, I got to ride an even older Royal Enfield (classic English bike), too. Never been up on a Vincent (ultimate classic English made machine), but there's still a little time.

A friend of mine once asked me how many miles I had on my butt on bikes. It came out to over three-quarters of a million. That was a while back. Probably up closer to an even million now. I guess that's what this is. Memories of a million miles. Memories of beautiful scenery and fine people. Memories of wrecks in the rain. Good memories mostly.

But the long range miles really started when I got my first BMW. I bought it shortly after I got discharged and divorced.

Some suspect a correlation between the cycle and the divorce. Still others think the discharge was at the core of it all. Might could be; I got discharged first.

BMWs (Bavarian Motor Works) are German bikes. In fact, the BMW people invented motorcycles. The machines are known for their durability. That first BMW was a brand new 1971 R75/5 (the R75 meant it was a 750cc, and the /5 indicated the first model like it put into production). They advertised it as The WunderBike, and The Obermeister of the Autobahn.

This one was gray, woops, I mean German Racing Silver. I dressed it with a handlebar fairing. A fairing is the big plastic portion that the windshield is attached to. Handlebar fairings are small, and attach to the handlebars. Frame mounted fairings are much larger, often covering the whole front of the motorcycle.

I can't recall the name of the brand. Yes, I do too. It was a Wixom. This was back when the only frame-mounted fairings were those English Avons, and they were lots more dangerous than a handlebar fairing. They were also real expensive, and I doubt they even made one that would go on the new BMWs. Nineteen seventy-one was the first year BMW made a bike without that big, heavy, Earle's fork front end. That fairing I got for mine was black. That was the color you could get. I also bought a real good pair of leather saddlebags, and put a tailrack and crash bars on it. A tailrack is a chrome luggage carrier that attaches behind the seat. Crash bars stick out low on the sides, and work sort of like roll bars on a car. In the case of BMWs, they protect the cylinders which stick out sideways from the engine.

It was one hell of a ride. Riders often refer to their motorcycle as a ride, a bike, a scooter, a machine, a cycle. And that really does rhyme with pickle. See glossary for details.

I rode way over two hundred thousand miles on that machine. Most of it long rides, trips of a few thousand miles, and more. His name was Charlemagne, but he let me call him Chuck. Only time I ever had to put any oil in that bike was in Nevada one time in a hundred and eleven degree temperature after we had run all day up around a hundred miles an hour. Chuck was a hell of a bike.

It was the finest ride on the road. Chuck took me to both borders and both coasts and a lot of places in between. The day I took delivery of that bike, it was a cold and dismal Michigan spring day. It was overcast and alternately spitting snow, sleet, and rain. As I got ready to leave the dealership, a guy, another customer, walked around my new ride and said, "Well, I guess these are OK, if it's what you want. But what you goin' to do if somebody on one of them big old Honda fours (new, hot, four cylinder Japanese imports, known for blinding speed, but not for endurance or reliability) comes up and wants to race with you?" Before I could reply, the man who had just sold me the bike laughed and answered. "Then you tell the dumb son of a bitch you'll race with him . . . to Los Angeles." I didn't have much to add, so I didn't try. But I have used the line a few times over the years since then. Always with a footnote. The man's name was Orin Gessell.

After years and a couple rotations of the odometer and some of the finest times I've ever known, I sold that bike for parts, and bought a new 1978 R80 next (again, the R80 indicates an 800 cc model). Cost just exactly, all the way down to the dollar, twice as much as Chuck. But only because Charlie Simms cut me a good deal. This one was black, and had a black frame-mounted Krauser fairing and plastic saddle bags. I put some crash bars and a tailrack on it. Came real close to doing 200,000 miles on it too. It was named Morgen. Bike names are funny. You don't name a scooter; it tells you its name. I had some great rides on that bike too. Then, in 1987, I sold it and bought a used, real low mileage 1984 R80/RT. I've got about 90,000 miles on it now. It's a real pretty dark blue, so is the fairing. Plastic bags with crash bars around them, sort of a Harley porch look, little, sporty looking, built-in tailrack. It's named RT.

Seems like all those rides and miles and roads and machines, and the time and fun involved ought to be worth something. As a young girl explained to me awhile back, the best part of me is my memories. Well, the restrictive, stifling, oppressive nature of contemporary society makes me long for the good old days. Many of the things, much of what you're going to read about here just flat don't happen anymore. And I miss it. And I have taken shit for years now because of my dedication to the old and the true ways. I'll admit to being some old-fashioned, but I am doing this on one of them damned computers. I commented about that all awhile back, with the line "Techno-Tiger takes to the nineties." Friend of mine, boy named Captain Zero who you will read about some, said that the fucking nineties had it coming.

So, I'm going to try to tell about some of it, write it down for posterity, and publication. In the very beginning, years ago, I began paying attention and taking notes and marking up maps so I could remember enough of it all so I could tell my Grampaw where I'd been. Every time I got back from a long ride, the Old Man would want to know where I had been to, and what I had seen. Wanted me to tell him about it. And then I also wrote chronicles of where I had been and when, so I wouldn't confuse myself later. Didn't work. But now I want to try to get it down in some kind of order. I'm sure it's going to be a lot harder than a damn poem.

When you read this, I'm sure it will turn out to be either instructive or humorous. Or maybe both. Maybe these stories will provide some details. There have been some real good times out there along the way. Some really funny stuff too. And there was some bad shit went down around it all. They are all damn fine stories.

CHAPTER TWO

**Birmingham Small Arms Commission,Ltd. **

I was in high school, putting in my time at the drive-in hangout with the other bikers and hoods and juvenile delinquents, bein' cool, when Charlie Wasson rode up on a brand new, yellow and black and chrome, BSA 441 Victor. It was probably the most beautiful thing any of us had ever seen. It was beyond beautiful. We all climbed off our own rides and crowded around Charlie and his new machine. God, but it was beautiful. Charlie was a little older than the rest of us. He had dropped out of school and gone to work in one of the auto plants. He had the peggedest pants and the pointiest boots and the sharpest duck-tail haircut, and he could keep a pack of Luckies rolled up in his t-shirt sleeve better than anyone else. He had money and a tattoo and a full-time girl friend. Charlie was cool.

And that brand new BSA was beautiful. We all made envious, congratulatory comments and vocally admired the hell out of Charlie's new ride. Somebody, I don't remember who, broke the code and asked Charlie if he could ride his new bike. Silence. Charlie bad-eyed the kid and told him he wouldn't let him ride his roller skates, and that if he was going to let anyone ride it, it would be me. I had an undeserved reputation as a good rider. Oddly, I think that was because I had already been run over and busted up and broken down, and for a high school kid, already limped badly, especially in bad weather. And Charlie's comment had just greatly enhanced that reputation. He immediately regretted saying it, because everyone expected him to let me ride it then. So he did. He had to; part of that code thing again probably. As I climbed on it, he looked at me with a look I later saw when people handed me their infant children.

For the younger among you, a BSA Victor was an English 441 cc single. It developed about eight million horsepower, and it probably weighed around two hundred pounds. It was a lightweight bomb with wheels. Surrounded as I was by a crowd of admiring adolescent peers, I felt obliged to do something dramatic, something that would insure my now rocketing reputation. I wound it up and let it go, and it came up on the rear wheel faster than anything I ever rode before or since. So I moved forward and tried to lay down on the tank. It was, in the mind of a sixteen year old kid, pretty cool to be doing a high speed wheel stand through a drive-in, in front of all your hood buddies and a whole bunch of other kids in cars, some of them girls.

If I had tried to stop it and drop it back down, everyone would have seen the brakelight. It would have been embarrassing and reputation damaging. So instead, I goosed it and shifted into second while the front wheel was still up high in the air, about eye-level. And the damn thing jumped. I mean it left the ground, leaped up and forward. It was very dramatic. It was very cool. It was also very fast. I was soon all the way to the end of the drive-in parking lot and at the street. In this case it was a real busy, four lane street. And I was on it way before I could stop. So I shifted into third and hit it hard and the damn thing jumped again. When it came down this time, it laid a patch of rubber that we all talked about for a long time. By now it was about to turn over on top of me, and I was going sideways through heavy traffic, still on one wheel, and I finally started to get scared.

Somehow, and we all talked about this too, and the best answer as to how was either dumb luck or divine intervention, I made it across the four lanes, and then into the parking lot of the hardware store across the street. And then through the length of the lot and into the chain-link fence at the other end. I buried the front wheel in the fence about two feet off the ground. I remember noticing that the bike was up in the air and my feet couldn't reach the ground. I also remember thinking I never did get the damn thing in high gear. Then I reached down and shut the bike off. Then I checked to see if I had peed on the seat of Charlie's new ride. It was pretty stable, stuck in the fence like it was, so I slid down off it across the rear fender and tail light. As I did that, I looked in the mirrors to see a crowd, it looked like most of the Free World, running across the street from the drive-in. It took four of us to get the bike loose from the fence. There was one bent spoke. That was it.

Charlie was shaking his head as he started it back up to leave. I was grateful he wasn't mad. All he said was, "Tiger, you stupid bastard, it ain't a fucking unicycle."

So, there's a scooter story. It was intended to be both amusing and pedantic. Perhaps nostalgic even. That was years and miles ago. There have been some other incidents like it, and even more that were nothing at all like it, since then. If you enjoyed that one, keep reading. It gets better.

When I decided to try to do this, I got to thinking about organization. I mean I could go at it chronologically, bike by bike, year by year. You know, The Early Years, and like that. But I'm too old and burned out to be able to do that shit. I've got to where I have trouble remembering my way home from work. Then I thought about doing it by categories. You know, like a chapter about terrible wrecks I've been in and around. That would be a huge chapter. Maybe do a chapter about truly fine rides, with no rain and no hassles. And there could be a chapter about funny stuff that happened over the years and along the way. Another pretty sizable unit. And maybe I could do a chapter with nothing but sage advice on how to stay upright and in motion. Not sure how long that one would be. Maybe some information about various kinds of motorcycles, and another one about other longriders I've come across. Or I could maybe do it kind of geographically by region, or state by state. See what I mean? This organization thing is a bitch. Typically, the answer to how to do it, is to get to it. Do the grunt work later.

Had the same problem with names and places. Names mostly. A lot of the people who figure in these stories don't associate with me anymore, so they probably don't want their names associated with me. So I left their names out. They are anonymous companions and nameless riders throughout this. And I decided to do this the way I've done most everything else: randomly. Or, as some who know me well enough think, all fucked up.

If you see chapters and sub-titles, it's a trick. I did it afterward. But that's the only trick. This is all true stuff. Even the part about setting out a rainstorm one time with the devil. Gospel stories.

Now go get you a map if you intend to read this. Get hold of a basic Rand and McNally Road Atlas, or one of those look-alike copies like Gousha's. If you can find one that shows topography, mountains and such as that, it will be even better.

CHAPTER THREE

*** Philosophy, Methodology, Zen, Deconstructionism, Crossing the Borderline, The Perfect Ride, and Ex-Wives ***

People who ride motorcycles are, for the most part, pretty individualistic. There are all kinds of people out there on bikes, but most of them are loners of one kind or another. When we were kids, they kept marking the space for Doesn't Play Well With Others, or Seems To Resent Authority, on our report cards. Riders are, for the most part, lousy team players. Way I figure it, if we'd wanted to be in a crowd, we'd have got on a bus. We didn't. We got motorcycles. And there isn't room for but one more person on it. Maybe that's where I should start this, with stories about people who've been up behind me. I suspect that would become an epic chronicle about ex-wives. Even when there are three or four people out riding together, each of them is alone. Robert Pirsig, in his classic *Zen and the Art of Motorcycle Maintenance*, discusses this all pretty well. That's a hell of a book. Ain't got much to do with motorcycles, really. Got more to do with madness than anything else. Maybe there's a correlation. Anyway, he explains that, unlike driving a car, riding a bike is a participatory experience. He says driving a vehicle is like watching tv. He's right. You can't settle in and roll the windows up and turn the air-conditioning on and crank up the tape player and put it on cruise-control and lay back with a soft drink and one finger on the wheel. No, you have to ride it. All the time.

And you know exactly how things look and smell and sound and feel and sometimes taste. You have to. You know when it's fixing to rain, and you know how old the road surface is. You can smell both those things. Like you can tell what kind of fertilizer or herbicide or insecticide they're spreading or spraying. Or if it's cows or pigs up the road. And how many calves are in that feed lot. And you know exactly how bad the bugs are; hell, you know how many per mile. You know to the decimal point how slimy the pavement is with a light rain on it. You know what's behind you, because you have to pretty much stay in your mirrors to stay alive. And you have knowledge about how many leaves the trees are shedding, and how much shade they're providing. You know with certainty how hard the wind is blowing, and precisely how hot or cold it is, and the specific angle of the sun, and exactly how hard it is

11

raining, and specifically how much damage that road surface could do to your person at high speed. You don't know or even think about these things when you're in a vehicle.

But a cycle is a whole lot different; it's much more intense. And it is entirely alone. If you're in a group with other riders, about the most you can do is holler at one another some. Even if you have a passenger up behind you, you don't get to talk much, at least not while you're in motion. It is a real solitary thing.

Another thing, one that Pirsig doesn't mention, is that most bikers are real superstitious people. Might come with the solitude. I know guys who won't ride lead, others who avoid being in the middle, and still others who prefer not to ride at the back end of a group. Used to ride with a boy who always wore a white helmet. I know people who are superstitious about the amount of air in each tire, down to the pound. There was a man I rode with a time or two who spit, always to the left, just before he kicked the sidestand up on his bike.

I have a little bell, I think it might be a camel caravan bell, that has hung from every bike I have ever owned. A woman gave it to me years ago. It wards off evil spirits. At least that's the way she told it to me. And there are other riders who have a specific way of loading and packing a machine. Yeah, some of it is good sense and load distribution, but some of it isn't. Some of us do things like offering the road some tobacco and coffee, sacrificing some blood to the highway, offering the air sage and woodsmoke, leaving water behind in the hot, bright sunshine. Most longriders have little rituals they go through like that.

Pirsig's other point about riding a motorcycle is probably even more important, at least to longriders. Without benefit of human interaction, you get a lot of time to think. Big, whole pieces of time. There are few interruptions. Like you aren't required to jump up and answer the phone, or the door, or interact, or change the radio station, or mess with the heat or air. All you have to do is stay upright and eventually find some gas. You get lots of time for contemplation. Lots and lots on long trips.

Sometimes, on an easy ride, you can roll for three or four hours without really having to take your mind off what you're thinking about, except to avoid the occasional wreck. If you get out in the right places, like along the Natchez Trace or the Blue Ridge Parkway, you don't even have to deal with stop signs. If you get lucky, and the traffic's light, you don't even have to interrupt your thinking to avoid being killed. You can take a thought, an idea, a curiosity, a problem, and chase it all the way to the end, or at least as far as you can take it, without stopping. Those opportunities are pretty rare anymore. So is the opportunity to be alone like this. Unless you have someone up behind you. Which brings us back around to second riders.

There are two main things to know about this topic. The first is that you really have the passenger's life in your hands, much more so than you do in a car. The second is that, with rare exceptions, riding up behind someone on a motorcycle is about the most boring activity on earth. It's right up there with watching a guy change his oil. It's lots different than being a passenger in a car. The passenger on a bike can't mess with the windows or radio, or take a nap, or carry on a conversation, or read, or do anything except sit there and occasionally, carefully adjust his or her weight around a little.

Which brings us back to ex-wives. A person really has to love you, trust you a lot in order to climb up behind you. And that person must really want to spend some time in close quarters if you're going on a long ride together.

I've been fortunate in that most of the women I've lived with have been willing to go on rides with me. One of them loaned me the money to buy Morgen. Another one found RT for me, but I found her two bikes of her own along the way, too. Still haven't found a woman who wants to spend all her time doing it though.

The first long ride I took with a passenger was back in about 1973. Her name was Elizabeth. That was one of the finest rides I've ever taken, and that was one of the finest women I've ever known. We rode from Michigan down to the Florida Keys and back. Stayed down there about a month. Spent some time out in the Bahamas. I remember it as a fine, fine ride, both ways. I hope she does too. Maybe not though. Women tend to want to stop more than is my normal habit. I'm likely to run out a tank of gas in between stops. On a BMW that's a couple hundred miles or more. Three, four hours, maybe longer. And women tend to remember things a lot different than I do, even when it doesn't involve a motorcycle.

I don't remember all the details of that ride. But she had never seen the Ohio River, or anything else south of there. She kept looking for that bluegrass in Kentucky. And I also do recall rolling through the Great Smoky Mountains in the sunshine, with wildflowers everywhere. There were waterfalls and splashing water in the sunlight. And I remember Lizabeth falling asleep behind me, and nearly falling off around one of those big sweeper curves in Tennessee. I still recall the way her arms felt wrapped around me, and her wonder at the new things I was showing her. I still remember the sound of her voice and her laughter behind me as she pointed out the rainbows and the roadside bunny rabbits.

And I recollect stopping in Atlanta to visit some friends. One of the almost constant fortunate things in my life has been people to stay with in Atlanta. One of the others was people to stay with down in Coconut Grove. I remember Lizabeth's reaction at seeing grapefruit and orange trees, and the ocean and dolphins for the first time. And I also recall riding down through the Keys over the bridges in the sunshine, with all the colors of blue in the world on either side.

One of my clearest memories of this one is of the ride back. We left out of someplace south of Miami early in the morning. It was summer, and it was already hot and sunny. Lizabeth begged me to let her wear her little halter top so she could put the final touches on her suntan. No, it really wasn't silly jealousy, or a misplaced modesty thing at all. She looked great in her jeans and little halter top, with or without a suntan. It was a safety thing. I've seen way too many people chopped up on bikes to be very comfortable with anything less than jeans, boots, leather jacket, and helmet. Don't misunderstand that. I think helmet laws are a travesty of everything American. I feel that way about the current federal government too. But I cringe every time I see a kid on a throwaway Ninja Jap bike with a pair of speedos, thong sandals, and a cut off t-shirt.

But it was hot and it had been a great trip, and more than anything I wanted her to be happy, so I told her OK. She coated herself with suntan oil and climbed on behind me. It was some kind of coconut suntan oil, and she smelled like a macaroon cookie all the way to Atlanta. I remember that clearly. We rode straight through from below Miami up to Atlanta that day. This was back when you could do such things. When we pulled in to our friends' place up there, Lizabeth was about the color of mahogany. Everyone complimented her on her tan, and she was very happy. Until we took a shower and most of her tan proved to be exhaust smoke and red clay Georgia dust, and went right down the drain.

Anyway, Lizabeth must have either liked the ride, or me, well enough to do it again a couple years later, this time from Michigan out to the Canadian Maritimes. That one was another great ride and a great time. The weather was terrific, the exchange rate very favorable, and lobster was a couple dollars apiece.

We ran into a guy getting on the Blue Nose Ferry from Bar Harbor, Maine to Yarmouth, Nova Scotia. They make you get in line in the pre-dawn darkness. Actually he sort of sought us out. He came up the line from the front, carrying his cup of tea, and told us that they loaded motorcycles first and we should go on up to the front. He was riding a beat all to hell 500 BMW with Louisiana plates on it. I asked him about that. He sounded real Canadian, not like anything I ever heard around Baton Rouge. It wasn't his scooter. It belonged to a friend of his from Louisiana who was staying at his house out on Prince Edward Island.

Sure enough, they loaded the scooters first, right up into the pointy end of the boat where a car wouldn't fit. They strung big ropes from overhead beams under the bikes and suspended them about an inch off the deck, where they swung and swayed slightly and gently the whole trip. It scared the hell out of me, and I must have run down belowdeck to check my ride out every ten minutes for the first hour or so of the trip. I've been on a number of ferry boats with bikes, and this was the neatest, cleverest way to handle it I've ever seen. I've had bikes tied down to the deck, and lashed to the rail, and had both the wheels chocked, and been told to stand beside my cycle and hold it up during the voyage. But that hanging them from the overhead beams thing was the best I ever saw.

Lizabeth discovered the slot machines and the favorable exchange rate about the same time. Over the years she saved me more money than I can count. One of her many attributes was a financial mind that figured things out that I hadn't even gotten around to wondering about. Anyway, she headed toward the slots, and I set and talked to the other biker. The man with the 500 BMW was named Emory Smythe, and he was a direct descendant of the guy who said, "It's an ill wind that blows nobody good." Emory had a hell of a story of his own. He was a hospital administrator in Toronto, or he had been. Seems that one day he and the guy from Louisiana who belonged to the bike went out into a park across from the hospital for lunch. The other guy was almost a doctor, doing his resident service or something. Anyway, they got stoned at lunch and didn't go back to work. Instead they went to Emory's place on Prince Edward Island to grow dope and bake bread. Remember now, this was in the early seventies. He invited us to stay at his place if we got to P.E.I., which we did later, after riding around most of Nova Scotia. The doctor/biker turned out to be a black guy from Slidell who had blown off a scholarship to bake bread. Years later, I heard old Emory had a career with a merry band of traveling minstrels who went around to Canadian schools with their show. Seems like he played the part of a banana, but I could have that wrong.

These guys saved us from becoming Canadians. Seems the ferry boat workers were about to go out on strike, and Emory heard about it ahead of time and tipped us off so we were able to board the last boat leaving P.E.I. for some time, and thereby escape to New Brunswick and avoid being stranded. They sent us off with our saddlebags full of bread and reefer.

See what I mean? This was supposed to be about riding up behind people, and it turns into a story about people I met along the way. Passing through. Get used to it.

The point of the Lizabeth stories was that she must have loved me a lot, because it couldn't have been all that much fun for her. I mean I'm sure she enjoyed a lot of scenery on the rides, and the Keys were beautiful back then. So were the Maritimes. But there were thousands of butt-numbing, mind-numbing miles involved. Endless hours of tedium with her arms wrapped around me and her face buried in my back. And I do recall that every bug in the Maritimes managed to take a bite out of that girl before we left. Bad weather, bad roads, bad food, bad campsites, bad motels, and setting out rainstorms under bridges gets old quick.

Must get older quicker from the back of the bike where you have no control, no function at all really, except to set still.

The last ride Lizabeth took with me was also up into Canada. We rode north along the Lake Huron shoreline the first day. It was spectacular. The sky and the lake were so many different blues, there were birds in the air, the world smelled of pine and wildflowers, and traffic was light. The ride across the Mackinaw Bridge was beautiful, the views majestic. That night we stayed in Saint Ignace. The next day dawned dark and wet. We got hassled at the border at Sault Saint Marie. That's a tradition. Maybe I'll have a couple chapters about great border hassles I've been in.

Anyway, it was raining hard by the time the Canadian Border Authorities got done with us. An hour or so down the road it was raining harder than I like to ride in. We stopped and got a weather report; we were screwed for at least the rest of the day. So, trying to be a considerate guy and a sport, I stopped at a motel. I don't remember how much they told me a room was, but it was way too much for the time and place. I explained to them that I was born at night, but it wasn't last night, and that I wouldn't pay that much for a motel room if it was a damn blizzard outside instead of a rainstorm. They laughed and we rode off down the road looking for another, more reasonable motel.

The next motel was forty miles and an hour away. The road and the weather were deteriorating. This motel was pretty sleazy, not nearly as nice as the previous one. And these Canuck bastards wanted ten bucks more than the other place, eh? We pressed on. It got darker and darker, and it rained harder and harder, and got muddier and muddier. The water found places in our rainsuits to penetrate, notably around the collars and cuffs, and a natural phenomenon known to all bikers, capillary action, resulted in our being soaked inside our rainsuits.

We finally found a place to stay. Actually Lizabeth found it. She said she was tired of being cold and wet, and that the whole world had turned to black and white, and that she wasn't having any fun anymore. She announced that she was staying there and didn't give a damn whether I did or not. It was very, very expensive, and the motel people there laughed at me too. The next morning dawned clear and bright. I was up at sunrise yelling at Lizabeth to get up so we could get to it. We were on vacation, burning daylight damn it, and we needed to get going and have fun. Count up some miles. I remember the look on her face from under the covers.

We checked out of that motel sometime after noon. Passing through, sometimes slowly.

The next couple days, the weather was clear and as warm as it ever gets in Canada. We rode down the east shore of Lake Huron, around Georgian Bay through some of prettiest country I can remember riding in. And then later that trip, another strange, but not unheard of phenomenon, this one an unnatural one, took us by surprise. Actually, two phenomena. The first was the transit strike in Toronto. I'd have thought they were in cahoots with the ferry boat strikers, but the incidents were years and provinces apart. And, yeah, right, why would a transit strike have any effect on a longrider anyway? This one didn't involve islands and ferry boats. Because every idiot with a driver's license was out on the road trying to kill us. That's why. Thousands, tens of thousands, hell, hundreds of thousands of people who normally rode the trains, the buses, the subways, the trolleys, the carpools, and the taxicabs, were suddenly out on the road in their own cars. It was scary as hell. It was like Florida in the winter when the elderly senile are on the roads. They were just no good at it at all. To compound things, I hit Toronto at rush hour.

And to make things worse, there was some kind of huge event going on in Toronto, one of them Expo things I think, and all the motels were filled. I know the motels were filled because I stopped at most of them. As I said, this was a couple years after the Maritime insect episode, and Lizabeth had made a deal with me—no camping. We finally found a room way the hell over by Kitchner. But it was cold and dark and miserable by the time we got to it. And most of the restaurants were closed.

While I'm at it here, I ought to tell a couple border crossing stories. Two of them involve Lizabeth anyway. One of the few redeeming things about living in Michigan was the proximity to Canada, especially Toronto. But Canadians have apparently seen too much U.S. tv, for they are suspicious and unfriendly toward bikers.

Then there was the added problem of Lizabeth being Chinese, and the border authorities' apparent fear that I was smuggling alien Orientals in and out of Canada and America. Lizabeth was something like third generation American Chinese, more American than Chinese, hell, more American than I am.

Before I get around to the border crossing debacle stories, I need to tell a Lizabeth story. Many of her things, clothing, cars, kitchen implements and utensils, were colored yellow. Yeah, I think it was a racial thing. Anyway, one day I burned up and melted her little yellow teapot. It was Roberto Duran's fault. And Liz was pretty upset at me.

So, the next day at work I started calling places to see could I get her a new teapot. Some of my students, coincidentally black kids, got in on it. Those kids thought the world of Lizabeth. And a couple of them ran right out to a store and got her a new teapot and brought it back to my office. It was red. When I explained about her color coded yellow stuff, they laughed like hell and turned around to go exchange the red teapot. One of them, a boy they called Sugarbear, turned and smiled at me from the doorway as he left. "Hey, Tiger, what color is all your stuff? Off white?" Then they all left amidst peals of uproarious laughter.

It got fucking weird at the border a few times. Like rolling off the damn Bluenose ferryboat into Yarmouth, Nova Scotia that time. Prettiest border guard I ever saw began asking us questions. When she heard we were from Michigan (Detroit is in Michigan), she searched me for my gun. She seemed real disappointed that I didn't have one. She didn't take us apart real bad. She just looked in the saddlebags and checked out our papers. You got to have your Very Important Papers in order at the border. Especially if you're with an Asian chick. They want proof that the bike is really yours, that you're really you, and that you have enough money to spend in Canada. And that you are just passing through.

I have to digress again for another couple Lizabeth stories. Both involve racism. We were someplace outside Minneapolis, I don't remember why. But someone told us to go to a particular restaurant. When we got there, it became a "private club," and we got bad hassled at the door. Last time something like this had infested my life was in South Carolina in 1968. This one with Lizabeth was like in 1975 or so, and about as far north as we could be and still be in America. It was long enough ago that I was ready to fight, but Lizabeth pulled me away. As we started back to the bike I heard one of the guys at the door say something about a "goddamn squawman." I looked quizzically at Lizabeth, who was looking quizzically at me.

Then it hit us. She had her hair in braids and was wearing an Aztec looking poncho. I turned around and told the stupid sons of bitches to pay better attention, she was Chinese, not Indian. Everybody has to have somebody to hate. And most places are real specific about it. These folks didn't have any Negroes, so they hated Indians. Like I said, this was awhile ago, and I was lookin' for a fight. And damned if they didn't apologize, immediately and with great sincerity. They insisted we come in and have dinner. One of them even insisted on buying us a drink. Lizabeth spent the rest of the evening charming the locals. Passing through.

The other incident was in the Upper Peninsula of Michigan. On our way out of a restaurant, some local jackpine savage in a cap with earflaps kind of got in my way at the register, blew beery breath all over me, and asked what kind of slant-eye that was I had with me. Wanted to know if she was a Chink or a Jap or some kind of Hawaiian (he pronounced it High Wawyon) gook, or what. I told him she was Viet Namese and still had handgrenades in her fucking pockets. Got away with it too. Lizabeth giggled behind me for miles. But then, I have always been a great source of merriment and amusement.

I got a couple other stories involving Lizabeth and some real ugly racism, but they involve the hatred that the Chinese in San Francisco and Toronto showed toward me for being with one of their women. Especially for having her in a leather, up behind me on a bike. Especially a real pretty woman.

But, this was about border stories. Coming back into the U.S. a few weeks later, after touring the Maritimes, was the second worst border crossing I've ever made. We rode to where you cross there into Calais, Maine early one morning and left the border station late that afternoon. I have no idea what touched off the guys at the border, but they damn near made me take the bike apart. It took them about five hours. They emptied both saddlebags, and both the bags tied on behind Lizabeth. They made us unroll our sleeping bags and tent, and they went through the cooking gear like they thought I was maybe smuggling oregano into the country. And then they got into the fairing compartments, and then they got up under the seat and made me unroll my tool kit. They gathered around and examined my extra parts, uncoiled clutch cables and put their fingers all over light bulbs, and scattered nuts and bolts. They went through my pockets and looked in the lining of my helmet. Made me take my damn boots off. Those of you who ride know, and those of you who think about it for about two seconds will have figured out that you can't carry much on a bike. You can smuggle even less.

I finally admitted that I had, in fact, pumped up a low tire back in New Brunswick, and that if it was illegal to transport Canadian air into the country, then they should take my sorry ass off to international criminal prison. For a minute, I thought one of them, a large, humorless boy, was coming after me. But the other border guards dissuaded him and told me I was free to go. Fuck I was. It took me about two hours to put everything back together. That was twenty years ago, and I still ain't got over being pissed off about it.

The same damn thing happened with a friend years later at Sault Saint Marie. They took one look at us and directed us to walk, not ride, both bikes to a nearby inspection station, where an unattractive, but overzealous Canadian customs official lady shortly had me unrolling my socks amidst a big but untidy pile of everything I owned. About an hour into it, she seemed to suddenly realize what she was doing, and kind of got embarrassed about it. She looked at the mess she had made of my gear, and turned to the other rider, who she hadn't checked at all, and told us to go ahead on. Fuck I could. Took an hour, and the other guy laughed the whole time.

Three weeks later, after a fine, fine ride all the way around Lake Superior, we crossed back into the U.S. over at International Falls, Minnesota. The U.S. Customs guy looked at us and smiled and asked what we'd been doing. My pardner told him we'd been fishing. He looked us over a little more closely and asked where were the fish. I told him we had eaten it, and he laughed and waved us through. I could have smuggled a Haitian family in on that ride. I've had more trouble crossing into California.

Speaking of California, Captain Zero and me once took a hell of ride with him up behind me. He currently captains one of those cable cars out in San Francisco. Remember I told you that you'd get to read about Captain Zero? Well here it is. The Captain wrote a story about it, called it "The Perfect Ride." If I had a nearby copy, I would just insert it here. Instead I will steal as much from it as I can remember.

We left New Orleans northbound up the River Road. Zero had been listening to his friends' old biker stories about riding around the country for years, and figured he ought to find out. I brought him my woman's helmet (by now we're up to another woman, this girl was named Nancy) and a brief note from her telling the Captain, at his request, how to ride behind someone. Nancy wound up with a lot of miles on her cute little butt too. I took that girl from the Atlantic to the Pacific Ocean, and back, one time.

She rode the Outer Banks and the Blue Ridge and the Keys and that recurring ride from Michigan down to Florida and all around the southeast with me. But those are all later stories. The note to Captain Zero said for him to set still, not to try to help or lean or steer, to keep his head above mine on hard curves, to keep his feet up until the scooter stopped and I shut it off, to get the hell away from the bike if it went down, and to yell at me hard and loud if he wanted me to stop for anything. Good advice. But it should have been. Nancy owned and rode her own 350 Honda, and later a 440 Kawasaki. Not for long, but long enough to know. And she put in several thousand miles behind me too. She got good at it.

Like I said, me and Zero started up The River Road one New Orleans morning. We had just finished a short week's work for a man, and done such a good job that he paid us in cash money, and then he took us to breakfast at Brennan's. Oysters Bernaisse and Eggs Benedict. Beignets and chicory coffee. It was August, so it was hot and steamy. Paul Simon was right. The damn river looks like a National Steel Guitar. At least down there in the Chemical Corridor it's real shiny and metallic looking. Our intention was to wander around for a week or so, eventually winding up back at my place in Florida. Then Zero was to get on a bus to someplace he had to be. Seems like it was Detroit. We really didn't have a plan, or a route, or a destination in mind. The Captain hadn't traveled extensively in the southeast, and I was going to show him some of it, randomly.

I don't recall how far north we got when he saw the first sign for the Natchez Trace. Told me he wanted to follow the sign to the Trace and ride some of it. OK, Zero. Well, it wasn't that easy. There wasn't any next sign. I figured to hell with it, we'd ride another road. But the Captain was adamant. He wanted to find the Trace, ride some of it, find out some about it, get it into historic perspective. Captain Zero has been around the world. He's been to the New Delhi bus station, he's listened to the yetis scream in the Himalayas, and he made a bunch of guys named Achmed scream in Tehran one time. He's braved the narcobulls on the Trans-Canada Railway, and the schemers and scammers in Thailand, and the German touroids on the San Francisco cable car that he operates. He wasn't about to be put off by a missing second sign.

It took four stops for directions, two at little gas station/stores, one at a bait shop, and one from a guy named Lonnie who was walking along a road with a cane pole and a stringer of catfish.

I don't recall what year this was, but the Natchez Trace wasn't finished yet. I mean it had officially been there since about 1790 I guess, and it seems like we learned that the Indians had created and used it for a thousand or so years before that, but the state of Mississippi hadn't finished the highway yet. I think it, like the Blue Ridge, is called a Parkway, and it parallels the original Trace. They hadn't even gotten around to putting up very many signs. We backtracked and sidetracked and took up an hour or so, but we found it. Zero was determined. It was a good thing. Like I said, back then the Trace wasn't finished yet, but big pieces of it were. You'd ride thirty or forty miles on it, and then they'd detour you around and get you lost good, until you got on the next piece. Lots of the exhibits were open, and there were some signs explaining the history already in place. We had a great ride, a fine time, and we learned a whole lot.

The historic Natchez Trace went from Natchez, Mississippi to Nashville, Tennessee. Boys would float giant rafts full of trade goods down the Ohio and Mississippi Rivers to New Orleans. When they had unloaded their goods, they'd sell the rafts themselves for lumber. Then they'd walk, or maybe ride a horse or more likely lead one packed with supplies, back north along the Natchez Trace. Seems like I remember that President Jefferson proclaimed it the First National Highway. The recent highway they built runs beside it the whole way. But back in 1981 or whenever this ride with Zero was, the end of the Trace was in Tupelo. So that's where we got off. We visited the Information Station there for a couple hours. One of the sweetest old ladies in the world was running the place, and she insisted we read the historic brochures, and view the displays, and see the little movie they had, and sign the guest book. And then she sent us off to visit the nearby Civil War battlefield, and Elvis' house.

I've ridden the Trace lots of times since then. Like the Blue Ridge, it seems like it was made for motorcycles. It's much flatter than the Ridge, and there are far fewer curves, and no hairpins at all. Like the Ridge, they make you go forty-five, and like the Ridge, they're pretty serious about that. But at forty-five, or sometimes even fifty, you get to see some beautiful stuff.

In the story he wrote, Zero said this was where they invented the word "verdant." Said he'd never seen so many greens or so much green anywhere. And that boy's been around the world. You don't get the long vistas and broad panoramas on the Trace that you do on the Blue Ridge, but you sure do get to see a lot of forest. Very verdant. And like most places I've been in the southeast, and the south generally, you run into some real nice people. Run into some nasty ones too. More about these kinds of things when I get into the chapter about New York, New England, and Defiance, Ohio.

Women are usually better passengers than men. They're generally smaller, and that helps. And they have more of their weight low on their frames instead of up around their shoulders. That helps too. And they have a tendency to get hold of you around the waist and snuggle up close to you. Guys don't. One time, up in New Brunswick, the guy I was with broke the whole rear wheel drive spline on his machine. We finally got it fixed, but not until I had ridden him up behind me for several hundred miles in pursuit of parts, and we had both learned the French word for "hammer."

He was bigger than me, and he was holding his rear wheel between us most of the time, at least until we figured out I should take a saddle-bag off and tie his wheel on that side. But despite the fact that he was a good rider, one of the best roadriders I know of in fact, it was tough. Might have been tough because he rode his own bike. Like maybe he was sub-consciously trying to ride mine for me. Maybe people who don't ride their own bikes are the best passengers.

It isn't like I resented having to ride the guy around behind me. Years before that, I had dropped my own bike, hard, out on The Million Dollar Highway in Colorado. Dropped it off Red Mountain. This story might be part of a whole chapter in itself, entitled Incredibly Stupid Shit I Have Lived Through. And this man rode behind another guy all the way from Farmington, New Mexico back up to Durango, Colorado holding my new fairing in his lap while he sat backward on the bike. True story. So I was happy to run him around rural Canada chasing parts.

But back to that Perfect Ride me and Zero took, on which he was, by the way, The Perfect Passenger and the Perfect Pardner. We eventually ran out of the unfinished Natchez Trace to ride on, and went from Tupelo over to Huntsville, Alabama just to get some elevation and to cool off some. And we got a sort of prototypical motel there. It was pretty crummy, the kind of place where you could change your oil in the parking lot and no one would notice or know. So I did. It looked like they all look, a long strip of rooms with an office at the end near the road. This one had a dry swimming pool and badly peeling blue paint on the building, looked like a couple of the pickups in the parking lot were there for good. The old drunk running the place gave us a deal on the room. I've found this to be nearly universal. They give bikers a deal on the worst room, and we wind up fixing the air-conditioner, the tv, the door lock, and the shower. Zero thought that was about the funniest thing he'd ever heard of.

We rode from there on down to the Gulf Coast, and then rode the coast road through the Redneck Riviera and on home, which was by now in west central Florida. We got back and hung out a couple days before Nancy jumped up and said that we had around eighty bucks loose money and that me and Zero should head back out on the road before we drove her and ourselves crazy. So we did. I still had a couple weeks before I had to be back to school for the fall semester. This time we rode over to the east coast and then up through Saint Augustine and Jacksonville, where we found a pretty neat ferryboat (stand by your ride and hold it steady; no ropes), and then on up to Savannah, and the Marshes of Glynn, and Charleston, and then inland to Columbia where the Captain finally caught his bus.

As I recall, I located an ex-wife of mine in South Carolina and we spent the night with her. I wasn't married to that girl long enough to take her on any long rides, but I do have a story about her dropping my Yamaha on herself and burning the hell out of her leg. And I had told her not to try to ride anything she couldn't pick up off the ground. I told her about wearing shorts too. Anyway, she treated us with all the Southern Hospitality a well-bred gentlelady from Charleston, where the Cooper and the Ashley Rivers meet to form the Atlantic Ocean, can. She turned us on to a couple real pretty roads outbound from her place too.

This really was The Perfect Ride. The only time we got into rain we were able to get under cover and watch it rain on the warm Gulf waters at Mexico Beach. The dolphins put on a show for us there. Captain Zero took the girl's advice and hollered loud enough to make me keep looking for The Natchez Trace. Zero never ever scared me, or even made me uneasy up behind me. And we got to see Elvis' house. And on every other trip I ever made that direction, I always stopped at the Tupelo Information Station for the Natchez Trace and visited with that sweet old lady. Last time I was through there, I was told she had retired. I left a copy of my poetry tape, and the guy who had her job promised he'd get it to her.

Zero insisted on stopping several times, and as a result I got to see some beautiful and historic places, and he got some terrific pictures, some of which I still have. He took one over my shoulder. It's a picture of the instrument cluster and handlebars. Got a hawk feather and an egret feather tied on one of the mirrors. Got my little bell warding off evil spirits on the other. The speedometer reads seventy-five.

I've never hurt anyone on a bike. Never dropped one while some-one was up behind me, never got hit while I had a passenger. Well, I did kind of lay one down on a dirt curve up on Mount Tamalpais, up at the north end of the Golden Gate. But I was going about a half a mile an hour, and Nancy was laughing as she tumbled off. So, while I have been a constant source of amusement, I've never hurt a passenger. That's one of the few things in this life I have to be proud of. And I am. I've worked at it. If someone has the trust to get up behind you, seems like to me that you ought to return the courtesy and work real hard at not hurting him or her, or their trust in you. Hell, I know a lot of people I wouldn't ride in a car with them driving it.

Zero is a good example of someone, a friend, who trusts you and loves you enough to find out what your life is all about. I'm sure he had a good time. That story he wrote is proof. The fact that he climbed back on after a couple thousand miles and did a few hundred more also seems an indication of his having had fun. But, you know, he never asked to do it again. Could be he was just passing through.

Weirdest passenger I ever had was a guy called Bill Dudley. Bill was the engineer and producer on my motorcycle poetry tape. Bill's a genius. He is also a perfectionist. When he caught on to what I was trying to do, he said that he wanted to get out on the road on the bike with his portable sound equipment to get the right sound effects. Nancy gave him pretty much the same advice she'd given Zero, handed him her helmet, and he climbed on with recorders strapped to his back and microphones dangling. He gave me various and assorted instructions, to run through the gears, or to slow down, or to downshift. At one point, we were going pretty fast, he asked if I would pull over and stop. So I did. He climbed off, took his helmet off, and sat down. I asked if he was OK, and he said yeah, but he'd never been on a motorcycle before, and it had just sort of briefly overwhelmed him. A few minutes later he climbed back on. Trust. Those of you who have heard the tape know what I meant when I said he was a genius. And he was real glad to just be passing through.

CHAPTER FOUR

**** Roadsongs ****

W hile I'm on the topic of that tape, I need to address the issue of music. That was another clever transition. This time to something about the roadsongs. Most longriders I've talked to hear them. Different roads have different songs. The road from Steamboat Springs through Rocky Mountain National Park and on in to Estes Park sounds different than the road into Big Bend down along the borderline. Sounds different in the Rocky Mountain Park than it does a little while down the road in the Big Thompson Canyon. Through the Park, it sounds like real fast gypsy fiddles and tambourines. Later, going through that canyon, the road has a song that sounds like white girl gospel wailers. Down along the Rio Grande, between Presidio and Terlingua, it sounds like slow guitars and castanets and trumpets. A corida beat. Might be a deguelia. Turns into a real slow Texas fandango when you make the turn north.

The music in the movie *Easy Rider* came pretty close to getting it right a couple times. And if you try to tell someone who doesn't ride about this, they just sort of look at you with that Pity The Poor Demented Old Burnout look, and nod and nervously smile. Burned out, but still smoking. Hah! Shows what they know. Better to burn out than to fade away. Neil Young said that. I think he believes it too. Then, other times people try to excuse themselves and leave the room. Sometimes they try to tell you it's the wind, or the air in your helmet, or the tires on the concrete or asphalt, or the drug and alcohol damage.

But it ain't. It's the road singing to you, telling you its song. Some roads, long ones, have different songs. The Blue Ridge sounds a lot different up north at the Skyline Drive than it does down south by Cherokee. It's a different road, a different kind of road at one end than the other. The northern end is a lot easier than the bottom end. Different song. Maybe just a different version of the same song. There are steel guitars and banjos on the south end of the Ridge, flat top guitars and lots of fiddles at the top. Sounds like the kind of music Doc Watson plays. And you can move over west one valley and the song is different. One of them has a road that sings a song about how the coal mines are dark as a dungeon. The Snake River Canyon sounds like a huge organ in a huge cathedral.

The Trace sings the same song to you from one end to the other. It's a waltz. That ride around Lake Superior sounds a lot like "The Wreck of the Edmund Fitzgerald." The Going To The Sun Highway sounds like the music in a Bible movie. The road out across the water down into the Florida Keys sings a kind of Reggae Cowboy song. U.S. 2 up in Washington and Montana sings a song a lot like "Ghost Riders in the Sky." Lot of harmonicas in it. Turns into a kind of a slow schottische across Minnesota and Michigan. The River Road down along the Mississippi, south of Memphis, sounds like the blues, all dobros, and steel guitars tuned in open D. The McClure Pass Detour was a damn dirge.

And it's a road in West Virginia, runs along the Tug Fork, sounds more like "Amazing Grace" than anything else I ever heard. I got on a long road through Philadelphia one time. Damn thing sounded like a Salvation Army Band playing on the sidewalk at Christmas. Snowflakes and French horns and tambourines whacking out "Silent Night," even though it wasn't. Between Austin and Abilene, the road sings you a slow polka with a pretty heavy oompah beat to it. It's a different song than the one with the oompah beat you hear in Pennsylvania, up around Lancaster and along the Susquehanna. And you get to hear a song like "Home on the Range" between Rawlins and Lander, Wyoming. Where the deer and the antelope play.

The road up the California coastline sings a different song than any east coast highway. That road up along the California shore sounds like Dick Dale Surfer Guitar Music. The Atlantic roads have different songs. Up north in New England, you get Sea Chanties. The New Jersey shore sounds like Bruce The Boss music. Some of the early stuff. The Carolina Coastlines are pretty Rock and Roll. Keeps on like that through coastal Georgia and down past Daytona too. Until you get to South Florida where U.S. 1 begins to sound some like Cuban salsa music.

Down around Ft. Sumner, New Mexico, out along the Pecos River, you can hear the road singing about Lincoln County and Armageddon. Down in the Cheat Mountains, along the Shavers Fork, one of the headwaters of the Monongohela, the road plays reels and jigs. The bridge out across Lake Ponchartrain is a jazz highway. Dixieland. U.S. Highway 64 runs sideways across most of Tennessee. It sounds like The Band. There is a road in Idaho sounds just like that old Steppenwolf music. Prettiest sounding road I ever rode was the one inland from Eureka, California, along the Trinity River. Sounded like Ry Cooder. I damn near cried when I got to the end of that road. I would have turned around and rode it back to the coast, but that was the trip east after I had busted my shoulder on Red Mountain, and I was still in a sling and sort of a slow hurry.

Somewhere across south Kansas, I found a road that sang a kind of duet with the wind there.

There's a road down along the Ohio River, I believe it's Highway 7, sings a song with calliopes and steamboat whistles. Rides along rivers are almost always real pretty rides. And you get to hear some fine roadsongs. The Yockanookany River, or rather the road that runs along it, which is Highway 12, around McCool, Mississippi sounds like "Dixie." Real slow. Riding beside the Columbia, it sounds like a march, or maybe a processional. Out along the St. Lawrence you get to hear roadsongs about London and other seaport towns.

There is a road down in south Louisiana, down where they filmed the final scene of *Easy Rider*, where you hear fiddles and accordions playing "Jolie Blon." The Million Dollar Highway is all bluegrass music. Mandolins mostly. The ride around the Cape Breton Highlands is bagpipes and a few snare drums. There's a ride up the east side of the Bay of Fundy sounds a whole lot like the song you hear riding from Grand Chenier up through Evangeline and on to Mamou out along Bayou Nezpique. A lament. Way down in southern California, and through most of south Arizona, too, you get a song sounds a lot like Woody Guthrie singing about deportees and the Los Gatos airport. There is a piece of road I know that used to be part of the Trail of Tears. You can hear drums and hawkbells if you listen right. Most interstate expressways are disco music, some are elevator music.

I've even had a couple passengers admit to me that they heard the roadsongs. But they were all women who were in love with me and willing to believe damn near anything I told them. Years ago, when me and ol' Cousin Doc first got together with him playing music behind my poems, he asked me what kind of music went with which part of the poem. So I told him about the roadsongs. He came up with a piece he calls "Tiger's Last Ride." Those of you who have heard the tape know that Ernie, like Bill Dudley, is a damn genius. He got it real right.

CHAPTER FIVE

***** Spectacular Wrecks,
Old Times,
and Mythical Places *****

Time to tell a story about a wreck. All I got to do is pick one. There are several. Worst one happened to me was up there on Red Mountain, up on the Million Dollar Highway north of Durango, Colorado. It has been referred to as my Downfall In Durango.

There are lots of reasons wrecks happen. I've seen guys go down on hard curves and wet leaves and loose sand and oil spots and railroad tracks and when the pavement ended and dropped a fast couple feet down to dirt. I've watched guys hit grease spots, and dogs and assorted other roadside wildlife, which then became grease spots. I've seen flat tires turn into disasters. I've seen people take turns too hard, and I've seen chains snap and damn near kill the riders. And I've watched people just drop it for no apparent reason. I didn't get to see it, but I heard a guy tell a story about how the wind got up in his fairing and lifted him up in the air and then dropped him back down upside down in the other lane. I believed him. It was up around the Straits of Mackinac. It was one of those old Avon fairings. I knew a guy who got clotheslined off his cycle by a downed telephone wire. They had to cut the bike off him in pieces. But most wrecks are the fault of bad vehicle drivers. Damn near everyone I know who rides has been hit at least once. Usually the bad driver makes eye contact and smiles as he hits you.

But my Downfall north of Durango was entirely unassisted. Well, the state of Colorado road construction people were at the heart of it, but I did it myself. And it was dumb. There were three of us on that ride. We were going out to the west coast to see Captain Zero out there in San Francisco. The wreck happened first thing in the morning. The road was all tore to hell with construction work, and we were probably going forty-five through it. I noticed a bird up high, over to my left. So I looked at it. Like most riders (and drivers too, I think), my tendency is to steer away from what I am looking at. So while I was looking up and left, up a cliffside, trying to see was it a hawk or an eagle, the bike was drifting over to the right.

Yup, you got it, I fell off the damn road. But I didn't fall down. I would have been a whole lot better off if I had dropped it right there, but

I didn't. I was still upright and in motion on the shoulder, in the loose dirt and gravel. And instead of just stopping, or even letting it fall, I decided I could get back on the road. The road was about six inches higher than the shoulder at that point. I got as close to a right angle on it as I could in the limited space and time I had, and gunned the bike. And bounced off the concrete and damn near wobbled into a fall right there.

Again, it would have been lots better if I had, and again, I skillfully and bravely held it upright and pressed on. Decided I wasn't going fast enough, and tried it again, faster. Only by now the pavement was a foot higher than I was down there on the shoulder, and the shoulder was getting mushy and crumbly and narrowing down to about a two foot strip. And damned if there wasn't a huge boulder blocking it.

Yeah, you probably figured it out again. I was going forty when I hit the damn thing. The guy riding behind me later told me there was a huge cloud of dust in the air with my tires poking up out of it upside down. He said the scooter was ten feet in the air. I tore a muffler off, and a mirror, and ruined a saddlebag, and broke the tail light lens and bulb, and shattered an entire fairing, and somehow ripped the centerstand off. Worse probably, I broke my glasses, and my shoulder, and my nose, and two fingers, and my thumb, and my face looked like I'd been through a dull cheese grater, and I shredded a brand new pair of blue jeans, and made a mess of one boot. You know you're in bad shape when your boot begins filling up with blood.

When the guy riding last got up to me, I told him I was OK, and to go get my bike and set it up for me. I've never, ever heard a biker say anything else after a wreck. Heard Evel Knievel say something like that after that Caesar's Palace mess. That movie he made ought to be mandatory viewing for all riders; the damn bike got back up and came after him and got him four different times after he had dropped it.

While my pardner was doing that bike picking up thing for me, I stood up and fell down, and the guy in the station wagon full of kids who had been behind me and had watched the entire fiasco, arrived with wet rags and his first-aid kit, and, oddly it seemed at the time, ice. I must have been a mess. He looked down at me with his hands full of bandages and ice. And I looked back at him through the grit and the blood and the dirt and the grease. I did this with one eye, the left one had swelled shut already. I grabbed the ice and told him it seemed a little early for a drink, and this was of a Sunday, but there was a bottle in the saddlebag that had survived, and did he have a Dixie cup? He sat the first-aid kit down and walked back to his station wagon to throw up on his tires and shoes. I later got a look at my face in my friend's rearview mirror as I rode behind him back to the hospital down in Durango. Damn near made me throw up.

One of the guys with me stayed up on the mountain with what was left of my bike. The other guy rode me back down to Durango, where I became fast friends with several people on the Sunday shift in the Emergency Room there. It was there that I got confirmation on that bad looking face thing. They handed a pair of needle nosed forceps to this little nurse-in-training girl they had there and told her to root around in my nose and see how much gravel and bone and like that she could find. She nearly fainted before she threw up.

It was at that point that the guy who brought me down the mountain spoke up and explained that my face never was my best feature, and that no one should really be concerned about that aspect, but that I had broken my shoulder, and that concerned him because I had a bike to ride. To the far left coast. He then left me and his bike there, and got a ride with someone back up the mountain. When, hours later, after arguing with everyone on two shifts, I finally got myself out of the hospital, my friends had found a pickup truck and brought my ride back down into town, gotten us a motel room, and even located some of the parts I needed and an old blacksmith who could work on the mufflers and the saddlebags.

I don't know what the hell I would have done without those two guys with me that time. The next four days were a merry series of limited events. I would alternately visit the busted shoulder doctor, set in the motel room in a codeine and Wild Turkey stupor watching reruns of "Zorro" on the tv, and wander out into the parking lot to watch the progress on my busted up scooter.

My buddies were chasing parts, and putting my ride back together for me. The doctor told me I was foolish, but to go ahead and see if I could ride. I was persistent about it. It had worked well with getting out of the hospital that first night. So my friends lifted me into the saddle, taped my left hand to the handlegrip, and walked beside the bike in the parking lot to make sure I could do it. It was a lot like training wheels.

Then we went to California. And along the way, these guys would have to pull into a place ahead of me and kind of catch me when I came to a stop to make sure I didn't fall over on my busted shoulder. Sometimes, on take-offs, they'd walk beside me until I got the bike going good. And they had to cut my food up for me, and help me put on my socks and boots. And they did. Hell, one day after that, on our way to San Francisco, we rode a thousand miles. You used to could do such things. A Nevada State Trooper blew by us that day waving and grinning at us. We were going about a hundred and ten. That day damn near killed me in my weakened condition. I climbed in a tub that night to soak my battered body some. And later these guys had to come lift me out of the tub. And they did.

Not sure what the moral of that one was. Improve your bird identification skills maybe. Pay attention better is always good. Take an easy fall in favor of a potential bad one? It took me another ten years or so before I got around to finishing riding the Million Dollar Highway. And it was snowing that time. I figure that damn road owes me some change.

I mentioned being allowed to return the favor to one of these guys up in Maine years later. I also was permitted to balance things out some when he blew off a curve on the Blue Ridge, on the Peaks of Otter. I didn't get to see him drop it, but the aftermath was the most spectacular I have ever seen. There were four of us on that ride. We left Michigan and headed over to ride the Blue Ridge south. The guy who dropped it was riding last in line, which was an error. Some guys don't ride last very well at all. We learned that on this trip. From then on he rode out front where he belonged. I ride last well. It's been a long time since I've had anyone to ride with, but back when we did, I almost always rode drag. I think I spend more time in my mirrors than most people. This is helpful when the local police are bent on harassment or taking some of your money. Or worse. Stories about worse to follow. There's a story about the guy who was in the easy chair, with me behind him, and his pack came loose and off his ride at about seventy-five. Thermos bounced once before it damn near tore my head off on the way past. But this one is about the Wreck on the Peaks of Otter.

Like I said, the guy was riding last in line. The tendency is for the bikes to stretch out as various guys take curves at various speeds. The last one winds up playing catch-up a lot. And he was doing just that when he went into the curve and hit a patch of loose sand. None of us got to see it. We were all three up the road a quarter mile around another curve. Took us another mile to realize we'd lost one of us. We stopped and waited and discussed possibilities and then rode back. The man was standing on the side of the road, helmet in hand, looking crestfallen and forlorn. His bike was nowhere to be seen. He was looking out over a steep and deep gorge. We all found places to park and joined him. His scooter was about fifteen feet away and another several feet below us. Hanging in a mass of grapevines from a huge, ancient tree there. Upside down. The windshield was torn off, gas and oil were leaking out, and it was sort of gently swaying in the breeze.

The guy who had put it there was frantic. He was unhurt, but he was concerned about his ride, and jumping around ranting and babbling a lot. He looked around and told me to get up there with a knife and cut it down out of the vines, and he'd ride it back up. Apparently I was to hold the knife in my teeth. He couldn't have flown it out of there. I still wasn't sure he wasn't hurt and asked him could he still ride. He got mad at me and explained that he damn sure could, that he was riding the fucking thing when he fell off it.

Fortunately, about the third car to show up was The Ranger. There are some local police on the Parkway, but the real cops on the Ridge are federal rangers, Department of the Interior people. And we found the guy who rode a BMW. Or rather he found us. He got over his amazement at the bike hanging upside down, apparently unhurt, and its rider, even less hurt, hopping around, offering bizarre solutions to his problem, worrying about his bike. He got all the bystanders on their way, told my friend to leave the bike where it was until he got back, grabbed me, and hopped in his car. We drove to a nearby equipment shed, got an axe and a bowsaw and a whole bunch of rope, and returned to the scene of the disaster.

All was well upon our return. My friends had even made a pot of coffee while we were gone. The ranger sent me down the precipice, and then back up the tree to a position above the bike. I tied ropes to it, and chopped the vines away. The other three guys positioned themselves below the bike to catch it as I cut it down. The ranger stayed up on the road and directed the work. He told me which vines to cut in order to first turn the bike over, back rightside up, and then to let it go on down to the ground. The other three guys caught it and eased it down like they had been doing that job for years. Then we tied a whole lot of ropes around the bike, and one to each of us and threw them back up the slope to the ranger, who had stopped every car with a big guy in it. There were about eight big guys pulling on ropes as I climbed back down out of my tree and joined my three friends as they kept the bike upright as it was pulled up the sharp incline. The incline was so steep that all four of us had to be pulled up out of the bottom.

The bike was hardly scratched. The windshield was gone, and it had lost a couple gallons of gas and a couple quarts of oil and most of the water out of the battery. But that was it. One of them highway miracles. My friend borrowed some oil, and the ranger gave him some water, and then we headed back down the road. We got off at the next inhabited exit of the Parkway to get gas and to begin making phonecalls to find a new windshield. Asheville, it turned out.

And this, not climbing the tree and cutting the grapevines, was where I really got to help him and pay back some of the left-over debt from Red Mountain and the Million Dollar Highway, and my own Downfall in Durango. The guy who needed the windshield was from Michigan, and had such a hard time understanding the woman on the phone at the bike shop in Asheville, that he exploded out of the telephone booth waving the receiver and hollering, "Tiger, come talk to this hillbilly bitch. I can't understand a goddamn word she's saying!" Tree climber and translator extraordinairre. It's on my resume. Along with just passin' through.

Both the bike and the rider came out of that one barely hurt. Another friend of mine hit a dog in North Carolina one time. He got hurt as bad as I ever want to see a man hurt. I was riding behind him at the time. It was the worst wreck I've ever been required to watch. The damn dog ran across the road, in front of a semi, and then back across the road, also in front of the semi. The second time, he got under my friend's bike and jammed his fat little Basset body between the front fender and the frame. Locked the cycle up like Fort Knox. First it went down, and then it went over, and then it went end over end. The dog, and then my friend, and then the bike all went under the oncoming semi's trailer. The dog came out of it all in two big pieces and several smaller ones. The bike and my buddy came out intact, but badly busted up. I pulled over and started out into the road toward my friend. He lay there looking over at his bike, then at me. I understood, and went to set his bike upright before dragging him out of the road. His next concern was that I kill the goddamn dog for him. I explained it was too late.

That was one of the few times I've seen the dog come out of it hurt. Usually you can get around them. When I was a kid, a boy I used to ride with back then bailed off his cycle at low speed and wrestled Mr. Duckworth's bulldog to the ground and bit it several times. This boy later got himself a Section Eight discharge, and was known to be over-fond of thorazine. But the damn bulldog never chased us on our bikes after that. One time in Rye, New Hampshire, there beside the sea, a big German Shepherd dog came after me and Lizabeth. The guys riding behind me slipped up on the dog, and the guy riding the second seat back stood up on his foot pegs, and kicked that poor dog in the reproductive organs hard enough to drop him right there in the road. I thought he had killed it until I saw the dog crawling toward the ditch in my mirrors.

Dead animals on the roadside always make me sad. Well, not that Bassett hound. He had it coming. But on a bike you, pretty typically, get to see more dead animals than you do in a vehicle. I imagine I've seen an average of one dead animal by the roadside every thousand miles or so. Time out while I get a pencil. Yeah, that's a thousand animals, unless I screwed up that trick decimal thing there. Now that I wrote it down, I bet it's lots more. Sometimes you see four and five raccoons or possums laying dead in a quarter mile. I once saw about six deer down, but the two pickups that had done the damage were loading dead and wounded deer as I rode by. And, once in awhile, out west mostly, you encounter a road-killed cow. Certain species of chipmunk-like animals eat their dead, and more of them get wasted during cannibalistic endeavors than running across the road.

Anyway, the sight of an animal lying dead alongside the road never fails to sadden me, sometimes to bum me out real bad. And not just because I hate to see senseless death, or wasted meat. Not because I hate to see somebody's fine looking bird dog, or a pet cat, or some little kid's cute little Benji dog wasted on the highway. No, it's because I know it could be me.

As my friend and I discussed the dead Basset hound there by the road in North Carolina, a car pulled over and a man jumped out and came up to us. He asked my friend how bad he was hurt. He still hadn't really stood up. Asked if he had broken anything, or if he was busted up internally. When a negative response finally came, he helped my partner get up, put him in his car with his wife, and told me he would be back soon with a trailer to get the bike. I set there for about two hours, until he showed up with a big flatbed trailer. We loaded the smashed up cycle and I followed him back to his place. We unloaded my friend's cycle in a garage that held three other BMWs.

Man's name was Ingraham, and he was a fine mechanic, and a hell of a good guy to have around when you needed to figure out how to improvise and make things up as you went. The other thing I know for sure about him is that he truly loved his wife. At the end of each meal, he would stand, walk around the table to his woman, bend and kiss her and thank her for feeding him. You could tell he meant it too. He'd been hungry before, and he was honestly grateful to be fed. His wife took care of my friend, and he was a mess, just flat beat all to hell, with road rash and cuts and bruises all over his body. And Mr. Ingraham and I fixed the bike. No, that ain't right; hell that's a lie. Mr. Ingraham fixed the motorcycle. I tried to stay out of his way, learned a lot, and ran for parts all over coastal North Carolina.

I lied again. Turns out I know three things about the man. He told me some incredible stories while we were working on my pardner's bike. The one I remember best was about how he rode an Indian Chief from San Diego Naval Base to Norfolk Naval Base. In 1937. In eight days. Mostly on dirt roads, the way he told it. I guess there just wasn't a whole lot of cross-country pavement back then. Said the mufflers fell off it somewhere around Yuma, and that by the time he got to Ft. Worth, where he could work on it, he had gone deaf. Third thing is I know Mr. Ingraham to be a hard man.

The details of his current repair work could easily take up a whole book. The headlight shell on my pardner's bike was smashed about as flat as a book of matches. What was left of it was full of dog hair and blood. Mr. Ingraham measured it and did some research, and found a guy up in Havelock with a wrecked Honda 450. Turns out the headlight shells are the same size. And, for a lens, Mr. Ingraham cut a piece out of an airplane canopy and warmed it in the oven so he could shape it properly. He had most of the BMW riders in that part of the state involved in rewiring the cycle.

Five days later, we lifted my buddy up onto his bike and walked beside him while he got it out of the driveway and onto the road. I had spent four of those days working on the bike and running up and down the state for parts, and one of them running my friend into a town with a hospital so he could get x-rayed. I suspect that was the day Mr. Ingraham got most of the work done on the cycle. After breakfast on the day we left, I asked Mr. Ingraham could I give him some money. We had spent five nights in his house, eaten fifteen meals and a number of snacks (Mrs. Ingraham was to be applauded as well as thanked for her cooking), taken advantage of his time and effort and local connections. And, of course, he wouldn't take any money. Instead he told me to scrape up the next rider I saw down, if I was in a position to help. Pass it on. Pass it around. If it comes around, it will go around. Passing through slowly.

It's a good thing most riders understand this, or I would be abandoned, dead, and forsaken along the highway years ago. First time it came around for me was back when I was a kid riding one of those Bultacos. I was broke down on the side of the road and a huge group of Harley riders roared up to save me. I told them I had the parts I needed at home, and could one of them maybe give me a ride down the line. That was the first and only time I was ever the fourth person on a bike. The guy riding lead insisted I ride with him. So I climbed on behind his old lady, who had an infant child in her arms. And they took me, all twenty or thirty of them, twenty miles out of their way to my house to get the part, which fucking terrified my parents, even though they should have been used to it by now. And then they took me back to my bike and sat there until I got it running. And they wouldn't even let me buy them a beer.

One time, awhile back, I screwed up and abandoned a rider I should have helped. Was over on the east coast of Florida, I think on I-95 over there. It was dusk and I was headed south with Nancy up behind me. Up ahead I saw a bike over to the side. If a guy has pulled over to the side of the expressway, he's in trouble, so I geared down and started to move out of my lane and onto the side. As we slowed down and got up to the broke down bike, I noticed two things. It was a Honda, one of those big Aspencades, and the guy was finishing up tightening his axle. I had no idea what the problem was, but it looked like he had it fixed. Second thing I noticed, as he straightened up and faced us and smiled, was that he had on a t-shirt that said "AC/DC." I kind of nodded at him, and swung back onto the road, and kept going. Nancy yelled at me what the hell was I doing. And I explained that I didn't really have any homophobic tendencies nor was I prejudiced against gays, but I just didn't feel obliged to stop and help him, and it looked like to me that he had it fixed already. She pounded me on the helmet some and explained AC/DC was a musical group, not a declaration of the man's sexual orientation. Honest, I thought it was identifying him as semi-queer. Just passing through, sometimes in the wrong decade, sometimes in the wrong century. Fortunately I've often had a good woman with me for a guide.

Here we go again. That AC/DC thing put me in mind of another story. I used to know a boy in New Orleans, a homosexual, who had three earned Ph.D.s. Gay or otherwise, he was one of the best teachers I ever worked with, a fine man, and a good friend. I rolled through there one time going somewhere and stopped to see him. He insisted I stay, and took me out to dinner and to a couple bars. Somewhere along in the evening, he said I looked nervous, ill at ease. And I told him I just wasn't used to being around that many homosexuals at one time, and I was kind of afraid I would offend one of them if they tried to hit on me. He laughed and explained that I wasn't attractive to homosexuals either. Told you he was a good man.

Same thing, kind of, happened in San Francisco. Was Zero's doing. Me and Nancy hit town late and hungry, and he sent us to a place down on Castro Street. Nancy later reported that the little sissy two tables away had been flirting with me all evening. Hell, I didn't know it. She said I didn't notice it when women flirted with me either. That bothered me, and I started paying better attention. She was just messing with me. It don't happen; the guy in New Orleans was right.

But this was about what comes around going around. And I have gotten to return the favors a few times over the years, but I think I still owe the pot some. I once saved a Yamaha rider with office supplies. His chain had come apart, and he didn't have a clip for the master link. So I made one out of a paper clip for him there in the shadow of the Mackinac Bridge. He was amazed and grateful. Amazed that another biker would have a fucking paper clip, not that I had fixed his ride.

Maybe that's one of the troubles with riding motorcycles. If this was about airplanes, I could tell you one about crash landing in the Arctic and spending the winter whittling a new propeller out of a cedar log.

On that ride around Lake Superior that time, I did get above the Arctic Watershed. Got a picture of the bikes parked beside a big sign telling you that it's the Arctic Watershed and where the water goes from there and all. Got a similar photo of the bikes parked beside the sign telling you it's the Continental Divide, I think up at Deerlodge Pass, and another one explaining that we're parked beside the Eastern Divide up there in Kentucky by the Cumberland Gap. Got a lot of pictures from a lot of long rides. Most of them are scenery, with bikes in the foreground. Too many of them are of places that no longer really exist.

A few years back I got a call at work one day from a boy up in Boston. Seems he worked for some big book publisher up there, and he had heard my tape, and called his local distributor for my phone number. He was doing research for a trip. He and some of his friends were going to ride down into the legendary Florida Keys. I told him not to. I explained that there were no more Keys, not really. That the roadside was so cluttered with condos and commercial endeavors that you couldn't even see the water along most of the road. Explained how Mallory Square now had a cover charge and a choice of several quaint little combos to listen to as you waited to watch sundown through a maze of rich people's boats. Told him the road was slow and often clogged to gridlock with Winnebagos and Rental Cars out of Miami. Informed him the road was loaded with sand and grease and trash and pedestrian traffic. Told him it wasn't there no more and not to try to ride it, especially around a holiday, or a weekend, or a winter.

There was a time, back in the early seventies, when that shot along U.S. 1 down out of Miami was about the prettiest couple hundred miles in the country. Used to detour out around some of Key Largo and take the Card Sound Bridge. Stop at Alabama Jack's for a cheeseburger and a beer. Jack sold out years ago. His old place is some kind of family restaurant/souvenir emporium now. It used to be a fine, easy ride in the sunshine. But that was back when you could ride down into Little Havana at midnight of a Saturday, park your bike anywhere along Calle Ocho, and wander away with absolute certainty of the safety of both yourself and your machine. Hell, this was back when you could take five dollars with you and have a fine meal and a good time. Now you can't. It ain't there no more. And neither are the Keys. Now they're scary and dangerous. Now they're crowded and real expensive. They might be a great place to take your big sailboat, but they sure ain't noplace to be on a bike. Not if you want to ride it.

While I'm telling sad stories of this nature, I have to tell you about the Outer Banks too. First time I came upon the Banks was 1973. Thought I'd gone to heaven. They didn't even have tv out there yet. I rode the ferry boat from Swan Quarter out to Okracoke, and had to look hard for a motel and a restaurant. That was a great ferry boat ride. I think they tied the bike down that time. There was a guy who lived on The Banks going home on the boat. Him and his big black Labrador dog. Nice dog. Can't remember the man's name, even though he told me a story about killing twenty-three geese with one box of shells. Dog's name was Zeke. And he was thirsty, and the guy didn't have any water with him, and the water on the boat tasted like it had been around way too long. So I gave the dog a drink out of my canteen. And the guy told me stories about goose hunts and fishing trips, and where to get some great seafood on Okracoke. The restaurant was clean, cheap, and had truly great seafood, channel bass as I recall. The other places I found were cheap and good too. I spent hours the next day, riding slow and stopping a lot, getting up to Nags Head. I doubt I saw twenty cars all day. The Outer Banks of North Carolina was the last place in the continental U.S. to get telephone service. It was so very pretty that I combined an Outer Banks-Blue Ridge ride every time I could.

Last time I was to the Outer Banks, a couple years ago, it looked like the Florida Keys. Insane, inept, jammed traffic everywhere. They've paved most of it. K-Marts and Kentucky Chickens as far as the eye could see. Overpriced, frozen seafood. Condos blocking any hope of viewing the ocean. It was gone. Disappeared like Ocean City, like the Keys, and any hope of riding through Yellowstone unharmed, gone like Gatlinburg, Tennessee, and the Black Hills of South Dakota. I got the best catfish supper I ever ate one time in Spearfish, South Dakota for three dollars. Last time I was there, they had casino gambling and cold six dollar hamburgers. It was gone. Gone like most of the ferryboats. Like Route 66. Crowded out like both shores of Florida. Gone like Big Sur, vanished like the Eastern Shore of the Chesapeake, and Big Bend. Growth and development. Plazamalls and paved parking lots and fast food places. Iranian dentists, Hindu motels, Afghani convenience store operators, German tourists, and Yankee real estate people. Handbaskets ain't big enough.

CHAPTER SIX

****** Funny Stories, Dead Animals,
Savior Waitresses, Ex-Wives,
and Other Women ******

One time on the Massachusetts Turnpike I rode through a swarm of bees so dense that it sounded like machine gun fire rattling on my fairing and windshield and helmet. A semi-truck full of hives had overturned, and the damn bees were staying in place and being real territorial about it. Took a long time to get their sticky little bodies washed off the bike. Another time, we were out west, either in Utah or Nevada, and a strange smell came upon us. We rode beside one another long enough to discuss it and insure that everyone had smelled it and no one was going crazy. We agreed it was the smell of bananas. Odd smell in the middle of a desert. Another ten miles or so into the wind and we came upon the disabled semi. The bananas were melting, and banana juice or oil or whatever bananas have was leaking out all over the road. The air was much fresher on the upwind side.

And another time in upstate New York I hit a groundhog. The damn woodchuck was a big one, forty pounds we estimated later. And I was going about fifty when I popped him. As luck would have it, I had a passenger who saved me from dropping the bike. The guy I was traveling with was burning his clutch out, so he took his old lady and as much other weight off his bike as he could, and put it all on mine. When the groundhog jumped out in front of me, all I could do was line the bike up straight at him and hope to ride through him. Both of which I did real good. But the impact of it drove me forward onto my tank, and positioned my testicles somewhere around my ears. I damn near passed out. Tears were in my eyes, and I couldn't see a thing. But the lady behind me could, and she just leaned and swayed and kept the bike upright from behind me. I eventually got it slowed down and over to the side of the road. She held it up for me while I got off and threw up and cried.

Up in Canada one time, the guy I was with must have gotten a bad walleye at the all-you-can-eat Elks Club fish dinner. A very few miles down the road I saw his brakelight come on, and then his turn signal. As I pulled up beside him on the side of the road, he sort of handed me his bike and bailed off it into the ditch, where he was real sick. Holding one motorcycle up while you are sitting on another one is a hell of a trick it turns out. Trickier when they're both running.

That woodchuck wasn't the only animal I ever wasted on a bike. I've managed to miss most of them, but I've run over a couple suicidal squirrels and prairie dogs, and an occasional armadillo. I once ran over a possum, lengthwise. And I don't think I hurt him much. And I've been assaulted by a couple of insane birds bent on kamikaze missions. Felt bad about every one of them. I've done told the story of my pardner killing that ridiculous Basset hound. There was a poodle with the dog he killed. I missed it. And I've always felt kind of bad about that.

I heard a story once about a guy killing a deer with his bike. Seems it was late at night, and real cold. The guy's wife was behind him, bunched up trying to stay warm and about half asleep. And the guy came out of a curve to find a half dozen deer frozen in his headlight. One of them, the biggest one as the story goes, stood still sideways across his lane of the road. And, as the story continued, he lined his bike up straight and turned it on hard, and rode right through the damn deer. Tore it stone in half. Tore the windshield off his ride was all that happened to the cycle. And his wife, once awakened and alerted to the situation, had the presence of mind to go pick up the hind quarters and carry it home. I ain't real sure I believe the story, but the guy who told it to me swears he ate some of the venison.

Another funny story that comes to mind here doesn't involve dead animals. In fact there are two funny stories a few hundred miles apart here. Me and Nancy were coming back from that ride to the west coast. We had come east out of El Paso and followed the two lane road along the Brave River of the Border through Lajitas to Terlingua and down into Big Bend. We were riding the empty, deserted road north from Boquillas up to Marathon. And it was under construction. Most of it. It was the damndest thing I have ever seen. There were holes in the road. The construction crew put them there. I have no idea why. But there were holes, about the circumference and depth of a pound coffee can, punched all over the roadbed. So many and so thick that you couldn't ride around them. They were set up in a tight grid. You had to ride over them, through them. You could do that at about twenty miles an hour, tops. And that made your teeth rattle like castanets. Years later, when I was diagnosed with arthritis and tendinitis in both elbows and hands, I told the doctors about this road.

There must have been forty or fifty miles of this shit. It was a hundred and some degrees. It was dusty. There was no place to get off and stop and rest. No place with shade anyway. No place where the shade wasn't already taken by snakes and gila monsters. No stopping. No resting. No water. Except for the tears in my eyes. And, oddly it seemed, damn little other traffic. The locals had been alerted. The few people who bounced past us either looked at us with genuine sympathy and pity, or they looked at me like I was the biggest idiot that side of the border, and/or a real son of a bitch for taking a girl out into it with me. Couldn't really blame them much either.

We eventually caught up with the construction crew, even got to see the weird machine that made those holes in the road. I still don't know why. When we passed out of the construction area and onto a decent surface, several of the workers removed their hard hats as we passed slowly by, some held their hats over their hearts. I must have looked like I just didn't get it at all. One of them, a Mexican boy, looked at me with sad, sincere eyes, like I was Jesus coming back in from my forty days in the wilderness, and said, "Damn, man, we never even thought about a motorcycle. We're really sorry."

The waitress, Betty Lou Thelma Liz, up in Marathon, took one look at us and brought a giant pitcher of iced tea and some nachos. She, too, looked sad and sincere on our behalf, and asked, "Y'all come up from down by the river?" When I nodded weakly and croaked a positive response, she told me the iced tea was on the house.

But that ain't the real funny part yet. That night, me and Nancy discussed that part of the ride and the road over chiles rellenos and wet burritos. She said she had been terrified that I was going to put it down out in the wilds someplace down on the far end of that road where there would be no one to rescue us. Maybe no one to even find us while we were eaten like roadkill by the buzzards and gila monsters. And I explained to her that my great fear had been that I would drop it in the middle of the construction crew at the near end of it all, and make an ass of myself in front of people.

This was a long time ago, and me and the woman ain't even together anymore, but she is still mad at me for that. And, like them holes in the road, I still just don't get it. She must not have been too mad at me. The next day she sat for a half hour with me, waiting until the Judge Roy Bean Museum in Langtry opened. In fact, Nancy knew how bad I wanted to see the place and insisted we wait for them to open. I do kind of understand why she is still mad at me for taking her through Death Valley on the way out to Captain Zero in San Francisco that time. But I thought she ought to see it. And I knew it would be hot. And, I knew that the gas at Stovepipe Wells would be real expensive. And I had enough sense to stop and get gas in Beatty, but I was in a hurry trying to get her away from the slot machines. And I did stop and buy her a soda pop and set in the shade there at Stovepipe Wells awhile. Parked the bike about five yards away from the overpriced gas pump, under that tree they got there.

And then I damn near ran out of gas before we got out of Death Valley. I'm talking real close. I coasted in to the pumps at Darwin on fumes. If I had been burning regular instead of high test, I would have had to have gotten off and pushed it the last few feet. And the last thirty miles of that ordeal, running on reserve and climbing up out of the Valley the whole time, Nancy worried about running out of gas in the desert, even though it was only a hundred and twelve degrees that day. Just in case you think I was bent on killing this woman in the desert, later that same day I took her through Yosemite. There was still ice in the Tuolumne River and snow piled up high beside the road in the Cathedral Mountains. We had to stop at the pass there at Tioga so Nancy could put all her clothes on. A woman has to be in love with you, and pretty brave, to get on behind you cross country. But then I did show her the Rocky Mountains and the Pacific Ocean.

But that wasn't the second funny story. The day after the road construction fiasco up north of Big Bend, we found ourselves in Del Rio, in need of maintenance. That road full of holes had shook everything loose except my front brake, which kept grabbing and holding and binding. Well, it turns out there's a place called Cycle Works there with a sign on it saying they'd work on BMWs. I parked and walked in and asked who was the BMW guy. A tall, skinny, long-haired freak said he was, and I told him about my brake problem. He said he knew just what to do and walked out and looked at my bike. Said he had to get a piece of two-by-four from around back of the building. So I walked down the alley with him. Nancy stayed with the bike and watched us walk away. A few steps into it, she giggled and hollered, "You two guys walk just exactly alike."

He smiled and looked over at me and didn't miss a stride as he asked me, "You always fall down on your left side, too?" Then he fixed my brake and wouldn't take any money.

Well, yeah, all to the left except for my last fall. I have no idea whether that is circumstantial, or indicates a particular brain hemisphere dominance, or what. But they've all been to the left. Hell, maybe it's political.

This next one might be a funny story. It was a long time ago, on Chuck, that first BMW I had, and I still have some trouble laughing. Happened late one night, early one morning. In the middle of downtown Flint, Michigan.

The people who were in control of such things there had screwed up the roads with all kinds of four and six lane one-way streets. It wasn't a dark and stormy night, but it should have been. I was going home and caught a red light. I was in the second lane from the right, the third lane from the left. And a car pulled up into the far right lane and stopped at the light, too.

This is where it can be didactic. I should have figured it out, but I didn't. I actually glanced to the right across the empty lane at the car, at the driver. And I still didn't figure it out. The light changed, I eased out into the intersection, and the woman in the car came across three lanes to get to me, but she managed it. She also managed to get moving real fast real quick and was going a serious twenty or twenty-five when she hit me. Caught me broadside with the left corner of her front bumper. Knocked me down like the guy on the tricycle on *Laugh-In*. She was drunk. And I should have known that. Hell, it was three o'clock in the morning.

Most of my focus was on getting out from under and away from my bike. But as I looked up, our eyes met through her side window. And then I knew finally. The bitch wasn't going to stop; she was taking off. Figuring that out was the last clever thing I did that night. The next thing I did was grab her door handle. The next thing she did was floor it and lay rubber back and forth across four lanes for about fifty yards, dragging my terrified ass along with her. That's when I decided to bail out and turned loose of her door handle and rolled and tumbled and skidded to a stop at curbside, just in time to watch her lose control of her car, hit a telephone pole, bounce off it, and then go across the street and through the window and down the lunch counter of the Woolworth store on the corner. I got up and limped back to pick up my bike.

The dark, empty street was filled with an array of red lights and sirens. Ambulances, fire trucks, wreckers, and cops. They had me frisked and cuffed before they figured out I was the victim. Then they got the drunk broad onto a stretcher, and out of the Woolworth store. One cop dropped five or six tickets on the stretcher as they rolled the unconscious woman out and into the ambulance. Looked like he was dealing cards. Smelled like a busted case of Seagram's on the way by. As the ambulance and firetruck departed, I finally noticed my shredded pantleg and felt the blood filling up my left boot.

Then the wrecker pulled her car out of the store and away. Then the cops left, one by one. And then I was alone there in the early morning darkness. And not one of them angels of mercy had bothered to ask if I was hurt or if my bike was busted up too bad to ride. In fact, after they realized they couldn't arrest me, they weren't much interested in me at all. My handlebars were bent and twisted, my brand damn new handlebar fairing was beat all to hell, and I'd torn a footpeg and a handlegrip off. Busted a tail light, bent a clutch lever, scraped up a good paintjob. Messed up a good leather jacket too. And that boot never was the same after that.

This here tale about the Empty Woolworth Store Lunch Counter Massacre, with no waitresses at all to protect me, and that other story about riding wasted into Marathon, Texas and being rescued by Betty Lou Thelma Liz the savior waitress, put me in mind of a couple other times I've been saved by the craggy, but benign local waitress. Once was in Vernal, Utah. Me and the two boys I was riding with had put in a long, hard day eastbound into Vernal. We were tired and beat and hot and hungry. Mostly hungry. The mental deficient at the motel told us where to go for a good steak. The three of us walked into the dark bar and restaurant with our helmets in our hands. And about forty heads with John Deere hats all turned our direction at the same time. It was just like synchronized swimming, only nobody was smiling. They had identified us as alien outsiders. It looked like trouble to me. But the friendly, protective waitress, WandaJo Melba LaVerne, damn near sprinted up to us, got between us and the crowd, turned to frown meaningfully at the locals, and led the three of us quickly to a dark table around a corner. The steaks were among the best I've ever eaten. Nobody tried to frown at us. And that girl got a huge tip.

The other time that happened was in Bernie, Missouri, my ancestral home. The summer my grandmother died, three of us had planned a ride out to the west coast from Michigan. We left a couple days after I buried Grammaw. Told the other two guys I wanted to ride south down along the Wabash into south Illinois where Grammaw was born and raised. And then I wanted to cross The River and ride through the Bootheel of Missouri where she and Grampaw got started. We rolled into Bernie early one morning, rode around long enough for me to get oriented, find the old house and the graveyard, and then find the only restaurant for breakfast.

Same thing as in Vernal, only these guys had on Massey-Ferguson caps. And they all turned, just like they'd practiced it for years, in unison, to observe, and disapprove of our entrance. And just like Vernal, this waitress, MinnieAnn MaudieJean, sort of ran over to the door to shield us from the frowns. She turned to the boys having their biscuits and grits, put her hands on her hips, and announced good and loud, "Y'all behave, and leave them be!" You could tell she gave a lot of orders. Then she walked us to the back of the room to an empty table. And not one of them boys looked up at us as we went by. Tipped that girl good, too.

One other time, in some godforsaken place in Montana like Choteau, I didn't need a waitress to save me. I wandered alone into the local bar and eatery, helmet in hand. This time a sea of cowboy hats turned my direction. I'm beginning to think this whole phenomenon has to do with headwear. Might be I should start traveling with a cowboy hat and a variety of farm implement caps. Maybe a yarmulke. Anyway, I was identified as an alien outsider immediately. I stood there long enough for the guardian angel waitress to show up. And she didn't. And I already had her named. Mary Norma Irma Lou. So I took my usual seat near the door. As I did, the cowboy hats all turned away from me and back to the big screen tv. There was a brown-out or a black-out or something such as that in New York City, and there were news specials all over the tv showing the rioting and the looting and the general urban merriment that had ensued. The tv would show a scene of a group of deprived sociopathic urban youth kicking in a store window and looting the merchandise. The cowboy hats were attentive. As each scene faded to another, they all briefly turned, in unison of course, back to me. Like maybe I was an urban looter on a scouting mission to Choteau or wherever the hell it was.

Finally, during a commercial, the Big Cowboy stood and walked over to me. The son of a bitch was about seven foot tall. I think I could have hidden in one of his boots. As he bowlegged his way through the mob of other cowboys, the only sound was his spurs and bootheels, and I wondered if he rode a Clydesdale or a Percheron. He got to me, sort of loomed over me a minute, spit some tobacco juice out the door, grabbed a chair, turned it around and sat facing me. He sat there looking at me for what seemed a real long time. I glanced to the door, and was figuring my chances of getting around him and gone. How fast could a man that big move? But several of his friends had by now gotten up and were ambling over to join us. Spurs jingled, and I thought of every Clint Eastwood movie I've ever seen. Then the Big Cowboy pointed at the tv and asked, "How come the boys who own them stores ain't standin' out front of them with .30-.30s keepin' them damn nigger thieves out of their merchandise?"

He really wanted to know. All of them did. They didn't understand it, and they wanted to know. And they figured they'd ask the only guy they'd seen in awhile who didn't have a cowboy hat on. After all, their people didn't let the damn Indians come in and raid the supplies at the trading post without a fight. But the main thing was that I wasn't going to have to fight. And no angel of mercy in an apron had saved me. I spent the rest of the evening trying to explain the urban mentality, insurance, ghetto youth, and cities in general to a real nice bunch of guys named Hoss and Hoot and Clete. I don't think they understood it, but then I ain't sure I do either. Sort of like them holes in the road in Texas, and why that girl is still mad at me, I just don't get it.

Once upon a time in the south, in a very wealthy suburb of Miami, I picked up the only woman I ever managed to pick up on a bike. It's pretty hard to interest women, much less pick them up, when your best, hell your only, line is, "Get on behind me." Think about it. I carried an extra helmet for years. It was an old half hat. One summer I just finally figured it out, and gave up and left the damn thing at Captain Zero's out in San Francisco. Now I carry a heating pad and orthopedic devices, prescription pain pills.

I only used that old helmet one time. That happened in Miami too. I was blowing through town, and there was a beautiful woman, with long blonde hair and short cut offs, hitch hiking. I damn near dropped the bike. I must have been staring, and probably had a goofy grin on my face. When I handed her that extra helmet, she smiled and was even more beautiful. And then she explained that all she wanted was a ride, and that she would be very grateful for the ride, but that all I was going to get was her thanks. It was pretty funny. She looked about mid-way between Candice Bergen and Cybil Sheppard. With longer legs. And she wrapped those legs and her arms around me tight and snuggled right up to me all the way down to Perine or wherever the hell it was she was going. Just to make sure that I knew what I was missing. And of course I took her all the way to her house. And she did thank me and smile at me again. And then she handed the helmet back, and left me to laugh at myself.

Actually I lied about that only ever picking up one woman on a bike part. The other one, I was really indoors, on foot, with the scooter out under a tree at the time. This other one happened down in Miami too, in one of the suburbs. I had been invited to a party by my friends in Coconut Grove. The lawyer, who had just gotten them off on a bust for littering in the trees (This is another one of those stories that could take up several chapters; they were hanging effigies in the few remaining coconut trees in the Grove in protest of the construction and development, and the authorities couldn't come up with another charge), was throwing a victory party. Mandatory attendance. So I rode on out to the prestigious suburb, and parked in the shade at the mansion. Left my helmet on the bike. One of the few times I knew I could safely do that. I went in, met my host, one of the only lawyers I've ever been able to be in the same room with for more than five minutes, mingled briefly, grabbed a drink and then went to a corner and leaned on the wall there. My usual party behavior.

And I hadn't been there two minutes when a real pretty lady walked up and stood in front of me and looked me over real thoroughly. She smiled. I looked behind me to see who she was smiling at, then I checked to see if my fly was open. She smiled again and asked me did I ride a BMW or a Harley. I don't know how she knew. I mean I didn't have an identifying t-shirt on, or a belt buckle, or my helmet in my hand, or a tattoo on my arm. I told her I rode a BMW, and she smiled bigger, and asked me where did I want to go? Said she had her helmet out in her car. We rode on down to the Keys. Came back four days later. If I try hard, I can almost remember how red her hair was, the way she freckled when she got too much sun, how her arms felt around me, the way the wind smelled in the Keys.

I ain't sure this next story qualifies for this picking up women category. More organization trouble. We were riding up the Blue Ridge, one end to the other. I was riding solo that trip. Must have been between women. Two of my friends and their ladies were along. I rode drag, like I almost always do. Riding the Ridge is always a fine ride, even if it rains. And riding with a bunch of friends is always a good time. As I've mentioned already, the bottom end, the south end of the Ridge is much steeper, and higher, and twistier than the more gentler, lower, northern end. The transitions between the two extremes on the ends are some of the best riding I know about. The five of us got off the Ridge and rode down into some little town down in a valley in Virginia. To get gas, and look for a motel and a meal.

Well, the little girl running the gas station store was a cutie, and took a liking to me, and me to her right away. She was a local lady, named Irma, or Edna, or Emma, I don't recall exactly. She went to school in Richmond, and came home to work summers. She talked to the ladies awhile, made friends with them, and sort of looked me over with that appraising look I get all too infrequently from pretty women, especially young, pretty women. She said if we wanted to wait about a half hour until she closed the store, we could all shower and crash at her place, and she'd take us to a place to eat. So we did. As she climbed on my ride behind me, I asked her about boyfriends. She said she kind of had one, but that he was leaving to go back to college that evening, and they had already said their good-byes. OK with me. Just passing through, little darlin'.

Well, it was a small town, and the boyfriend was alerted, and came bursting into the restaurant. She calmed him down, and he joined us. He didn't eat anything, he just glared at me a lot. He did let me buy his girlfriend supper. Then he took her home in his car and spent the night with her, while the rest of us slept on sofas and floors, occasionally waking up to giggle at my plight. We got up and gone before dawn, before Edna or Emma, and her boyfriend had a chance to tell us good-bye. Just passing through, by myself.

That was the beginning of that trip going to hell. Three days later, we crossed the border into Canada in a rainstorm. Damn near drowned while the customs officials spread our gear out in puddles on the ground. Once they made sure everything we owned was soaked, we were free to go. It continued raining. Everything between Niagara Falls and Sarnia was mud. And then it kept raining, and Michigan was the same mud. Fortunately some of us lived there so we were able to find shelter. Good damn thing too. It rained for eleven days.

Sometimes, there just ain't no passing through.

CHAPTER SEVEN

******* Riding in the Rain, and Worse *******

Weather, usually rain, on a bike can make life miserable. Hell, enough of it can make life a near-death experience. One of the worst ones I ever got in to was in Kentucky in mid-April. I was headed down south out of Michigan to Coconut Grove and the Keys. First day out was real nice and I rode down through Cincinnati and across the river there. The weather changed at the Ohio River. I've seen that happen more than once since then. One time, crossing one of the smaller bridges, I hit a gust of wind that held the bike stationary in one place for a couple seconds. Anyway, by the time I got out of Covington, I was wet. It wasn't going to get any better, so I bailed off and got a room someplace, seems like it was Dry Ridge or Corinth. I changed out of my wet clothes, took a long, hot shower, and then walked through the rain from my motel to the restaurant across and down the road. It was raining harder by the time I got to the restaurant than it was when I began that walk.

And an hour or so later, when I left to walk back, it was sleeting. Hard. By the time I got the quarter mile back to my room, the sleet was sticking and the road was getting slippery. Later on, about midnight, I stepped out of my room and damn near fell on my ass. There was a glaze of ice over the whole world. I managed to work my way out to the road and looked back toward the expressway. It looked like I-75 was devoid of traffic. It was just as devoid the next morning when I got up. The sunlight on the ice was blinding. Everything was covered with ice, the buildings, the road, the trees, the wires, my bike. I walked carefully back over to the restaurant and dawdled over breakfast, and drank a lot of coffee waiting for the ice to melt. It didn't. It spit some rain, but it didn't get a bit warmer. By ten o'clock I was wired too hard to set still any longer. It was raining, kind of gentle but steady, and I figured that would melt the ice and I'd be OK. Boy, was I wrong. I wasn't even close.

The rain turned to sleet before I had gotten out of the parking lot. That took about a half hour. Then it increased in intensity before I got to the expressway. Within a mile or so, my plastic rainsuit had frozen. And

I was out there on that road all by myself. I never got out of third gear. I never picked my feet up off the ground. I was on the road nearly an hour. I got eleven miles to the next exit. And then I slowly and carefully got off the expressway and found my way to another motel. All without falling down. That was the important part. When I got the kickstand down and stepped off my bike in the parking lot of the new motel, my rainsuit shattered. Pieces of it exploded all over the place. Then my faceshield shattered when I took my helmet off. And then I put on a skating exhibition that would have rivaled anything Peggy Fleming ever did all the way to the motel office. The lady running the place told me it had dropped about fifteen degrees in the last hour, and the weather guys said it was going to continue like this awhile, and how many days would I be staying? Two, it turned out.

One time me and two other guys rode on out to San Francisco, hung out there with Zero awhile, and then two of us started back. We left San Francisco in the pre-dawn darkness, got across the Bay Bridge before it got lethal, and headed south down The Valley. The first sprinkles came upon us down by Paso Robles. As we rode into Kingman, Arizona, it got utterly Biblical. We beat it for higher ground and sat there in an abandoned gas station while it flooded all around us. It kept on like that all the way to east of Memphis. Whole damn ride eastbound was in black and white. We lived in our rainsuits. We had to stop to light a cigarette, and then we had to seek cover in order to keep it lit.

It was raining in Winslow, and it was raining in Gallup, and in Tucumcari, and then it was raining in Amarillo and in OK City, and in Little Rock, and in Memphis. Rained on us mostly. Finally, the rain let up some in between of Bolivar and Savannah, Tennessee. We rode beside one another for awhile and grinned and laughed. Then we touched hands, and he rode north and I headed south. When I talked to him on the telephone a week or so later, he told me that he had ridden right back into massive weather before he got to Nashville. Me too. Couldn't hardly see going through Montgomery. Just passing through, in the rain.

The next day, however, was one of those truly beautiful ones you get once in awhile. Maybe one day out of six or eight on a long ride turns out this pretty. I followed the Gulf Coast home, crossed the Suwanee River in the bright sunshine. Damn near made it worthwhile. Had another day like that up on the Ridge one time. Got into a hailstorm up high there around Mt. Mitchell. A bad hail storm. I couldn't see to my windshield. The road was about an inch deep in hailstones the size of marbles. I pulled over and found a little bit of cover for me and the bike up under a tree. And I didn't take my helmet off until it quit hailing. Didn't get going again until it melted. It melted pretty fast because it began raining right afterward. But the next day was one of those spectacular days. The road was clear and the sky was too, the flowers bloomed, the waterfalls had rainbows, the animals frolicked on the road-side and didn't try to die under me.

And I remember one time out along the Kansas-Missouri line when I got into some local tornados. I damn near launched and orbited a BMW that day. I finally found an abandoned gas station and kicked in the door and rode the bike in. About a minute later the whole front window exploded outward. It was raining too hard to see good, but I am pretty sure I saw livestock in the air out there.

I almost forgot to tell about the time I really did run out of gas. It was on, of all places, the Florida Turnpike. The Florida Turnpike costs money to ride, and it has little in the way of places to get off for gas. I have no idea why I was on that road. I haven't been since. That was a terrible day. I pushed a quarter ton of motorcycle, and another couple hundred pounds of everything I owned fourteen miles to the next exit. Three cops drove by me. Two of them smiled and waved. When I pushed it off the exit, the guy taking tolls felt so bad he wouldn't take any money. Good damn thing. That one was a hard lesson. I haven't run out of gas since.

Longriders spend a lot of time up under cover. Or at least I always have. Finding shelter in a storm is frequently more difficult than it would seem. And, if you got your woman with you, you want to find some real class shelter. I mean, big deal, find a bridge, or a roof, or an awning, or something, and get up under it. Right? Nope, not always. As often as not, the rain is coming at you sideways, and a roof just isn't enough. Oftener than that, you just can't find a sheltered place that you can get your bike into. And nobody wants to set through a storm watching his ride and everything loaded on it, often everything you own, get wet.

One of the many problems with riding the Interstate Expressways, and, by the way, I blame interstate highways for all the bad things that television isn't responsible for, is that there are few places to hide from the weather. Stopping under an overpass is often the only option, and it's a poor one. The best it is is scary and dangerous. Them damn cars are whipping by at great speed, frequently mere inches from your left handlegrip. Besides dangerous, it's usually damn near as wet as being out in the rain. If you try to move over farther right, the slope is too steep. Great design for draining water, but it ain't worth a damn for keeping a bike upright. And it's hard to leave your cycle there on the roadside, inches from Winnebagos wobbling by, and climb up under the bridge where it's dry.

And, anymore, getting off an interstate to look for cover is about as chancy as voting in a presidential election. About the best you can actually hope for is a coin-operated car wash. But sometimes you can get lucky, and there will be an abandoned business with an awning to get under. Or maybe the whole building will be gutted and available. I once set out a long rain in an abandoned revival tent on the outskirts of Waycross, Georgia. Current Interstate highways are a lot like plazamalls. Homogenous. Interchangeable. You can poison yourself at McDonald's/ Wendy's/ BurgerKing, or you can get somebody to sort of wait on you at Jerry's/Denny's/Golden Corral, and get some help poisoning yourself. You can buy overpriced gas and get overpriced nearfood at several interchangeable, homogenous combination gas/food emporiums.

Or you can drive to the next interchange and get off and encounter exactly the same things. Doesn't matter where you are. The sameness is scary. Much of the time you can't tell if you're in Ohio or Oklahoma. Oh, you get some local differences. Waffle Houses in the south, Pancake Houses in the north, better burritos at the Taco Bell in Douglas, Arizona, really good hot sausage on the McBiscuits in Tuscaloosa, Alabama, really scary egg rolls at a place in Boise. But basically, there is about as much variety as you find in the clothing at a military installation, or an IBM office. It's all such a dreary sameness, right down to the employee uniforms. Econo-this, Save-U-that, Rapid and Fast and Not-Really-Very-Cheap. Nothing without hyphens. It's tawdry. It's tacky. Neither of which really bother me much, but it's so damn predictable and devoid of any kind of character or difference or taste or flavor. And it is entirely the fault of the Eisenhower administration and their damn interstate highway system.

Used to be a motel chain out in the middle part of the country, not on interstates, called Mom and Pop Motels. Hell, they might still be in business, but I doubt it. This wasn't a chain like Econo-Lodge or Motel 7. It was a group of independent motels that were part of an organization, sort of like the old IGA grocery stores. The only things these motels had in common was that they were all clean, and they were all reasonable. I guess most of the rooms were pretty small too. Not cramped or tiny, just not ridiculously big like you get in some places. Most of them didn't have a tv in the room. If you wanted to watch a tv real bad, there was generally one available for everyone to watch. It was either in a common room, or sometimes in the owner/managers' house. There were always lots of books in the rooms, and more books available wherever they kept the community tv.

You know, when I started writing this, I was afraid it was going to be a long letter. I mean I just didn't know whether I had enough stories to write more than a dozen pages. Oh hell, that ain't true. I knew I had the stories, I just wasn't sure I could remember them good enough to tell. And what's happened is that each story has touched off memories of other stories, and they just keep on coming. About damn time that domino effect theory proved true.

I got into the middle of a motel price war one time up above

Gatlinburg, Tennessee. This was back when the only thing going on in Gatlinburg on a Saturday night was going on at the VFW post. And I saw a sign advertising motel rooms for $5.50. So I stopped and walked in and asked if they really had motel rooms for five and a half dollars. The guy at the counter smiled and said no. That sign belonged to the motel next door. This man explained that he just used it to suck guys like me into his own motel. He had motel rooms for five dollars. It was only about five in the afternoon, but I knew a deal when I saw it and shut it down for the night right there. Nice room too.

I also got into the middle of a drug war down around Bailey's Switch, Kentucky. It's the sinus capital of the world, and the drug stores in the area had specials on everything from Dristan to Afrin. Bet you thought this was going to be a story about Colombians with guns, didn't you? Hah. Was a trick. But I did get a goodly supply of aspirin and Sudafed pretty cheap.

Once, after a poetry reading, back probably in the early 1970s, I got interviewed by a newspaper reporter lady. I don't remember many of the details. I was still drinking a bit back then, and I was more intent on hitting on the pretty lady reporter than anything else. But I do recall telling her that if someone would just give me twenty dollars a day to stay in motion, I could devote all my time to riding and writing about it. Last summer I spent that much on gas every day I was out.

Been awhile since I've found a decent place to sleep for under twenty bucks. Hell, I found a campground a few years ago that wanted eighteen dollars for a place to park and set up a tent. And it's got to where it's easy to spend twenty bucks a day on food. You can damn near do that on a snack some places. Back in the mid-eighties, me and Nancy took that epic ride out to California, and back. That one cost me about fifty bucks a day on the road. Last summer it cost me damn near that much all by myself. And it's got to where, especially if you're running alone, you don't feel real good or safe about trying to crash for a few hours on a picnic table in a rest area. At least not at night.

Used to be, you could stop someplace and buy your gas, or some food, and ask the people there where might you be allowed to pitch a tent for the night. Chances were real good they'd tell you to camp out back. Used to be, back when there were gas stations with garages and mechanics, instead of gas stations with convenience stores and guys in turbans, that the guy working the night shift would tell you to go ahead and climb up in the wrecker, or in the back seat of a car he wasn't working on, and just crash there. Help yourself to the bathroom. Often, you would run into local bikers, and they'd ask you to crash with them. Times change. People do too. But used to be they'd take care of you somehow, either right there, or they would turn you on to real good place.

There was a store out in the Daniel Boone Forest down in Kentucky. I don't remember the road or the year. Yes I do too, just now. Was near a town named Thousandsticks. And you could buy two slices of white bread and bologna or whatever you wanted by the slice, and make a sandwich. I was hungry and had three slices of I believe it was pickle-pimento loaf. Cost me thirty cents. The Royal Crown Cola was a dime. Mustard was free. Moon pie was a dime, too. I inquired of my genial host about a place to set a tent up overnight. He sort of squinted at me a minute. I don't think they had many longriders blow through there. He asked me a couple questions, engaged me in conversation. Finally, he apparently decided I was OK, and approved of my wandering reasons. And he sent me to a campsite on the Red Bird River that was one of the prettiest places I ever woke up.

But this wasn't about bitching about inflation and prices. This was about bitching about riding in the rain, or actually I guess not riding in the rain. I set out a rainstorm one time with the devil. Gospel truth. Satan rides a red Harley. Drinks his coffee black. And in the summer of 1995, I encountered one of the mysterious Highway Witches while trying not to ride in Hurricane Erin.

But sometimes you meet some real nice people while you're all hiding from weather. One time northbound from Florida up to Michigan, I kept running into a guy and his kid. We were running from and through some bad weather. The man was riding an old 750 Honda. And the kid, who I think was too young to legally have a license, was doing it on a Kawasaki 185. There might have been a time when I could do that, but I doubt it. I'm pretty sure that kid grew up to have arthritis worse than mine though. He already limped pretty good, for a kid.

One time running south down through Indiana, I wound up riding with a guy on a Harley with a crossover pipe and snuffers, and all the noise coming out on his left side where I was riding. It was raining on and off, and we stopped on and off, and he had a bottle of Jack Daniel's, and by the time I got to the river and into Louisville, I was mostly deaf, especially in my right ear, and too damn drunk to be riding a scooter.

Back when I used to ride with the same two or three guys on a regular basis, we had it down to a science, no an art. When the weather would come upon us, we'd split up and each run a mile or so in various directions scouting for cover. Then we'd reconvene and head for the most comfort the local roadside provided. If we couldn't get the bikes up under cover with us, we'd cover them and head for personal protection and refuge. One of the more popular sites was quarter car washes. Nobody washes their cars in rainstorms, so it's an easy place to hide from weather. When the three of us were riding together, one of us carried a coffee pot, one of us had a little butane stove, and one of us carried the traveling Scrabble set. Usually Oreo cookies to go with the coffee. We had some real good times beside the road, up under awnings, and parked in picnic areas under a pavilion, setting up under a porch of an abandoned dwelling, or in the lee side of a building. Some of them cut-throat, buck a point Scrabble games got a little weird and intense sometimes, but we set out a lot of rainstorms like that.

Most of my riding has been in the south, in the summer. So I've had lots of experiences with rainstorms. Summer of 1994 I got into that mess in Georgia that Tropical Storm Alberto caused. It was typical. The first sprinkles fell on me just about at the Georgia line. I was northbound up to Atlanta, riding I-75. By the time I got to Valdosta, I had to stop and set out some hard rain. I got lucky and found a fireworks stand out of business that I rode right into. The next few hours were a series of ten and twenty mile rides through a light rain, and then having to get off when it rained hard, and spend an hour waiting it out. I just didn't feel like getting into my rainsuit or getting determined about riding. Besides that, when the rain got serious, it rained damn hard, it being a tropical storm and all. I spent some time in a real nice rest area up above Adel. Then I had to get off again around Chula. There was noplace to get under, so I settled for the east side of a convenience store in the lee of the storm. I finally figured out the error of my ways and got off at Sycamore. I'd seen a sign for a cheap motel. It was only four or five o'clock or so, but it was obvious the rain wasn't going to stop.

Well, according to the Hindu at the motel, the sign actually said several dollars more than what I thought I had seen. I knew what I had seen, and I had seen this particular third-world trick before. I explained that I could read English real good. It was my mother tongue and the area of my academic pursuit and interest. I continued that I wouldn't stay at his damn roach infested, curry smelling, dog hovel even if it were free, and snowing instead of raining. Velly good, you dot-head motherfucker. I got a motel at the next exit at Arabi. After a shower and a cup of coffee and a dry cigarette, I waded through the parking lot to the nearby bar-b-que joint and had supper. Damn near had to swim back to the room. I moved my bike up next to the motel door. That gave it another couple inches of elevation. By now high ground was important. I alternately watched the Weather Channel on the cable tv, and the rain coming down outside the window. It rained all night long, and it didn't let up a bit. Around midnight, the weather people named it Tropical Storm Alberto. I just hate it when they name the weather I have to ride through.

Having accepted that I was screwed, I got into my rainsuit and headed out into it next morning pretty early. It was a real mess. When you have a wet windshield, and then a wet faceshield, and then a pair of glasses, also likely wet, all bouncing around in front of your eyes, you sometimes can't see as well as you'd like to. Fortunately, traffic was light. Just me and the semi-trucks. And I-75 was under water. But all the trucks got off, some of them suddenly, and damn near all of them eastbound, at Cordele onto U.S. 280. So I went with them. There will be other stories in this about truckers. Damn near all of them will be stories of praise and gratefulness. For the most part, these guys are professionals; they know what they're doing. Most of them know how.

So I believed them and bailed off along with them. And not fifteen miles east, we all broke out of the rain and I was able to take my rainsuit off. Rode in the sunshine all the way to Highway 441. Most of the trucks swung north, and I headed that way right along with them. Thirty miles up that road, we came upon I-16. And damned if most of the trucks didn't get on it back westbound. So I joined them. Figured to get back on I-75 at Macon. It was still sunny and nice.

Three exits later I knew I had screwed up. I was out there alone. All the trucks had gotten off. By the time I got into Macon, it was an island. It took me three hours to get out of town. I-16 shut down behind me. I-75 was three feet under water there, 475 was even deeper. One twenty-nine was closed and swamped and barricaded. The bridge over the Ocmulgee River in town was still open, but the crowds of people out watching the flood crest made it a mess and a hazard. Upper River Road was under water. Forty-nine was more a torrent than a road. There was a cop waving traffic off U.S. 23. It looked like enough water to surf on. I told him I needed to get to Atlanta, and he told me probably not today. When I stopped the bike to talk to him, I put my foot down and water ran in over the top of my boot. I finally found some backroads and then Highway 80 south and east out of town. Then I found a way to get back on I-16. And then I backtracked and rode back east to 441, got on it northbound and approached Atlanta from the northeast much later that same evening. Good thing too. If I'd been in Macon much longer, I'd have been eligible to vote.

I set out a couple days with some kin in Atlanta and then, tired of watching it rain out a window, I saddled up so I could watch it rain through my windshield. Spent the next five days dodging rain in north Georgia, South and North Carolina, and a little piece of Tennessee. I was off on the backroads the whole time, so I found some good places to get out of the weather. Once you get away from the interstate highways, people get some friendlier and more tolerant, or so it seems. Like if you pull up under a roof over gas pumps at a place on the interstate, they get bent that you're blocking their pumps or something. Lady in Six Mile, South Carolina told me I could set there under cover until winter if I wanted to. There was a convenient, scenic rest area up around Mineral Bluff, Georgia that was so peaceful, I not only sat out a rainstorm, but I slept through most of it, dry and warm.

That reminds me. I got to be instructive on that ride. On the way back south, I got into some weather up in north Florida. This time it was named Beryl. I really do hate it when they get to naming the weather that's beating the hell out of me. It was raining pretty good by the time I got to the rest area on the interstate. None of the picnic facilities were in use, which is usually the case in bad weather. And I have only been told to get my bike out of such a place by the authorities one time. And I know damn good and well that woman was kin to the bitch on the ferry boat in Texas down on the Sabine that time.

Anyway, I picked out a covered table at the far end of the rest area and headed toward it. I picked it because it was remote, and because there were trees around it to block the rain. As I rode through the parking area, I saw a big road bike with out of state plates, a brand new bike, parked in the rain with a cover sort of badly thrown over the load. Then I saw the rider and his lady cowering in the lee of the building so they could watch their bike. I noticed their youth right away. And as I rode by I waved and motioned back to where I was headed. Then I rode up under the roof, right up tight to the picnic table where it was nice and dry, and parked. They were looking at me pretty hard by now. I saw the lady engage him in heated conversation, pointing and gesturing toward me occasionally. As I was getting my stove and coffeepot out of a saddlebag, I saw the guy head for his bike, and his lady head for a nearby picnic table with a roof. I could tell it was going to be a long rainstorm, I was right too. So I made coffee and something to eat. Got out my book.

The wind shifted and drove the rain in on my bike at one point. I got up and threw my cover over it. Again, I saw the lady looking my way and trying to tell her old man something. Finally she covered their bike while he sat with his back to me. When the coffee was done, I held the pot up and motioned for them to join me. She did. Girl ran through the rain and hit the cement around the picnic table apologizing for her old man. She looked back and forth from the book I had up there on the picnic table, *The Assassination of Jesse James by the Coward Robert Ford*, to me a number of times. It seemed to confuse her, but only briefly. Then she began thanking me for showing them how to find shelter from the storm. He still sat at his own picnic table, with his back to us. I told her I understood him perfectly. It was a guy thing. Sort of like asking for directions. She got all serious and frowny faced at the mention of that.

This was one of those women you come across all too infrequently; she was nineteen, going on forty, or maybe fifty. When I excused her boyfriend's bad behavior, she jumped right in and said it was bullshit. She asked what I would do if I was lost and needed orientation. Apparently they had gotten, and remained, lost for some time, crossing the Virginia-North Carolina state lines repeatedly, both directions. And she was still steamed about it.

When I allowed as how if I get lost, I report myself to the nearest authorities, announce in a loud voice that I am inept and confused, that I probably ought not be allowed out by myself without supervision, and that I am desperate for help. Tell the folks there that if they don't help me, my continued bafflement and imminent death will be on their heads. Made her laugh. Then she pointed out that apparently refusing to seek help was not a guy thing for all guys. And I had to explain that it was a Young Guy thing. Old guys ain't got many things left.

They had just gotten the motorcycle a couple months before, and this was their first long ride. It was a big 1100 Kawasaki, that model that most of the CHiPsters out there in the Golden State ride. And I recall they were from somewhere in Virginia. They were headed down to his sister's place down around Vero Beach. Can't remember that girl's name though. She sat and drank coffee with me, ate some of my cheese and crackers and apple. Listened to some of my old highway stories. Took good notes when I mentioned places and things to avoid, and some to be sure to see. She asked about my little propane stove, and the coffee pot, and did I cook my own food, and did I camp or stay in motels, and how the hell could she keep from getting her nose sunburned.

She also complained that her boyfriend not only refused to ask for directions, but that since they had gotten lost so bad, he now refused to ride anywhere but on the interstate highways. I asked how long he had been at it, and she told me he had a little Honda before this one, and this was their first time out of state on a bike. So I got my maps out and showed her some real empty parts of Florida between where we were and where they were going. Told her to somehow get him out and let him get some easy experience. Then I told her about the Blue Ridge on their way home. I'd give a little money to find out if she ever got him to ride the Ridge.

I ought to be able to recall that lady's name. Not only was she remarkable in that she was real bright and mature and perceptive, but she was one of those rare women who gets prettier while you're sitting there looking at her. Like a basically plain looking girl ran through the rain and joined me there at my picnic table. She wasn't unattractive at all, just not especially good looking. But she was so damn clever, and bright, and discerning, and honest, and basically a nice person, that she was stone pretty by the time she got up and rejoined her boyfriend. She was some drier, too. I've had a whole bunch of women tell me and bemoan the fact that it's hard for them to be pretty, or to look good on a bike. Ain't true. Maybe it was because she was drier. But I don't think so. I think it was one of those rare things, like the occasional woman who looks better at fifty than she did at thirty.

Anyway, this lady in the rest area, thanked me for the coffee and the conversation, asked if she could take some of the cheese and crackers and apple back to her boyfriend. That was the second most impressive thing she did there in the rainstorm. I told her to take him a cup of coffee too. And I spent the rest of that ride wondering where the hell that girl was when I was nineteen.

The rain slowed down and was petering off to done when I saddled up and headed out. As I rode by them, there at their picnic table, on my way out of the rest area, she did the most impressive thing of all. She didn't even turn to look at me, much less wave at me as I rode out. As I review this, I will not only bet that she didn't get him to ride the Ridge, but that they are no longer together. I just don't think the boy was deserving of a woman that good. I believe she was just passing through.

Probably the worst weather mess I ever got in was the McClure Pass Detour, north of Paonia, Colorado. Three of us were riding west. This was another time a woman impressed me greatly. Nancy was with me, the other two guys were riding alone. We had met in Missouri, at The River, at Cape Girardeau, and were going to ride west together awhile. Me and Nancy were going on west, out to San Francisco. The other guys were going to break off and head south down into Texas.

And we had come up into Colorado Springs because one of the guys was having carburetor problems, and there was a BMW shop there. Boy, was there a BMW shop there. I have to interrupt the McClure Pass Detour story here to tell the Doc Baum story. The three of us pulled up in front of the shop, turned the bikes off, and walked in. An old guy behind the counter smiled and said that the second bike that shut off had a torn diaphragm in the left carb. We all looked at each other. We were in the presence of genius. Doc Baum. He was right about the carb. And he had invented a way to fix it for a couple dollars instead of that BMW fetish for replacing whole, expensive parts. And he was the kind of man who was happy to show us how to do it.

About then Nancy came skipping in announcing that there was a Bultaco shop down the street. Doc Baum smiled at me and asked if I used to ride them. I told him yes, and he smiled knowingly, and told me to go on down the block and look at what they had. It was neat, highly nostalgic. It even smelled like old times.

But it was not nearly as neat as hanging out an hour or so learning things, mechanical, philosophical, and practical from Doc Baum. He maintained a highly tidy shop. He told us how to ride the Rockies. He explained how our machines, any machines, would lose three percent efficiency for every thousand feet of elevation. He told great stories. He gave great advice. Damn shame sometimes that you're just passing through.

The next day there was a blizzard in Leadville. I mean the damn snow was piling up on our windshields and faces. We were in Leadville because the pass at Aspen was snowed in and closed. That was after the one at Crested Butte was snowed in and closed. We got scared and rode north up to I-70 westbound. Interstate 70 was only flooded in places. Never saw so much rain and mud in my life. Seems like most of it was under construction too. Looked like a damn war zone. It was a wet mess all the way to Glenwood Springs where it was a genuine flood. We got off and dropped south down to Carbondale and then 133 south.

I described the McClure Pass Detour in a poem once as twenty miles of hell on an incline, and another thirty miles of mud. It was worse than that. Most of it was under construction. All of it was mud. It was narrow and steep and full of flooded holes and ruts and hooks and hairpins and boulders that had fallen on the road in the current deluge. It was raining pretty hard the whole way. I bet I did five or six miles of it with the bike damn near sideways and both brakes locked up slipping downhill. Nancy was terrified, but brave. When we finally got to our friends in Paonia, she talked at some length about finding an airport and catching a plane bound for the coast. Meeting me in San Francisco. But she didn't.

This was a lot of years ago, but I still have vivid memories, and sometimes bad nightmares, of parts of it. We encountered a trio of Suzuki riders along the way on the McClure Pass Detour. They were north-bound. We were all going slowly enough to damn near leisurely chat with one another as we passed. They encouraged us, loudly and sincerely, not to continue, but to turn back and follow them back out of it. They had stunned, yet knowing expressions on their faces. Looked like Charlton Heston when he came down off the mountain with the Ten Commandments kind of. We couldn't turn and join them. I doubt we would have if we could have. But we could neither stop nor turn around. We created a place to stop finally. We just stopped at a comparatively flat place, shut the bikes off and took deep breaths. We couldn't get off the road. Hell, we couldn't get off our bikes. There wasn't any Off The Road. But we had to stop. Just to regain our perspective and courage. Sat there in the middle of the damn road for a long time. There wasn't any other traffic.

There was one stretch where the road ran along parallel to the river, the North Fork of the Gunnison I believe, for several miles. The water was running down the road so hard and fast, and the river was running so high and close, that you couldn't really tell where the road and the river started or ended, or which was which. As often as not, there was an inch or so of water up over most of the road. Dead cattle and deer were swept by. Trees, lots of real big trees, bobbed down stream. Like I said, it was pretty scary.

Like most of these stories, this one has a happy ending. We arrived in Paonia, where we were given towels and food and warm, dry places to keep the bikes and ourselves. Our friends there noted that we had a stunned, beatific, almost rapturous look about us. We had to stay there three or four days. Paonia became an island. It was that kind of flood. I keep getting into these Biblical rainstorms. Anyway, we washed the McClure Pass Detour mud off our rides, ate elk steaks and antelope chops, toured the area in our friends' truck, and eventually got outbound again. Our friends there rode out with us from Paonia down through Montrose and Ouray, and then they turned around and went back home, and we continued south and west.

That was the day Nancy claimed I tried to kill her with snow and freezing temperatures after I had failed to kill her with rain and mud. The Million Dollar Highway is one of the prettiest roads I've ever ridden. On the way into Durango, we rode by the place where I had tried to kill myself identifying eagles in that construction zone years before, and reviewed the scene of my unfortunate downfall there. Made my shoulder and my nose hurt. Didn't do much for my pride or ego or self-respect either. And I still think that Million Dollar Highway owes me some change. But a little highway humility is good for you sometimes.

It's a good damn thing too, because just about every time I get to thinking I know what I'm doing, and that I can ride the box the damn thing came in, I get a dose of that humiliation. Fortunately it ain't just me. Worst one I ever saw was up along the Thunder Bay River in northeast Michigan. Me and an old biker buddy were up there fishing, wading the river. And a bunch of kids riding dirt bikes, Chinese chainsaws mostly, rode down to where we were. They rode around our big, old, ugly highway machines that we had parked there beside the river. They were all kids, maybe fifteen or sixteen, and real full of themselves. They made a lot of noise and put about a ton of dust in the air. Then one of them, the biggest one, rode up to the river's edge and motioned across a narrow stretch to the far bank as he revved his bike loudly. It was about fifteen or twenty yards.

"You think I can make it across there?" he asked, his voice full of macho bravado in front of his friends. The route he had indicated had a huge and real deep hole about mid-way across the river. We had been pulling smallmouth bass out of that hole all morning. It was easy twelve or fifteen feet deep. Before I could warn him, my friend sort of chuckled and said, "Kid, I don't know what the hell you can do. I know I could make it across there."

I didn't even bother to watch. The noise was plenty. As I reeled in my line and walked out of the river toward my bike, I heard the kid wind it up like a cheap clock, and turn it loose like a rocket. Then there was a huge splash and a real loud gurgling and hissing and popping noise. Then splashing and choking. Then screams. My buddy joined me as we broke down our gear and got on our bikes to leave. I asked him if they needed any help, and he said they about had the kid out of the water and were already talking about a truck to pull the bike out.

Sometimes I drove the truck to the rescue. Friend of mine broke down once way up at the Straits of Mackinac in Michigan. He called, and I headed north with my truck to get him. It's a long drive. By the time I got there he and the Indian with the broke down Pontiac were both drunk. Huge puddles of oil under both machines. I couldn't do much to help the broke down Indian except leave him some cigarettes. But we got my friend's bike loaded on my truck and headed back south. Got within a hundred miles of home when my truck blew up. Yup. So we made a phonecall, and when the next wave of the rescue squad showed up, we were both drunk. As I recall, we left the bike up on my truck and just towed the whole mess back home.

When I was a kid on them Bultacos and like that, we used to tow bikes, sometimes with other bikes. Pretty stupid upon careful retrospective scrutiny, but I don't remember anyone ever getting bad hurt that way. Well, there is that part about how bad I limped by the time I got out of high school. I remember my dad telling me that if I would get off motorcycles, he would somehow find the money to send me off to airplane pilot school so I could learn to fly and just kill myself outright. I was on a first name basis with most of the emergency room staff in two hospitals by the time I had a legal driver's license. But, this was about towing bikes. Usually we'd loop one end of the rope around the car bumper and try to hold the other end while we kept upright and got towed to help. Sometimes we'd tie the rope to the neck of the bike. I have no idea why no one was killed.

I also wonder why none of us got killed when we were doing some of the other stupid kid things we did on bikes. Like polo. It involved a croquette ball, and mallets we made with shortened hoe handles and pieces of two-by-four nailed to one end. Yeah. Use your imagination. There also used to be a game, or sort of free-for-all tag, that we tried a couple times. And this was a long time ago, back when bikes were dangerous enough without making up dumb stuff to do on them.

Those Bultacos were two-stroke bikes, and sometimes they'd start and run backwards on you. Yeah, they would just go backward, the bike would take off in reverse when you let the clutch out. Pretty scary, even for kids. That first BMW I owned, Chuck, damn near killed me on an early ride. The drive shaft came apart and then locked, at about 75 miles an hour. First it went into one of those classic tank slapper wobbles, then it went sideways. I burned the sole off my left boot all the way down to the sock keeping it upright. Then it unlocked itself and went straight again. By the time I had it over to the side of the road, the truck driver who had been behind me watching the whole thing was walking toward me with an open bottle. The repair on the driveshaft was all on warranty, and it only cost me some time. And that boot. Highway humility.

I just went back and looked over some of this. Sounds like all I ever did was run up and down the Blue Ridge and the Natchez Trace. Those are still two of the prettiest roads I know of, but there is another one in the extreme northwest corner of the country that I hope to get back and ride again some time. The run around the Olympic Peninsula is a monster. And the time I rode it, we got a ten day window of sunny weather coming up out of San Francisco. All that damn sunshine about terrified the folks in Seattle, but it made for a great ride. But then we had it coming. Boy, did we have it coming.

Me and one of my old highway bloodbrothers rode out to California to collect a guy we had left out there a few years before. We had a fine ride westbound, especially considering that this was 1988, The Year Of The Great Drought. We crossed The River at Refuge and headed west. We had to ride across Texas, sideways, at night. Took about damn near forever. It was a hundred and seven degrees at the Bend in the Gila River. The humidity was eight percent. The sun sucked our eyes dry between Blythe and Barstow. We rolled through Bakersfield like dried out tumbleweeds. But along the way I got a personal tour of the museum in Tombstone. Another one of those sweet old women took pity on me.

I finally figured this one out; I remind them of their grandson, the one who went bad. There was no one else in the place, so she took my dollar and walked me all around the displays. I've seen carbine rifles with shorter barrels than that Buntline Special of Wyatt Earp's. And Doc Holliday's dental tools looked more deadly than the six guns. Another fine history lesson. Got to stand awhile in the OK Corral. The sweet old woman even showed me where the Clantons were standing and everything. Hung out there on Boot Hill awhile. And we got some great burritos and frijoles down south of Douglas. Got to visit the site of Geronimo's surrender. Although it seems like to me that he just finally fucking gave up to it all. Still felt like a holy place. We rode slowly.

Anyway, we eventually got to California, made the turn north at Buttonwillow and rode on up into the Kettleman Hills, headed up to San Francisco. And damned if it didn't start raining on us up around Los Banos. It was a cold, steady, relentless, coastal kind of rain. Kept on raining like that all the way on into The City. We got to Captain Zero's place up on Russian Hill, unpacked our gear and ran indoors. The next day it was raining harder. And the next day too. The newspapers called it The Storm From Hell. It was the second worst weather in the history of recorded weather there in the San Francisco Bay area. Made the headlines. The good part is that I was indoors, dry, well-fed, and among friends. The bad news is that my scooter was out on the street, uncovered during the whole mess. My seat absorbed several gallons of really cold rainwater. Those among you with hemorrhoids know how this story ends.

When we finally got outbound from The City several days later, there were four of us. The guy we had ridden out there to get had joined us, and the guy I rode out with had found a woman in San Francisco. No mean feat. Especially when you're just passing through.

The next couple weeks were some of the prettiest weather and best riding I've ever heard about. We rode the west coast north from San Francisco up to the Olympic Peninsula, and then around it, and then on in to Seattle, partly by means of ferryboat, without seeing a cloud. Even the traffic was light and cooperative. We rode along the cliffs above the ocean. We rode through redwood forests. Hell, we even rode through a tree, got pictures of it someplace. Cost us each a dollar. We rode through a half dozen mountain ranges. We rode over a lot of rivers, including the Columbia. We had about the best ride possible.

The Olympic Peninsula, like most pretty places, is usually infested with tourists. But that doesn't detract from its beauty a bit. It is one of the most geographically varied places I've ever been. Like you're riding through a primitive, giant redwood forest awhile, and then you blow around a curve and there is a glacier. And then there is a desert. Then a meadow full of wildflowers and elk. And then a big mountain, and then an inlet of the ocean. Like I said, it's real pretty. And I do hope to get back out there and ride it again. In fact I would like to ride the whole of the Pacific Coast again. There are long stretches of uninhabited coast once you get north of about Lompoc. And between San Francisco and Seattle there really aren't any sprawling urban disasters to deal with at all. Just lots of road along the ocean. Lots of beaches, cliffs, forests, miles of empty.

CHAPTER EIGHT

******** Cities, Truckers,
Winnebagos, Cops, Shriners, More Bad
Weather, More Ex-Wives,
and Fort Jackson, 1968,
or maybe it was '69 ********

S ome places ain't a fine ride at all. New York City comes to
mind. It was an error. I made a wrong turn and wound up well
on my way into The Big Apple before I could avoid it. That was my first
mistake. The second one was thinking I could handle it once I had made
that first mistake. I should confess outfront that I don't do cities well at
all. I just don't see any excuse for them.

And New York is the Mother of All Cities. One of the reasons I
stayed so bad lost there was that I couldn't see the sun for all the tall
buildings, and I was unable to orient myself to escape.

Traffic, driving customs, weather, infrastructure, and attitudes dif-
fer in different places, different cities. Los Angeles kind of overwhelmed
and intimidated me. Miami continues to baffle me. Washington, D.C.
makes me angry. Tucson is the biggest truckstop in the world. Houston
is really scary. Last time I did Dallas-Fort Worth was in the dark of the
night, and we damn near got killed by the holes in the road, the breaks
between the slabs, and the repair work going on around them. Anymore,
Orlando makes me want to mutilate mice. Atlanta amuses the hell out of
me. St. Louis just makes me wish I was upwind of it. Phoenix makes me
thirsty and tired. Toronto is OK once you find the river and get situated,
and figure out that trick, pink and blue money. Oklahoma City makes
me want to be someplace else. El Paso usually makes me want to stay
awhile. Minneapolis always makes me want to flee before the blizzards.
San Francisco causes me to park my bike and become a public transit
enthusiast. But New York City flat fucking terrified me. You can't see
the sky, can't see the sun, can't get oriented, can't get gone. Just passing
through, or trying to.

One of the worst places on earth to be on a bike is Florida, especially in the winter. The whole damn peninsula is over-populated by the
inconsiderate senile elderly. Most of them are taking their medicine regu-
larly and are pretty heavily fucked up most of the time. Those that aren't,
and many of those who are, are bitter, bored, angry, hostile people. They
drive, at best, erratically. And then, in the winter, this is made much
worse by the tourists, most of whom are lost and think that driving badly

will help. I guess I've been lucky. I've lived in the state for fourteen years now and only suffered one wreck at the hands of the sedated elderly. And it was as much my fault as it was the fault of the blind, senile, spastic old bitch that caused it. I mean I could see the blue hair, and she was going the usual fifteen under the speed limit. So I hung back away from her. Just not far enough. First, she stopped. For no apparent reason. Then, several seconds later, and remember we're talking old people time here - it's like the opposite of dog years - she put on her left turn signal. Then, several more seconds after that, even though there was no oncoming traffic, she made a slow, halting yet leisurely, casual left turn. She made eye contact with me in her mirror. Smiled. But by then I was down, and damn near underneath her. That was the only time I ever dropped it to the right. And it didn't matter. I still verified The First Law of motorcycle wrecking - a skidding wheel will pass a rolling wheel every single time.

Me and the bike went down and spun around like a top two or three times and then I managed to somehow set it back upright, facing the other direction. Which was OK, because I was going back home now anyway. Busted a mirror off, scraped a valve cover up real deep, made a mess of a crash bar, screwed up a saddlebag some. And I was roadrash and deep bruises from my shin to my ear on my right side. The school nurse and the basketball coach at work told me I had a hip pointer. I pissed blood for a week. My dick turned purple, on the right side. So did that testicle. I hurt real bad. I hurt for a long time. That was the time I learned that aloe will suck gravel out of human flesh.

The sad thing about it all, and leading to one of the lessons to be learned here, is that it was the first time I had been on my bike in about a month. Me and Nancy had gone down to Mexico and the bike had just sat for the month we were gone. I suspect some kind of condensation got into the brakes. The first time I got on them real hard was when the old woman decided to stop and stand her ground in front of me. I should have known there would be some water in the brakes. And I should have known that the goofy old bitch was going to try to hurt me. Sometimes they just don't want you passing through.

Cities are, generally, no place to be on a bike. Some, like L.A., are better than others. San Francisco, while my own personal favorite urban area on earth, is one of the worst places to be on a bike. The hills are part of the reason. Just way too many stop signs and lights with the bike pointed more downward than forward. They got some weird surfaces in that city too, ranging from semi-soft, tacky asphalt to sandy concrete to cable car rail infested cobblestones. And then there is the weather. Mark Twain, typically, was right about the coldest winter he ever spent was a summer in San Francisco. I've never ever been over-warm in that town. But the hazard to riding a cycle is the moisture. People in San Francisco are weird about the weather. They pretend it's warm when it ain't. And they pretend it ain't raining, and refer to the mist, and the fog, and the dew. Either way you wind up with streets that are absolutely fucking slimy. And there is way too much traffic blowing way too much exhaust all over the street surfaces. Combine all that with mostly inept drivers and Eurotrash tourists in rental cars and you're in real trouble on a bike.

Some of the most inept drivers in the world live in Atlanta, Georgia. They just ain't no good at it, most of them. I don't know why. I've wondered. Atlanta is worse than a lot of other places, but everywhere is pretty bad. Besides the million motorcycle miles, I've done about twice that in old pickup trucks from coast to coast and border to border. And in a former life I drove a truck for a living. And my impression and conclusion is that about three-quarters of the people out there driving around on the road shouldn't be. They can't. Just absolutely inept. For the most part, in Atlanta, they are amusing, rather than dangerous. Detroit drivers, on the other hand, are among the most skilled. Washington D.C. has the most hostile people in cars I've ever encountered. Don't blame them, really. I'd be angry too if they made me live there. Miami used to be a pretty safe place on a bike. Now I doubt that you'd be safe in a tank. Last time I was through there, they made several attempts on my life. In all fairness, one of those tries was made by a tourist in a Winnebago, and another by a confirmed Marielito, so I can't blame Miami. I don't know who to blame for idiots in Winnebagos, and I use the term generically. But if I ever find out, I will gladly go to jail after I kill the son of a bitch.

I hate Winnebagos. Most longriders do. They have less business on the road than tugboats. Most of the people driving them can't. I was there when the damn things flat gridlocked Yellowstone. I was there when a guy got one sideways on a street in Chinatown in San Francisco. Dumb bastard managed to get it on both sidewalks. I was there when the guy who had tv cameras instead of rear view mirrors (honest, I ain't making that up) backed over three motorcycles in a campground south of St. Augustine. I was there behind them while they were riding their brakes going uphill in Rocky Mountain Park. And I was behind them again on the Oregon coastline when they tossed a week's garbage out the window. I was there when they parked in the middle of the road and abandoned their vehicle to go pick blueberries in Maine. I was there when two of them met coming from opposite directions and shut the road down all day long in Cedar Breaks, Colorado. And I was there for the all night screen door slamming festival down on Islamorada. I was there when one of the clowns got a flat tire and decided to go ahead on and cross the bridge over Lake Ponchartrain on the rim. I've been kept awake all night in my tent by their air-conditioners and toilets and televisions and cb radios. I've been excluded when they organized pot-luck dinners in the campground. Good damn thing, too. Only thing in this world I hate worse than Winnebagos is multiple bean salad.

Winnebagos are the antithesis of truckers. I've never had a Winnebago help or assist me or drive well anywhere around me, and I've only had one trucker ever try to do me harm. Well, two, if you count the pickup full of drunk Indians between Shiprock and Gallup, but I don't think you can count that. Besides, the number on that road is 666, so I might have had it coming. I have no idea why the other guy tried to kill me. And he was in an eighteen wheeler, not a pickup. Must be I looked like somebody he didn't like. Or maybe he just didn't like the way I set my ride. Wasn't like I did anything to piss him off. It was someplace in south Georgia, on I-75. I don't know how it got started, but I began paying attention when he came around me and cut me off as he slipped back into the right hand lane.

Now just because I'm funny looking, it don't mean I'm stupid. I'm probably not real bright either, but I'm not a slow learner, and I have figured out that in contests between motorcycles and vehicles, bikes lose. It's one of The Laws, like that skidding wheel thing. Every single time. And the odds are even worse with semi-trucks. So I backed off and let him have it. Figured he misjudged me in his mirrors. Wrong. Turns out it was on purpose. He slowed down to where I had to go around him. And as I did, he swung out and tried to force me off into the center of the expressway. No place for a bike. I jumped all over my brakes and got back away from him again. He slowed down again. And I stayed back behind him. I may have made a couple of rude gestures, but I stayed put. It was the only safe place on the road. And then I got off at the next opportunity and got a cup of coffee. Sometimes they really don't want you passing through.

More than lots of times I've had truckers wave at me or flash their lights and save me a ticket. One time outside of Terre Haute, Indiana a truck driver stuck his arm out the window and waved me back as I started around him. I dropped back in behind him, and rolled by the police shooting radar up the road going about three under. A couple miles later, the guy waved me up beside the truck. I hollered my thanks, and he smiled and held up a jacket with a BMW emblem sewn on it. Then he waved me in front of him, I was dead in the middle of an eight truck convoy. We blew through Indiana and on into Columbus, Ohio at about ninety miles an hour. Passing through.

If you're broke down on the roadside, it's either going to be another biker or a truck driver who stops to see can they help. You just don't hardly ever get saved by a yuppie in a Volvo or a minivan full of kids being taken to ballet practice. Same thing if you're hurt. And most of the time truckers know more about the local weather and the local road and the local police than anyone else around.

Speaking of police, it's time to tell my Defiance, Ohio story. I was headed back north to Michigan, I believe from a trip out to Kansas. And the rains had come upon me in the night. I was in full rainsuit and face shield. It was raining hard, but the traffic was pretty light, so I was rolling along pretty good out there all alone. Except for the local cop. He caught me on his radar and then turned on all his lights and sirens and bells and whistles and tried to scare me to death as he raced up behind me at great speed. The son of a bitch wouldn't get out of his cruiser to bust me in the rain, and he wouldn't let me in the cruiser because I was soaked and he didn't want to get his car any wetter than he wanted to get his little cop suit. I stood beside the cruiser in the downpour while he yelled at me. Told me I was going sixty-one miles an hour. He made it sound like I was a serial mass baby napper raper stabber murderer. Pissed me off. So I told the dumb bastard I was trying to go sixty-one miles an hour, and to give me the damn ticket for going six miles over the limit.

This was back in the mid-seventies when Richard Nixon had hidden all the gasoline and lowered the speed limit to fifty-five. Or so I thought. Turns out that in Ohio the speed limit, on non-interstate expressways, at night, was fifty. I was eleven over, and Officer Opie was going to make an issue of it. Hell, he'd already made an issue, now he was going to make it an ordeal. Told me to get back on my bike and follow him into town. He made it real plain that if I tried to escape, he would pursue and shoot at me. He wanted to real bad, you could just tell. He took his gun out and put it on the seat beside him so I would know that. Turned his flashing red lights on.

So I followed him back into Defiance. Where every other cop on duty, every jailer on duty, every clerk working that night, and about a half dozen guys locked up in the big holding cell told him he was an idiot and way out of line for stopping me, much less for arresting me and making my already lousy experience in a rainstorm worse. The other cops told him it was a stone chickenshit thing to do. The jailers and clerks called him a pussy. The prisoners called him lots worse than that. But he was adamant and I got a twenty-six dollar ticket, payable right there, before you get to leave. When I asked him what exactly it was that I was getting for twenty-six dollars, he frowned at me and said, "Loose."

I paid the money so I could leave. It took him about two hours to do the paperwork. It would have been an hour, but he was as busy defending his chickenshit action to his jeering colleagues as he was getting it all down on paper. I stood in my rainsuit dripping all over the floor for the first hour. After that I was dried out and done dripping. When I finally got released for good behavior and cash money, it was after midnight. And it was raining lots harder than when I had first bedampened the doorstep of the police station. Lots harder. I had to walk past Officer Idiot's squad car on the way to my bike. He was still in the building, filing my papers and fondling my money. I got my knife out and punched holes in both the tires away from the curb on my way past. Never missed a stride, just bent down some and stuck them rascals. Made me feel better, but it wasn't twenty-six dollars worth of entertainment or revenge. It wasn't twenty-six bucks worth of knowledge, finding out that trick thing about Ohio non-interstate expressways in the dark either.

But that wasn't the worst one. Worst one was in New York, way upstate someplace. Two of them got me that time. Came at me from different directions, surrounded me, and had me on the roadside within seconds. And I didn't know what the hell I had done. I wasn't speeding or anything. I was being a good tourist, stopping periodically to spend money as I went, wearing my helmet the entire time. Maybe they'd just seen too many biker movies. But they threw me up against the cruiser and frisked me and roughed me pretty good. One of them opened a saddlebag and looked around in it. They both kind of walked around the bike a few times. Laps, I guess. One of them went back to the car to call me in on the radio and see was I maybe an escaped mass serial baby napper raper stabber murderer or something. While the other guy frowned at me and hoped I'd make a run for it, I asked him what was it that I did that I was being persecuted for. Asked him twice. When the other guy got back, I asked him. He walked around to the back of my scooter and kicked the tail light all to hell. Then he told me my tail light was out. Then he wrote me a ticket for it while the other guy stood with his hand on his gun hoping I'd attack his partner and try to stab him to death with his own pen. I think that one cost me fifteen bucks for the ticket and another ten for a new tail light.

Years ago, on Chuck, with Lizabeth, I dined at The Original Kentucky Fried Chicken place in Corbin, Kentucky. Lizabeth was bent on going there, and she was so good to me that I felt obliged. But it was damn near as bad as that time she made me take her to the Betty Crocker Museum up there on Red Spoon Drive. I would've done damn near anything for that girl, but being surrounded by about a thousand high school home ec. students all giggling and pointing at me was about my limit.

But this is about the Original Kentucky Fried Chicken Dining Misadventure. Took awhile. They still had The Original Waitress there. Ida Jean Mildred Louise. The weather was bad, turning off cold and fixin' to rain. So we decided to set inside and eat our chicken. And the local constabulary took umbrage. He parked in the lot beside my bike and frowned at us through the window of the restaurant as we ate. Cops are funny about bikes. Either they got one themselves and they pretty much let you be, or they hate you and the iron you rode in on for no particular reason. I don't know, maybe it's something they teach them in copschool.

Anyway, this particular law enforcement officer wasn't real happy about us being in his jurisdiction.

I wasn't all that damn thrilled about it myself, but there was no reason for him to cop an attitude and sit there and bad eye us while we ate. So when we finished, I told Lizabeth that when we got out to the bike she ought to get her sweatshirt out of the pack and put on some warm clothes. She did, and I did too, and in the extra ten minutes that took, I thought the damn cop was going to have a stroke. Finally he burst out of his car and began screaming at us that we couldn't just tarry around like that, and if we had finished our meal, we should be moving on. Just passin' through, marshall. I learned that lesson years before down in Daytona Beach, so I didn't say a damn thing to him. Just got Lizabeth up behind me, started my ride and departed. And the bastard followed us all the way out of town, all the way to the expressway, all the way to the county line. Passing through some more.

That time down in Daytona was at a damn McDonald's. Normally I'd sooner have a bad rash than eat at a McDonald's, but we were in a hurry and hungry. Waitress there was named Jennifer Tiffany Amber Heather Tami. And about mid-way through the Big Mac the damn cop showed up. We were eating outside at a picnic table so we could watch the scooters. And the cop walked up like Clint Eastwood. He swaggered and ambled, and his gun barrel banged against his ankle. The goofy little bastard looked like Pee Wee Herman, and was dressed like a bird colonel in the Vatican Guard. If it hadn't been for the gun, I would have figured he was the Hamburger Rent-a-Cop. But he was real, and he was very, very serious about his job. He perceived his job as keeping migratory riff raff out of the local McDonald's. He got up to our table, put one foot up on a bench and announced that we were free to finish our meals, but as soon as the last tasty morsel of near-food had passed our lips, we'd have to move on. OK, marshall, just passin' through.

Well, the guy I was with on that ride has a very strange sense of humor. He leaped to his feet, and flung the remains of his McBurger in the air, causing the heavily decorated local gendarme to step back and reach for his gun. My friend then delivered a long and heartfelt rant about how he had just traveled a thousand miles for the express purpose of hanging out at the McDonald's on Daytona Beach, and please, please officer couldn't we be allowed just a few minutes of loitering, apr'es burgers. The cop, he was as young and stupid as he was overdressed and overgunned, only understood about every third word, but he sensed he was being fucked with. And damned if he didn't call for backup. We got escorted up U.S. 1 all the way to north of St. Augustine that time.

But that wasn't the worst one. Worst one was in Iowa, back in I think it was 1973 or '74. I was eastbound on U.S. 18 across the north end of the state. The first cop picked me up on the east bank of the Big

Sioux River. He must have radioed ahead, because I got a new cop escort at the county line. They kept passing me on from cop to cop, county to county, jurisdiction to jurisdiction all day long. It was weird. It was silly. So, around Nora Springs somewhere, I got on it hard enough to get out of sight of the cop that was behind me at that point. Pulled into a cemetery and hid in there. Country cemeteries are usually pretty good places to stop and sit awhile. Good place to work on a bike too. Quiet and peaceful usually. In the time it took me to drink a cup of coffee and smoke a couple cigarettes, I counted seven different cops drive by, sort of frantically looking for me. When I got back on the road, I rode west awhile, then cut back south, just to fuck with them some more. Worked good too.

One summer, three of us were headed to California, and we got surrounded by four cops in Uvalde, Texas. The guy riding lead had a radar detector, and had jumped all over his brakes about thirty seconds before the police all came upon us. They came from three directions and surrounded us at an intersection where about eight roads all come together there. I think the fourth cop had been sitting there in that spot shooting radar. They were much more surprised at encountering one another than we were. But then, we had the fuzz buster. They sort of looked at one another with sheepish, embarrassed cop looks as we rode past them going a few miles under the speed limit. Just passing through, officers.

Went and wandered off into a bunch of cop stories, didn't I? Ought to tell one more. This one happened back in the early seventies, in Tennessee, on I-75 somewhere around Chattanooga. In the rain. The storm came up of a sudden, and about twenty bikes all piled up under the same overpass bridge seeking shelter. Only time I ever saw more than about three bikes wind up together like that. It was weird. And within a very brief time, we were all drunk or stoned or both. And all real good friends. It was proof that, if you do it right, the road goes on forever and the party never ends. One of the guys, a Gold Wing rider, had a tape player on his cycle, and he kicked the tunes up loud enough to hear, even in the rain. Leon Russell, Marshall Tucker, and Delaney and Bonnie. Was a hell of a party.

A state cop drove by us real slow and shook his head. After that, there was a cop went by one direction or the other about every fifteen minutes. A couple of them went by on the road overhead. They all slowed down to check us out. None of them hassled us; there were too damn many of us to hassle. That's one advantage to numbers. I've never really been harassed or messed with or even stopped when there were three or more of us. Well, once. But not this time. This time I think the police were afraid we were organized, or maybe that we would organize. We were too screwed up to find our bikes, much less get back up on them. We had about as much chance of organizing as politicians have of getting into heaven. But the authorities were concerned. And by now we were making a mess of local traffic as every car that went by slowed down and gawked. A couple of them stopped and took pictures. And one of the biker's ladies, she was with a guy who had a coonskin, head and all, glued on his helmet, held up her little makeup mirror so the good citizens could observe themselves observing us.

That was when the Shriners showed up. There were six of them, all on big, tricked out Harleys. And they were as drunk as we were. Years before this, I had watched a Shriner on a Harley lose his parade and get his bike stuck in a wrought iron gate down in New Orleans. Jammed that rascal in all the way to the handlebars. Took about a dozen guys to pry him loose. These guys were that drunk. They joined us and brought provisions with them. By now all the police going by were slowing down even more and all talking to one another on their radios. It was the best spontaneous party I've ever been to.

A few hours later some of us figured out that it had quit raining. Others among us figured out that it was getting dark.

The Shriners led us out. It took awhile; every time they'd all get saddled up, one of them would fall over and the others had to get off their bikes and help their fallen comrade. But we eventually got them all going, and then we joined them. Looked like one of those Hells Angels movies. Looked like the low-speed O.J. chase out in L.A., only with fewer cops in the escort. We rode about twenty miles and then got off the interstate and found a bar-b-que joint, where most of us sobered up enough to go about what it was we were doing before the rains came upon us.

Speaking of Hells Angels, I encountered them once. I've come across Outlaws, and Nomads, and Scorpions, and Disciples, and Gypsy Jokers, and Bikers for Jesus, and what I am pretty sure was the motorized Royal Canadian Mounted Police one time around Ottawa. And for the most part, they're pretty nice people. We ran into the Angels between Needles and Bakersfield. It was just me and Nancy, coming back east from a visit to the left coast. We hadn't seen any traffic for a long time, very empty out there that day. The Angles were westbound, about fifty or sixty of them. I tried to count, but got overwhelmed with numbers and gave up. Nancy tightened up like a coiled spring behind me. We had the only two helmets on the highway. She'd seen some of those movies too. And she had already braved the blizzards and floods and The McClure Pass Detour and Death Valley and Yosemite and the Streets of San Francisco. I held her hand and told her to be cool and smile. That girl had a real pretty smile.

Every single one of those guys, and most of their ladies, looked us over and checked us out pretty thoroughly. They all stayed in their lane. I really didn't know what to expect, so I just held my place and kept on at it, occasionally making eye-contact or nodding at one of them as we went by. And the last one of them, the one they had riding drag, he smiled and waved as he went by. I guess we passed inspection. Just passing through, anyway.

I've never felt threatened or anything by other riders, even the ones they've made bad movies about. And I've never had anything happen that changed my feelings. I'm lots more scared of the sort of thing that befell Captain America and Billy in *Easy Rider*. I rode that road one time. The road they killed them boys on in that movie. We were in west central Louisiana and had to stop for gas. I walked into the station to pay the man, and he began telling me about how Hollywood was right there at his gas station back in 1969. Said he had met Fonda and Hopper and all. Told me how to get to the road where they filmed that last scene in the movie. So that's where we went next. Sort of a pilgrimage. Last movie made me cry before that one was *Old Yeller*.

The next day we crossed the Sabine River on a ferryboat. And the little girl in uniform who was in charge of taking money and making people miserable decided that it was an exact-change-only situation. And the damn fare was some kind of weird figure like a dollar and seventeen cents. And the poor bastard in the car in front of us, he was a traveling salesman, sold electronics parts, didn't have the exact change. And the little girl in the uniform in charge of exact change decided it would look good on her resume to note that she hassled the poor schmuck. Refused to break his dollar bill. Told him he would have to go back and get change somewhere, and then cross the river on the boat's next trip. So I walked up and gave her the money for the guy's fare. She went nuts. I mean she lost it. I thought she was going to make us all walk the plank, or keelhaul us. It took awhile to calm her down and make her understand that there were no laws being violated here. I could pay the man's boat fare without fear of jail or nautical punishment. The bitch let us all on and took the money and scowled at us all the way across the Sabine. As we rode off the boat, I handed her another dollar. Told her it was a tip for being so damn pleasant.

Since then I've done that a few other times. Paid the toll road fare, or the tunnel fare, or the bridge fare for the guy behind me. It never fails to confuse the toll taking people as well as the guy behind me. Only exception to it was the Chinese lady in charge of the Golden Gate Bridge tolls. She laughed like hell, and told me I looked like a throwback timewarp, and wouldn't take my money. White boys can't jump, or dance, but we're pretty funny. And once in awhile you run into a sport out there who appreciates it. More often than not, they're just superficially entertained and amused, but once in awhile you get some genuine appreciation out there.

But then I recall a little squirrel in a Smoky The Bear hat who wouldn't cut us no slack going in to the Grand Tetons and Yellowstone. And we promised him we wouldn't even take our feet off the pegs, or look at a buffalo or nothing.

Oftener than sports and squirrels, you run into all kinds of criminal deals and illicit propositions. I don't know if this happens to bikers generally, or maybe just to guys who look like me. On three separate and distinct occasions in Florida, and once in Texas, I have been approached to join in some massive dope smuggling deals. Usually it happens at little out of the way bars and cafes along the coast, usually late at night. I'll be sitting there, drinking my coffee, studying my map, and minding my own damn business, when a guy comes in, looks around, finds me, and then sits down beside me.

I don't know if it's the sunglasses, or the ponytail hanging all the way down to my skinny butt, or whether there is just some sort of basic criminal aura about me. Whatever it is, it's been real consistent. On three of these occasions, they offered me a whole lot of money to help unload a boat. The other time it was an airplane. Maybe I just always look like I need money. It happened in Key Largo in 1972, up above Port Lavaca in 1975, and in Daytona in 1978, and then again up in the Panhandle around Panacea in 1983. It's good to have some regularity and stability in your life. But I turned all those deals down. Jails scare the hell out of me. Even passing through them.

One other time, down in the Big Cypress, in a town named Gator Hook, I was offered a lot of money to kill a man. Guy just came up to me while I was eating supper and asked did I want to make a lot of money. When I told him I didn't have a gun, he was real disappointed, acted like I'd let him down.

I once had to buy a rear tire in Spokane, Washington. I was outside the shop, just sitting in the shade smoking a cigarette, when a guy who looked like a poster boy for the mafia walked up to me. It was about a hundred and ten degrees out there, and the guy had a broken nose and a cauliflower ear and he was wearing a black suit and tie, and a little snap brim gangster hat, and had a gun lump under his left arm. I didn't ask, but I know he was named Guido. Asked me where I was headed. I told him east. Said he had a small package that needed to be in Chicago. I suggested UPS. He suggested I could maybe use a thousand dollars. Told me I could have a couple hundred now and the rest when I delivered the package. I explained that I wasn't going anywhere near Chicago, maybe never, and that I thought I heard my mom calling me. Like I said, jails scare the hell out of me. So do guys with gun lumps in their suits.

I've already told about getting rained on from Needles to Memphis, and iced over in Kentucky. Damn near burst into flame one time in South Dakota. This was during that ride through The Great Drought of nineteen and eighty-eight. We'd gone out to the coast the southern route, and were coming back the northern way. That was a twenty-one state, ten thousand mile ride.

And just about the second we dropped down eastbound out of the Rockies, the drought and the heat got us. Coming east out of the Badlands, the sun got behind us and into our mirrors. Our arms burned up like meat. The asphalt was erupting and exploding and the pavement was buckling all up and down the road. And there just wasn't any shade to hide in. Wasn't any fresh water either. The crops were gone already, and livestock was dying as we rode by. They were cutting grass out of the median of the interstate to try to feed to the cattle. Minnesota and Wisconsin were even worse. The Mississippi River was a trickle and the Vermillion was a memory. There were fires everywhere. It was a hundred and eleven all the way across South Dakota, then it went to a hundred and twelve in Minnesota.

And a couple days later we were riding in a rainstorm that was threatening to turn to sleet in the Upper Peninsula of Michigan. It was forty-three degrees according to the bank in Manistique. And then when we crossed the bridge into the Lower Peninsula, it was beautiful, pleasant, balmy even. I went through more costume changes than the chorus line in Reno.

One time we rode through Lassen Volcanic National Park on our way north to meet some other boys up by the Oregon line. Was right after Mt. St. Helen blew up north of there. Got to the gate at the Park, and the lady taking money told us that there was a blizzard up in the mountains there and that the snow was piled up beside the road twenty feet high. Told us not to go up there. We asked her was the road open and she allowed as how it was. We asked if there was some kind of rule about snow chains, and she said no. So we told her we had to try it and that if she didn't see us coming back southbound, or if she didn't see the rescue vehicles headed that way, then we'd made it through. She said we were foolish, but that if we were going on up, she couldn't take our money.

She lied. The damn snow was thirty feet high alongside the road, and we had to shut it down and set and wait for the snowplow twice. But we made it. Hell, compared to the dirt road we had to ride to get to the fish camp, the snowstorm was a snap.

Worst dirt road I ever got on was in Canada, up above Lake Superior. It started out as a paved two-lane. Then it went to a paved lane and a half. And eventually the pavement gave out and gave way to local soil surface. In this case the local soil was dust and rocks. And damned if it didn't keep on deteriorating like that until it just sort of ended in the forest north of Thunder Bay. Had to back the bike up about twenty yards to find enough room between the trees to turn around to get out. Sometimes the best thing you can get is out. Like that deal in Defiance. Like the one down in Big Bend.

One time I decided I could ride across a muddy field with a highway machine. Got the rascal stuck all the way to the seat. I'm talking sticky, wet mud, the kind with serious suction to it. It took about three hours to get loose that time. I hiked to a house a mile or more away and explained my situation to a woman who wouldn't open the door, but talked to me through it. I could still hear her laughing. She told me there was a shovel in the barn, and to help myself and bring it back clean when I was done. I found the shovel, and grabbed a piece of lumber, a length of one-by-six about four feet long, and headed back to the bike. It was still right there where I'd put it.

So was Lizabeth. I forgot to mention that Lizabeth was with me and had watched me make an ass of myself in the mud and the muck and the mire. But she's central to this story, so I have to admit that I did this with an audience. I dug and dug and sloped a hole out, and put the piece of lumber in there to make a ramp to ride out of the hole on. Told Lizabeth to get behind me and push. Got on, put it in third gear and spun mud and muck and slime everywhere as I slowly emerged. I bet I put a metric ton of mud in the air.

Unfortunately most of it wound up on Lizabeth. When she took her glasses off, the circles around her eyes were the only part of her not covered in about two inches of mud. She looked like an Oriental raccoon. We stopped at the farmhouse and returned the shovel and one-by-six, after I had found a hose so I could wash them both off. I hollered my thanks through the door of the house, and rode off in search of a quarter car wash. Spent four dollars in quarters, a dollar and a half to get the bike clean, and two and a half dollars washing Lizabeth off. Told you she loved me. Think I told you she was a hell of a sport too.

Fell asleep on a bike once myself. It was back when I was riding those old Bultacos. In retrospect, I must have been seriously fatigued to fall out on something that little. But I did. Came awake in a hurry when the carfull of nuns blew their horn at me to keep me from forcing them off the road. It was real embarrassing. But I suspect they prayed for me, so it probably worked out. Friend of mine fell asleep while we were rolling down an expressway one time. I was behind him, and saw that he was sort of drifting off into the passing lane. At first I thought he was getting away from a bad road surface and onto something better. Then I saw his head sag. It had been a long day, and mostly it had been a hot one. And I've heard people refer to BMWs as Interstate Easy Chairs. I managed to run up beside him, got between him and the median and woke him up in time to sort it all out and avert disaster. Woke him up by whistling at him. Years ago I learned that's the best way to communicate at high speed. Hollering just don't get it most of the time. Maybe it's because the guys I used to ride with were the same guys I used to hunt with, and they were used to listening to me whistle at my dogs. But I think it's easier to hear, that it stands out better in the middle of all the other highway noise.

I was down in Mexico one time, on an island off the Yucatan. And the Indians down there, I guess they are Mayas, the ones who run boats for the tourists, and ferry boats, and fishing boats, they whistle at one another across the water. They do it a lot better than I do. They actually have a language. I mean they have different whistles that mean different things. It's pretty neat. Years later I got to spend some time among the Mayas down in Belize. And they whistle to one another in the rain forest, too. About all I ever did was try to get the attention of the guy in front of me. Then it's a question of either sign language or getting close enough to talk or at least holler.

Most of that stuff comes real natural, evolves naturally. Point to your belly if you want to stop to eat, at your gas tank for that, gesture like taking a drink, and so on. Somewhere along the line we developed a system for passing that involved signals too. It's hard to ride in a group if the road is full of curves and hills and traffic and other things that make it hard to see up the road very far. The guy riding lead would signal and pull out and pass the semi or the schoolbus or whatever. Then, if it was safe for the next guy, he would stay in the passing lane with his left turn signal on. If not, he would put on his right turn signal and get back in the lane. Then, when the oncoming traffic was gone, he would drift back out in the passing lane where the next guy back could see him, and put his left turn signal on again. Then that guy would do the same thing to get the next guy around, and so on. Worked good. Nobody ever got hurt that way anyway. And I don't recall ever discussing it, or making it up. Just happened. Just evolved.

If you put in enough miles together, you get to where you can predict what one another is going to do. Or maybe you're all just reading the signs the same. You know when it's time to stop for gas, or for a drink or food. You know where to stop too. It's like everyone is agreed before any of you even think about it. It's a real good feeling. Like I said, it's been years since I rode anywhere other than alone, but I was permitted to put in some long miles with some good friends for a long time. Got to where I trusted them. You have to at high speed. Longriders either ride alone, or they run in packs with other longriders. That might could be one of those Laws, too.

Besides that telepathy thing, where you all know what's going on without talking it over, you get to where you feel real safe with friends around you at high speed. Charlie Simms once said that he had never been pulled over, or treated badly, or hassled, or pushed around when he was in a group of three or more. He's right. Charlie is, among other things, the best mechanic I ever watched pick up a wrench. He's creative and clever and inventive and thorough. A lot of the things that I admire so much in others. Probably because I lack such attributes. There will be more Charlie Simms references and stories along the way here. Anyway, as usual, Charlie was right. People are a lot friendlier toward three bikers than they are with one. Even if you've got your woman with you, you're likely to get hassled if you're on one bike. But people get real courteous, and friendly if there are three bikes. I've wondered about it for years, since before Charlie said that. No, I don't have the answer as to why, I just still wonder. Might could be fear. You know, strength in numbers. Or maybe they figure if there are three of you, you got some social skills anyway. Serial baby napper raper killers don't travel in groups?

One time, back in my youth, we put together a group. There were sixty-four bikes involved. The police counted us. And frisked and roughed us. And every damn one of us got a ticket for having a parade without a permit. Honest. It took all the cops and sheriffs and deputies and the little helpers auxiliaries in three counties, but they got all of us. Had a damn assembly line set up to ticket everybody, and then they made us leave in twos and threes at ten minute intervals.

Just remembered a real good rainstorm story. In Weiser, Idaho. I was eastbound, and had been rained on from someplace before Burns, Oregon. The weather report said the next day was going to be real nice, so I shut it down in Weiser. From there, I was going to ride north to the border, up along the rivers, to Coeur d'Alene and Bonner's Ferry, and then back down around to Missoula. And I wanted a pretty day or more to do it. Pulled into a motel in Weiser, and while I was talking to the lady at the desk, a voice drifted from the living quarters in the back. Asked me where I had come from, and I said west. He asked how far back west it was raining, and I told him. He said that it would rain there most of the night, and that then tomorrow should be a real nice day. Said there should be three or four nice days once it quit raining. He asked was I headed north to ride the Snake. I told him that was my fervent intention. He mentioned some other roads that I should run. Then that voice from behind the wall asked me what I was riding, and I told him. Then he told his wife to give me the conference room. Told me it had a big set of double doors, and that I could ride right on into the room and keep my ride out of the weather. Said he never knew a BMW to leak anything, so he wasn't worried about the floor. I thanked him and took the key from his wife and started back out the door. That's when I heard the squeak of a wheelchair. His wife had about the saddest look on her face that I have ever seen on a woman not at a funeral. And I knew I'd been talking to another fallen rider. Made me real sad too. And I was just passing through.

One of the things you have to look for at a motel is an overhang or an awning up over the door, along the outside of the motel. So you can get your scooter right up against the building, ideally in front of the window of your room. So you can watch it. And to keep it out of the weather. One of the things you don't want is an upstairs motel room. Carrying all your stuff up a flight or two of stairs is about the last thing you want to do after six or eight hundred miles. And carrying it all back down in the morning is no way to start a day. Most of the time I don't even have to ask. I think it has to do with that limping thing I was developing in high school. Even the clowns they hire to run cheap motels don't want to send an elderly cripple up stairs.

And you have to take ALL of your stuff. You can't just leave it strapped on with bunji cords, even if you cover it all up good. Bunji cords were a great invention, right up there with the safety pin for my money. But they ain't worth a damn as a security device. Several years back I was tying a load down on my truck with a length of rope. A young friend was helping me, and he asked me if I had learned how to tie knots in the navy. I had to explain Viet Nam, and 1968, and the fact that they didn't draft anybody into the navy, to him. He listened politely, and attentively, and absorbed the history lesson. And then he asked me where the hell did I learn to tie knots. And I told him that back in the olden days there were no bunji cords and you had to tie your gear on your bike with rope. He believed me about Richard Nixon being the ultimate personification of pure evil, but he was skeptical about there being a time before bunji cords.

Anyway, you can't abandon your ride and wander off. Bikers miss a lot because of that. Like you can't climb off it in the parking lot of a zoo, and go spend a few hours looking at wildlife. Somebody is going to: a) steal something off it; ii) vandalize it, cut the seat, throw sand in the gas tank, or something; 3) knock it down; D) steal it outright (I got a story about that which still frightens me); or, several of the above. So, you can't go into the Wright Brothers Museum at Kittyhawk. And you can't park in the shade and go on any of the Nature Walks in the Everglades. And you can't leave it, with all your worldly possessions piled on it, in a parking lot while you spend a couple hours at the Smithsonian. And you ain't going to park it out in the light of day while you explore Mammoth Cave or Carlsbad with the tourgroup. Or Graceland, or Old Faithful, or SeaWorld, or any place in any big city, or the Chickamauga Battlefield, or walking the beach up around Mendocino, or trying to see the seals down in Big Sur. Like I said, bikers miss a lot.

That's another advantage to traveling in groups. Three of us rolled in to Browning, Montana after having spent much of the day looking for Chief Joseph's grave. We found it, too. No, I ain't goin' to tell you. Go find it yourownself. Browning, Montana is the home of the Museum of the Plains Indian. And we wanted to see it. And it just wasn't one of those places you wanted to leave your bike and all your gear standing out in a parking lot while you admired native handicrafts. But we really wanted to see it. So we went in in shifts. Left one guy out in the lot guarding the bikes while the other two went in. It was great. Hell of a place. And I would have missed it if I had been alone. While I was on duty watching the rides, and the other two guys were in the museum, it cost me three cigarettes to get the drunk Indians moving away from the bikes, but that was about it. And I would have given them the cigarettes anyway.

Probably missed more than a few good meals because of my mode of transportation too. You really don't want to eat at a place where you can't watch your bike. Sort of like truckers eat at places where they got room to park, where they don't have to back up. Scootertrash eat at places where they can watch their rides. Sometimes you can get lucky and find a nearby place to hide your ride up under cover and out of sight. But most of the time you need some windows. And some of the time, especially if you're alone, it's a good idea to sit down real close to the door. That one might qualify as another one of those Laws.

Before I forget, I got another bad weather story. When I was a kid, I had a couple cars, but mostly I had cycles. Was cheaper, especially for teenage insurance. First time I ever bought insurance on a scooter, it cost me twelve dollars. Seems like that was about 1963. At the end of the year, I hadn't turned in an insurance claim, and they refunded four dollars to me. Anyway, I used to ride year round. I lived in Michigan. Yeah, we're back to use your imagination. And again, this was back way before face shields, and frame mounted full fairings, and full face helmets, or Damart long underwear. What we had was a silk scarf up around your face and goggles and big mittens. And the first year I went to college, they made me take a phys. ed. swimming course, in the winter. At night. Class finished up at ten o'clock, and I rode a long road home in some real cold weather, some of it sub-zero. Many was the night I would sit for a half hour or so in front of the tv as my hair thawed before I could take my helmet off.

The other thing they made me do was take classes at eight o'clock every morning. It was one of the things they did to try to get rid of the draft dodgers. January in Michigan is real cold at eight in the morning. Sometimes it was real slippery, too. One morning, riding my fourteen miles from where I lived to school, I kept getting tangled up with an idiot in a dump truck. He passed me about five times, then got himself hung up and screwed up, and behind me. Then he'd come roaring past me again on down the road. There were bad patches of ice everywhere that morning, and it had me pretty scared. Just wasn't a good day to hurry. And he didn't seem to know that.

It was a left turn into the parking lot of the school, and I got over in the left lane way ahead of time because of the ice. There was always a frozen area in front of the entrance to the parking lot. I had geared down all the way to second and was about ten yards from my turn when I saw him in my mirrors. He was going fifty. He sort of bounced up and down in his seat as he came up behind me at high speed. Later on, I figured out he was jumping on his brakes. If I stayed there, he was going to run over me and I was going to die. But there were still a couple cars coming toward me, and I couldn't make my turn just yet. The truck got closer. I could see that the driver was wearing a green cap.

That's when I stuffed it into first gear, leaned hard right, and turned it on all the way. I shot across the lane and into the curb. I bounced twice, and then me and the bike came to an almost graceful stop among the shrubs around a house that was owned by some real nice people. The dump truck hit the ice going about forty, with all its brakes locked up tight. It went over sideways to the right, in a weird kind of slow motion. And then it began spinning down the road real fast. It was like it picked up speed as it spun down the road losing its load as it went. It was carrying salt. The kind they put on the roads to get the ice off. Maybe that was why he was in such a hurry. I don't know because I didn't talk to the guy. The nice people in that house I was sort of parked at had seen the whole thing. And I was not only a hero, but a traumatized one. I got cocoa and a donut and didn't much care that I was missing a geology class. Putting you in geology classes was another one of the things that they did to try to get rid of draft dodgers. The next winter I moved much closer to the school. Much. In fact, I walked there a few days.

Now what happened there was that a combination of the winter weather riding parts of that last story, and the mention of trying to dodge the draft by identifying metamorphic and igneous formations at eight in the morning, well that put me in mind of another winter ride tale.

What happened was I got drafted. And one winter at Ft. Jackson, South Carolina, it snowed. It snows on Columbia, South Carolina about as often as Richard M. Nixon told the truth. The indigenous locals panicked. And then the army canceled itself and sent us all home. I was living off post, in a commune full of closet hippies in uniform, and I started home on my cycle. And I was the only thing in motion that knew what I was doing. There were fender bender wrecks about every half block. The roads were closing down because of traffic snarls. Now you got to understand that this was a South Carolina blizzard; it looked a lot like there was a thin sheet of paper all over the ground. And the locals were turning it into a destruction derby. And the municipal authorities' reaction was typical. They dispatched guys with pickup trucks full of sand who created mud hazards all over town. Honest, me and that motorcycle were the only things moving steady or safely in that whole damn city. All that passing through in the winter practice up north paid off.

Did it again. Writing about riding through the snow in South Carolina reminded me of another story about motorcycles and the army. There weren't very many motorcycles on Fort Jackson in 1969. Maybe a dozen. Probably not that many. Oddly, most of them belonged to officers. I got real friendly with one of them. An old major who was never going to make any more rank. Can't remember his name, but he had a 1956 BMW 500, and a real good attitude. He used to drink a bit. He used to do much of it with me. That was the first BMW I ever rode. He was a real nice guy, and he had a kind of bent sense of humor. One night, over a couple refreshments, he decided that saluting on a scooter was dangerous.

Earlier that year, he had asked for permission to shoot trainees before the Viet Cong had a chance. He convinced several of the other gentlemen officers who rode motorcycles about this saluting and safety thing, and they petitioned the commanding general for permission to not salute while in the saddle. The commanding general was a pretty weird guy in his own right. When, in a BBC interview, he was accused of slaughtering Vietnamese livestock, he replied that they were communist ducks. Anyway, he saw the wisdom in the safety argument that you ought not take your right hand off the throttle. But I doubt that there is a general in any army in the world that would give a subordinate permission to not salute.

So this highly decorated leader of men passed an edict that all motorcycle riders in uniform would henceforth salute left handed. I thought that was pretty communistic, but before I had a chance to voice that opinion, it got real funny. Officers, who had for years returned right hand salutes right handed, get badly confused when presented with a left handed salute, even an authorized one. Several of them dropped briefcases and so forth in order to match us with their left hand. We began riding by the PX a lot just to watch them drop packages. Others among them went for sort of a half salute with each hand. One brand new little second lieutenant damn near beat himself to death out in front of post headquarters one morning.

And yet another riding in uniform story comes to mind! Those who suspected senility were wrong! The M.P.s, like good cops everywhere, had it in for bikers. I think it was made even worse because most of the riders on Ft. Jackson were officers, and it must make an enlisted man's heart soar and sing to bust an officer. Fort Jackson has some roads on it that should be ridden. Empty, tempting roads that you almost need to ride hard and fast. Unfortunately, most of them had a speed limit of 35, maybe 45.

Well, I found myself pulled over to the side of such a road one late night. I was about half drunk, and the M.P., angry that I wasn't an officer, decided I was doing over a hundred. I don't think so; last time I looked, the speedometer said ninety. Anyway, he was explaining how much time I was going to do for this one, when I took a pen and paper out of my pocket and began writing down his name. He flashed his light in my eyes and screamed at me. Asked what the hell I thought I was doing. Like I said, I was pretty drunk, and wasn't all that sure myself. But I asked him for his service number next. His eyes bugged out like a roadkilled gopher, sweat and veins popped out on his forehead. He spit all over me as he asked again what the hell was I doing. And I explained that I worked in the finance section, and I just wanted to make sure that he got his paycheck on time, and for the right amount, and all his appropriate allotments, and so forth. I thought he was going to hit me for a minute. Then he about faced and marched back to his squad jeep and drove off. Only time I ever got away with something like that in my life. And while I did not work in the finance section, I did know a guy who had before he shipped out. Apparently the M.P. figured that out. I led him on several merry chases through the night, never considering pulling over again. I found lots of places to hide. And then we, that's me and that major with the BMW, found a guy, who, for a case of beer and a bottle of Johnny Walker Black, put that M.P. on levy to Korea. Passed him right through.

CHAPTER NINE

********* Ghost Towns, Wondering,
        Questions, Answers,
and The Girl With The Paisley Paint
        Job *********

Once upon a time in the west, it was 1977, it was New Mexico, down around Tularosa, we encountered a ghost town. Well, it was more like a ghost village. There were maybe five or six buildings. All deserted, hanging open and empty, or fallen down completely. It was real authentic. Tumbleweeds rolling down the street. Cactus and a few cottonwoods. There was even a hitching rail and a water trough. Seems like we stopped so one of us could work on his bike a little. Maybe that was just the excuse we used to stop and play cowboys. We approached each other from opposite ends of the short block that was the town, and outdrew one another in mock gunfights. One of the guys I was with stepped into one of the buildings, it was more like four walls and a door, to relieve himself. And the damndest rattling, buzzing noise I ever heard erupted from inside the shell of a building. I never saw a man with his pants down around his ankles move that fast before. Never saw many people move that fast with their pants up around their waist. He said there must have been a hundred rattlesnakes in there. We believed him. None of us looked in the door to count them. We just believed him. And then we got out of town. Just passin' through.

I hit a snake one time in Texas. I have no idea what kind of snake it was. Like that bird up overhead on Red Mountain there on the Million Dollar Highway, the snake remains unidentified by specific species. Anyway the damn thing crawled right out in front of me real fast. And I hit it. And as I did it, I wondered about running over it and flinging it upward and having it bite me at seventy miles an hour. And who the hell would suck the poison out of my butt?

Sometimes you think about weird stuff like that out there in motion. Wondering while wandering. Like have you rode this road before? And wondering just exactly how much damage that concrete could do to a human body at high speed. And what ever happened to all those old Burma Shave signs? And that sure did look like a wallet laying there alongside the road. Or did that sign say Park and Ride or Park and Hide? And what the hell do you suppose they call that color? And what would be happening to you right now if you had never gotten on a bike to begin with? And about that first little German guy who invented the damn things in the very beginning. Or South of what Border? And what kind of animals were those? And wondering what ever became of that red haired girl down in Beaumont. And was that a fifty-three or a fifty-four Plymouth just went by? And what a sad, defeated look that guy in the station wagon with all the kids had on his face. And you wonder what kind of flowers those were. And have you ever heard two words in any language any sadder than She's Gone? And does anybody really care how far it is to the Wall Drug Store? And do you know anybody in Idaho you could crash with? Or which way is north? And how the hell did you ever live to tell about that mess on Red Mountain? And what did that sign say? And is it possible those pretty ladies in the convertible were smiling at you? Or can you make it through Charlotte before rush hour? Or why on earth did they name Muscle Shoals Muscle Shoals? And what the hell kind of birds were those? And how long would it take you to do the legendary Four Corners run from Key West to San Diego to Seattle to Bangor, Maine? And then back to Key West. And how do they fish that river? And what kind of animal looks like a tiny little sheep, only brown? And how much money would it cost to ride the Four Corners? Or what does it look like around here in the fall? And how much longer can you stay gone on the forty-one dollars in your pocket? And why wasn't she listening when you tried to tell her how much you loved her? And what the hell did she mean with that too old and ugly to take out in public comment? And have you rode this road before?

In Miami, in 1974, I figured out that part about why I needed to ride a motorcycle. Involved alcohol and drugs and having to pull over to the side of the road in the night for a few hours to get it all back into order and perspective. Turns out it has to do with nomads, and probably horses. Somewhere back in my genetic ancestry, there was a wanderer. And I got it. Gypsy genes. Nomad racial memories. Pirate DNA. Explorer-Crusader-Cowboy-Migrant crossbreeding. It all came to me there beside the highway. I mean I didn't grow up around scooters. Wasn't like I had a heroic Uncle Rapid Ray, or a Harley freak older brother. Sure as hell wasn't early peer pressure. Scootertrash are outcasts even in high school. Nope, it's genetic. Some of us just belong to total up the milepost signs. Need to run wild and free. We can't help it. Ain't our fault.

Seems like I said I was going to tell a Jawa story. This is as good a time as any I guess. And it's a short, sad story. Jawas were real hot on the dirt tracks for awhile, some guys were winning enduro races with them too. This was back in the early and middle sixties probably. I have to digress to tell a dirt track story. It's even shorter and sadder than the Jawa story.

It was a hot Saturday night in July at the dirt track. I was there with a date, I can't remember her name. I do recall the beehive hairdo and helmet problem. The boys from the Bultaco shop where I had gotten my bike were there, and had been doing real well all night. And then the guy who was riding for them, the son of the owner of the shop, got tangled up with another bike and broke his foot. I was close, so I helped carry him into the pits, and drag his bike off the track.

That was when his daddy asked would I take their 360 Pursang out in the last heat. Told me I didn't have to race or anything, he just wanted to get his dealership's advertising out there on the track again. And his kid's jacket with the Bultaco ads on the back would fit me. Again, for the uninitiated and young, a Bultaco Pursang was hotter than that BSA Victor I told you about back at the beginning of this. These things would stand straight up on the back wheel and then launch themselves skyward if you weren't careful. And dirt track racing is real easy; turn it on and lean left, no brakes, steel plate on your left boot.

Somewhere, along about the third lap, I found myself leading the pack. No, I don't know why or how, but there I was in the lead. I managed to get right in front of the grandstand before I dropped it. No, I don't know how, or why, although I suspect I was trying to glance into the bleachers to see if my date was being appropriately impressed. Anyway, I just fell down. Unassisted. And about nine bikes ran over me on their way through the straight away. In front of my date.

But back to the Jawa story. It was the summer between high school and college, and I was riding through northern Indiana on one of those Bultacos. I had stopped someplace for something, I don't remember where or what. But I was away from my bike, and when I started back toward it, there were two guys walking around it, pointing and talking in a language other than English. As I walked up, they turned and smiled at me. They both had on the same suit. The same one the Russian hockey team coaches all wear at the Olympics, cheap and black and shiny. One was bald, the other had coarse black hair combed severely straight back. They both had white shirts, plain black shiny ties, and matching brogan shoes. And they both had gold tie tacks that looked like Jawa motorcycles. I always think of them as Boris Badinoff and Vladimir Dracula. They both smelled faintly of garlic and foreign tobacco. Really scary commie stuff back in 1964. In Indiana.

Neither of them had much English. Hell, between them they didn't have much English. But their English was superior to my Hungarian, so we spoke in bad English. They were representatives of the Jawa Motorcycle Company. And Jawa, breaking a long tradition, had decided to make and market a road bike. I have trouble with numbers, even in English, but I think the machine was supposed to be about a 450 or 500 cc. We talked windscreens and saddlebags as best we could. They were real impressed that I was out moving around as far as I was on a small bike.

They offered me a job. Wanted to give me one of their new road bikes, and just sort of turn me loose on it. The Perfect Job. They would supply the scooter and maintenance and repairs and insurance on it. I had to buy my own gas and food and lodging. Change my own oil. They just wanted me to go ride this prototype for them and report to them about it. That was part of the deal. I had to make monthly accounts, tell them how many miles I had put on it, gas consumption, performance, etc. And after a period of time which I couldn't determine, again those troublesome numbers, my job was done and I got to keep the bike.

Pretty sweet deal for an eighteen year old kid, huh? I wanted to do it so bad I could taste it. Unfortunately the taste of being drafted was much stronger, and I had to decline their kind offer in favor of going off to college to get a draft deferment. Told you it was a sad story. The epilogue is sad too. I got drafted right after I graduated from college. Damn near in the same ceremony.

Only other time something like that came around, I also had to pass on it. I was in Coconut Grove, out in my friends' front yard washing my bike in the hot sunshine, when a shiny new Cadillac swept up to the curb, and came to a halt. Then, from the back seat, exploded a Cuban guy wearing one of those guayabera shirts, enough gold chains to anchor a boat, and a big Panama hat. Carlos Suarez, he announced himself as he shook my hand. He was looking at me funny. All I was wearing was a pair of cutoffs, and it was hot and I was sweating hard, and he kept kind of looking at my body with too much interest. I stepped into the shade, nearer the porch where there was an axe, and asked him what he wanted.

The son of a bitch wanted to know how much I weighed. Kept on looking at me too. I've been the same size since about late puberty. Real skinny. I got drafted and discharged at the same weight. Got issued pants the same size I'm wearing. In fact, I am wearing those pants right now. I would put some weight on, but then I would have to pop for fifty or sixty bucks for a new wardrobe. Got married and divorced at the same weight. Got my high school diploma and my doctorate at the same weight. Figure to collect my first social security check at this weight if I live that long. I weigh about a hundred and twenty-five pounds. I'm about five ten, and I weigh about a hundred and a quarter, and I have a hell of a time finding a pair of pants. So I told him how much I weighed, moved over some closer to that axe, and asked him to quit looking at me like a sandwich.

He laughed like hell, in fact he got to coughing and his chauffeur got out of the car and pounded him on the back. When he caught his breath, he explained that he owned race horses and he was looking for a jockey. I said I thought most jockeys were about two foot shorter than me. He said they were, but weight was all that counted. Nobody ever measured a jockey before or after a race. He was talking real fast, and I suspected either a recent overdose of expresso coffee, or a cocaine habit. Carlos continued that he had several especially hard-to-handle horses in his stable, and he needed a strong man to ride them. He said I was obviously stronger than most midgets, and that a biker would make a natural jockey, and would I consider his offer? He had stopped looking at me like a cupcake, so I took his card and told him I'd think about it.

I thought about it. But by then, I had a regular job that let me have my summers off to ride. And, while I've been around horses a lot, I've never had a real good experience at a racetrack. Or around a junkie. So I put his card in my billfold, and every once in awhile I would take it out and play What If with myself. Kind of like I do with that prototype Jawa highway bike.

Every once in awhile I wonder about that girl on the Triumph with the paisley paint job too. Over the years I have seen a number of women riding their own cycles. There was a tiny little woman up in Michigan who used to ride a 450 Honda. She was so short that she had to jump off the damn thing when she stopped for a light, and stand beside it holding it up. She could no more have reached the ground with her little tiny feet than I could have touched the sky. But she rode that damn thing. When the light changed, she would stick it in gear and trot along beside it briefly and then jump back up into the saddle. I mean she rode the damn thing. Was another lady up there, a hooker, who rode a big Yamaha. She looked and dressed like a prostitute, and rode her cycle barefoot. Even in cold weather, she would have on her little halter and mini-skirt and be out there on her motorcycle, working, barefoot.

You run into more women riding their own bikes anymore than you used to. Seems like most contemporary women riders are riding with their husbands or boyfriends. Like the lady has a 500 and is out there with her old man on his 750 or 1100 or whatever. I mentioned that one of my women had her own scooter. She rode the hell out of a Honda and then later a Kawasaki. But I don't ever remember the two of us going out on the road together on two bikes.

That Kawasaki is a story all by itself. It has gone through three women owners. I think it's up north in a garage, sort of quietly rusting now, but it sure got rode some on its way there. A woman I have known for about forever said to me that she wanted to buy and ride her own motorcycle and I had to help her. Well, she's been a good friend longer than almost anyone else, so I jumped into that breach right away. Begged her not to do it first. I mean why the hell would she want a bike to begin with? Because she so admired the way I limped, and wanted to emulate that? I told her horror stories and showed her old scars and took her around to some other guys who did the same thing. We all explained to her all about the quarter ton of high speed iron and the quarter mile of cold concrete. But she was adamant. With or without my assistance, she was getting her own motorcycle.

We shopped around a lot. Finally we found the Kawasaki 440 LTD. It's a low slung model to begin with, and then it has a scooped out banana seat that sets you even lower. This is a little, short girl we're talking about here, and my first concern was that she get her feet on the ground. This Kaw let her flatfoot both sides, at the same time.

So we moved on to stage two, my second concern. I talked to the guy at the dealership, and he caught on right away. We pushed the bike out into a grassy field and gently laid it down. Told the girl to pick it up. Showed her how to crimp the front wheel and lock the front brake and get up underneath it with her knees bent, and lift. And damned if she didn't do it. I masked and muttered my disappointment, and the guy who wanted to sell her the bike asked me if she had ever rode anything before, and I told him other than behind me, no. Well, he wanted to sell her a motorcycle, but he didn't want her death on his head. In fact he even changed handlebars for her for free. The model she had been looking at had a sort of mock chopped, test tube Harley look to it, high apehanger bars.

He went back in the shop and came right back out with a little 185 Suzuki, and he and I spent the next several hours with her out in that field. She's a real smart person, and has better athletic skills and coordination than I had suspected. She rode her new Kaw 440 home by herself that afternoon. Put several thousand miles on it up and down the Atlantic shoreline of Florida, and then, a couple years later, she got tired of it and called to tell me she was selling it.

My woman was just about to use up a Honda 350 she had been riding, so I told her I'd buy her this 440 Kawasaki if she could sell the Honda. She found a kid with some money that day, and had the Kawasaki later that week. Then she put a few thousand miles on it around the interior of west central Florida over the next couple years. And then her knee went to hell and she got tired of it all, and sold it to a girlfriend of hers up north. That girl put another few thousand miles on it around northwest Michigan, and then she got tired of it. Must be she doesn't know another woman who wants to ride for a couple years. She's still got it even though she doesn't ride it. Hell of a bike. If I live to get old and feeble (older and feebler?), that's the model I expect to move down to. Hell of a bike.

But back to that lady with the Triumph with the paisley paint job. It was somewhere in the mountains down around where Virginia and West Virginia and Kentucky and North Carolina and Tennessee all come together. It was a long time ago. Back when I started riding, about the only women who rode their own bikes were your screaming butch leather and chrome bull dyke lesbians. You just didn't see very many girls on their own scooters. Kind of like you don't run across many black bikers.

I've wondered about that. There used to be a black bike club/gang in most major cities. I mean there was a bunch of brothers on their over-dressed Harleys in Detroit, and in St. Louis, and in Los Angeles, and so forth. They never went very far, singularly or in a group, but they had bikes. There was a pretty sizable crowd of African-American bikers in Wheeling, West Virginia for awhile. But, as a rule, black folks don't ride motorcycles. And I have always wondered why.

I mean I understand why there are very few black tennis players, or polo players, or golfers, or swimmers, or sailboat racers. It's a money thing. But motorcycles aren't a rich boy thing at all. When I was in Ann Arbor going to grad school, there was a bunch of black guys on bikes. They weren't an official club with jackets, or a gang with colors, but they were sort of semi-organized. I hung out with them a lot, rode with them some, got to be good friends with a couple of them. They called me the Omega Man, and even got me a couple of patches with an Omega on them. Made me sew them on the back pocket of my jeans. One of them, a boy named Norris who I was in several classes with, told me that it wasn't a comment on me being the last guy, or a statement about that Charlton Heston movie. No, it turns out the omega is the symbol for resistance.

Anyway, I talked to them a number of times about why there are so few black bikers. They had lots of opinions, beginning with theirs is not a mechanical sub-culture at all. Black folks don't, as a group, become mechanics, work on their own cars, pull the motor out of their Ford pickup truck and hang it from a tree limb out in the yard. They even went so far as to say that most brothers just ain't no good with tools. Norris thought it was a fear thing. He said most black folks are scared of high speed, especially when you are exposed like on a bike. Damn few African-Americans in any kind of races I know of, except on foot.

Another guy, he was called Fancy, said it was a fashion thing. Bloods like to look good, wear their finery, put on their ankle length leather coat with the fur collar, and their wide brim hat with feathers in the band, and their trousers with the knife edge crease, and their silk shirt and their fine shoes made of Spanish leather about as thin as a five dollar bill. And you can't do that on a bike. Another one of them, a great big guy named Tyrone, said it was an easy question and an easier answer. He said black men didn't ride motorcycles because black women would not ride on one. I believe he was a philosophy major. And I suspect he was right. You don't see many Jews on scooters either.

But this was about that girl with the paisley paint job on her Triumph. It was a mostly red and yellow paisley. It was a big Triumph Trident, that 750 triple that they made for awhile. One time, outside of L.A., I ran into a whole bunch of ladies on their bikes. The leader had the biggest bike, a Honda Dream. They were a club of some kind, and they were on a fieldtrip someplace, I think it involved shopping, and they were a combination of scared and disgusted by me, so I didn't get much of a chance to talk to them. But I suspect they had a fieldtrip ride like that once a month. They sure were dressed for it. Pink helmets and a whole lot of patent leather. They probably went as far as twenty miles on some of their rides. Used to see a lot of that. People, men and women, black and white, used to get a bike and then spend all their time washing and polishing it, and then ride it to a local drive-in restaurant, or to a nearby bar, or back to the shop, and then park it. Used to be you could hunt hard and find a bike that was maybe five or six years old and had three thousand miles on it. Never left the neighborhood. You don't encounter that behavior much anymore. I guess maybe The Varsity Drive-In, or Jolene's Bar and Grill, or the A & W, or their equivalent, in every town in America have become extinct and replaced by plazamalls and McFood and fern bars.

That girl on the Triumph was beautiful. And, based on the way she smiled at me, she was straight too. Never had a lesbian smile at me like that. Neil Young sings a song about a blonde on a Harley-Davidson with the wind blowing in her hair. I think maybe Neil ran across this lady on the Triumph. But he couldn't rhyme desert island with Triumph. Actually I guess it was a meter, not a rhyme, he needed. Anyway, she had long blonde hair blowing out behind from under her helmet, and long legs that reached all the way to the highway pegs, and her gear tied up behind her, an out of state license plate.

Used to be you'd see other longriders out on the road. Anymore, damn near everybody you encounter on a bike is local to that area. Check the plates. And, I've noticed another weird phenomenon that seems to be growing in popularity. A lot of people are trailering their bikes across country, and then unloading them and riding them around in one spot for awhile. Living in Florida, I get to see a lot of that. Often, if I get on an expressway, I see more bikes on trailers than on the road. One time, out in California, I had a guy who had obviously trailered his bike out there, look at my Florida license plate and say to me, "Goddamn! You RIDE that thing all the way out here?" I told him I had flown out on the airplane and had the scooter UPSed to myself in Chico.

The beautiful lady on the Triumph Trident with the paisley paint job, blew out around me on a two-lane, seems like it was around Clinch Mountain. I'd been watching her in my mirrors for some time and several miles. She was even pretty in my mirrors. She had come up behind me, and then sort of settled in back there. Solo riders are apt to join one another out there. Or a single rider might drop in behind several others and stay with them awhile. It was obvious she was a woman right away, even in my mirrors at high speed. Women set their ride different than men. I don't mean all women set their scooters the same way. Nor do all men. But you can tell. Sometimes, with helmets and jackets and all, it's the only way you can tell.

One time I was heading back up to Michigan, and around the Ohio line, another rider got on the interstate behind me and then dropped in and stayed there. Took me about a mile before I recognized him. I knew who it was by the way he set his scooter. It was a guy I knew who had just incidentally gotten on the road behind me. Actually, I never really liked him a whole lot. Didn't think much of the way he treated his woman, and he set his ride all wrong. But, I slowed down and motioned him up beside me. We exchanged greetings, determined we were going the same place, and rode on up the road together. When we got to where we were going, he said he knew it was me way before I waved him up beside me. Said he could tell it was me by the way I rode my ride, the way I set it.

One time, out between Big Oak Flat and Chinese Camp, California, three of us were sitting beside the road waiting for another guy to show up. There wasn't a specific, designated meeting place. We just said we'd encounter one another on that road someplace. He was riding east, out of San Francisco to meet us and escort us back into The City to a garage he had arranged to hide our bikes in while we were there. The road through that part of California is full of bikes. The Sierra Nevada and Yosemite and Lake Tahoe and Truckee are one way; the Valley and the Bay and The City and the Pacific Ocean and the coast road are all in the other direction. Hell of a road for bikes. And there must have been a hundred of them blow by us. And when Fast Eddie appeared in the distance, we all stood in unison. He was way too far off for any of us to have seen any colors, or recognized him by his helmet or jacket, or to have been able to tell what kind of bike it was. But we could see the way he rode his ride, even at a great distance, and we recognized him immediately.

Charlie Simms, I got to tell you some Charlie Simms stories, once got behind a bunch of us out on the road, he was driving his van, and identified all five riders, each one by name, way before he got up to us. His wife verified this, and Mildred never told a lie in her whole life.

But this is the story about that beautiful lady rolling past me on her Triumph up by Clinch Mountain. Ernie, remember my pardner Ernie, does a banjo piece called "Clinch Mountain Backstep." It always puts me in mind of the pretty girl on that paisley cycle. Took a backstep myself that day she rode by all smiles and dimples and blonde hair in the wind.

Charlie Simms had a BMW dealership in the area of Michigan they call The Thumb, for obvious reasons. His shop was in a tiny little town far, far from anything else except sugar beet fields. And people came from Chicago and farther to get Charlie to work on their motorcycles. I had heard stories about this little shop up in the middle of nowhere for years. Word of a guy like Charlie gets around. So me and another guy took a ride up there one day. It was the classic Mom and Pop scooter shop. Mom handled parts and inventories and the money; Pop handled working on bikes. There was always a pot of coffee on. Charlie was the kind of mechanic who wiped his tools off and put them back where they belonged when he was done with them. After our first visit, neither of us ever let anyone but Charlie touch our bikes. And we each bought a new bike from him a few years after our first visit.

A few years after I started hanging out with Charlie, I told him I would like to buy a bike from him. I'd about used Chuck right up, and was to where I needed a new ride. Charlie told me he had a pair of new, 1987 800s left, and that he would hold them for me and my pardner, the guy who fell off The Peaks of Otter. Told us he would cut us a deal. He did too. Then he told me he knew a guy who wanted a 750 engine, and would pay for it quite handsomely. Told me to take Chuck apart and sell the engine to this guy and part the rest of it out and I would do better that way than selling it whole. He was right again. And he let me take the engine out in his shop. He yelled instructions to me from across the room. About a week later, the boy who had paid handsomely for the engine called and wanted to pay handsomely for the transmission and rear end. Seems he'd blown his up. I gave the frame and carbs and headers and front end and damn near everything else to Charlie for letting me use his shop and tools and yelling instructions at me. Gave the seat to a friend of mine who had the worst seat I ever heard about. Damn thing was like an ironing board. Gave the tank to another boy. He had a late 1972 model with a small tank and was tired of being the guy who had to stop and get gas. Sold the fairing and bags to another boy who had a bike he kept in his garage and polished.

You kind of got adopted as much as became a customer when you started frequenting Charlie's place. I've eaten there a few times. And, if you paid attention, you learned something by being around him. I always learned something, and I always had a good time around him. I can't say that about many people.

One time he had a supply of a new product called Armor All, and he was trying real hard to sell some. A man we didn't know rode up and while shopping around in the dealership got to bitching about how high Charlie's prices were. They weren't, but the guy had ridden a long ways to bitch, so Charlie let him. Tried to sell the man a bottle of Armor All, and the guy didn't want any. So Charlie walked him outside to his bike and Armor Alled one of the guy's saddlebags. It was beautiful; it gleamed like new in the sunshine. By comparison, the other bag looked old and worn and mismatched. When the boy asked Charlie if he was going to do the other saddlebag for him, Charlie told him fuck no, and walked back inside. Yup, you got it again. The guy bought the Armor All. Charlie was as clever as that girl on the Triumph was pretty.

I used to know a woman who claimed that alcohol made her pregnant. I know what she means. Beautiful women make me stupid. So maybe it's just as well that girl with the paisley paint job blew on by me before I had a chance to be stupid. Like I said, she rode behind me for awhile, maybe twenty miles or so, and then she swung out into the passing lane and started around me. As she pulled up even to me, she turned and smiled. Some women got dimples that can do more damage than a gun. She stayed there, riding beside me, smiling at me for a couple minutes and a couple miles, and then she took off. It was an invitation. An ancient one.

Well, I didn't want to appear discourteous, so I gunned my ride to catch her. And ran out of gas as I wrapped the throttle on. Choked and coughed and sputtered and slowed down a lot. Oh, I had gas. I had to reach down and spin the petcock to open my reserve. And in the time it took to open the fuel line and get back up to speed, she was gone. I looked for her for over an hour. Broke every speed limit in the area. And damn near ran out of gas for real. Guess she was just passing through.

CHAPTER TEN


```
********** Alligators,
     Famous People,
  The Perfect Job, and
 Desert Rats **********
```


Riding the rim ditch around Lake Okeechobee one time I came upon the biggest alligator I ever saw. And I've seen some good big gators. There used to be a place called the Lakeport Inn on the west shore of the lake. I say used to be because I imagine it's gone like most such places. Might could be it's still there, but I bet it ain't. Stopped there because there was a dog looked an awful lot like my dogs hanging around out front. Hell of a place. There must have been a couple hundred bass mounted on the wall there. I doubt any were under eight pounds. And there were stuffed bears and deer heads, and otter skins, and boar hogs mounted alongside rattlesnake skins eight feet long, and gar fish longer than that. Alligator skulls and ducks and quail and a few birds I had to ask for identification on. Some of those fish were a lot older than me, but it was a spectacular display. And the catfish special was outstanding. The waitress was also a classic. Rachell May Agnes Roberta. If there had been a crowd of locals ready to turn in unison, I suspect all wearing Zebco or Shakespeare hats, and frown at me, this woman would have saved me. But the place was empty, and I didn't need an avenging waitress.

Some down the road, after I had stopped at the reservation for cheap cigarettes, a smell came upon me out there by myself. Then I saw the buzzards. Lots of buzzards. Enough of them to indicate a large, dead animal. So I found a little trail, just barely fit to ride, and rode it until I came upon the biggest alligator I have ever seen. Also the ripest. It had been there long enough to bloat and turn a kind of slick purple color. I couldn't get close enough to pace off the length. The buzzards were too full and fat to get up and fly, and they just sort of hopped and flopped around. There was buzzard shit a foot deep everywhere. But from a distance, it looked like a sixteen or eighteen foot alligator. Big enough that, even dead, it scared me some.

Second biggest alligator I ever saw was south of there, down along the Tamiami Trail. Long time ago, real early seventies. Used to be Miami didn't extend nearly as far west as its present limits. Used to be the Everglades extended a lot farther east. Used to be a bar and grill called

Frog City out there in the Glades. If the place is still there, it's in the middle of Westwood Lakes or Sweetwater or some other nasty new suburb.

Anyway, I rolled into Frog City mid-morning one summer. Parked in the shade and went in to find the place deserted. I stood in the door a minute, and then a woman's voice came from the kitchen. Maybelle Joy Theresa Anne. Told me to help myself to some coffee, she was biscuit dough to her elbows and would be right with me. I got my coffee and told her to take her time, I didn't want anything to eat anyway, and coffee would be just fine.

A few minutes later, she stepped into the doorway, biscuit dough to her elbows, and said she was making a mess of pancakes, and if I would stick a dollar in the jukebox, she would feed me some of them and not charge me for it. Well, I might be funny looking, but I'm not dumb enough to pass up free food. I slammed four quarters in the jukebox and began punching buttons. Johnny Cash mostly. Some other similar stuff. When she came out with the pancakes and sat eating with me, she asked if I liked Cash, and I allowed as how I did.

Then she told me a story about growing up in Arkansas in the same little town as Johnny Cash and his family. Said her family and his spent most of a flood in the same tree together. Said they were real nice people. I got to hear a couple other Johnny Cash in his youth stories, thanked her for the pancakes and coffee and stories, left a dollar tip, and started for the door. Held it open for an elderly gentleman on his way into the restaurant. He was wearing one of those beautiful, multi-colored jackets the Seminoles make. The waitress, having no one to rescue me from, hollered at me to come back and meet this man. Erwin Rouse, fiddler extraordinairre, and the man who wrote "The Orange Blossom Special." I set down to another cup of coffee and some great stories, most of them centering around how they ripped his song off and he didn't get any money at all for it.

Later that day I found myself in a restaurant way over on the west side of the state. After a cup of coffee and some time telling my story about Erwin Rouse to the waitress, Betty Jo Bobbie Lee, I started to leave. Looked out the window and saw afternoon weather starting to boil up on the horizon. Asked the waitress, who hadn't been impressed a bit with my Erwin Rouse story, if she thought the rain was far off. She told me I'd be lucky to stay dry for much more than a couple miles and if I had good sense I'd set back down and drink some more coffee and wait it out. I ignored her and saddled up and headed out. And I was drenched before I got in high gear. And it was raining so hard I damn near hit the gator crossing the road. His chin was on one shoulder of the road and his tail was on the other. Seems like I'd have enough sense to listen to waitresses, don't it?

Old Erwin Rouse was the only famous person I ever ran across out there on the highway. Well, except for that Canadian who claimed descendency from the guy who said an ill wind blows nobody good. I did, however, encounter the guy with the Perfect Job. It was out in Oregon, in the middle of the state around Burns, in that high desert plains that looks like wherever it is in Italy that Clint Eastwood made all those spaghetti westerns. It was getting on late into the summer, and Labor Day was about to make itself known with insane traffic and I was kind of hurrying east to avoid it. I was setting in a little roadside rest area around Drinkwater Pass, making a pot of coffee. It was one of those places where you can hear things from about ten miles off, and I heard a BMW coming toward me from the west. As he rode by, he glanced into the little picnic area, saw me and waved. I had a cup of coffee in my hand and held it up in a salute. Then I heard him gear down, and then he turned around and came back. Rode right up to me and asked if I had another cup of that coffee.

I don't recall his name, but he was the Vetter Products representative for the eleven western states. Go get your Rand and McNally out. Everything from the Rocky Mountains to the Pacific Ocean. Everything from Canada to Mexico. He went from shop to shop, dealership to dealership, selling Vetter fairings and saddlebags and whatever the hell else old Craig invented to go on a motorcycle. And he pulled his route on a bike. In some of the most magnificent country to ride on earth. He told me he usually started up north, just before Labor Day, around Kalispell and Spokane, he was coming out of Spokane that day in fact, and worked his way south during the winter. Told me he would wind up down around Tucson and Yuma around New Years, and then head for San Diego and then up the coast. I remember asking him if he needed an assistant. He told me he would add my name to his list. I never heard from him, but it's probably just as well. Anymore it seems like old Craig Vetter spends more time writing for magazines and being a literary figure than he does passing through anyplace.

There is a road runs north out of Phoenix to Wickenburg, and then north, through more nothing than should be in one place, to I-40 up by Kingman. Out in the middle of all that nothing, and after the clusterfuck that Phoenix/ Mesa/ Scottsdale/ Tempe/ Glendale/ Peoria/ Sun City/ Chandler have become, a little more nothing is damn welcome, and there is a roadside rest area. Me and two other guys were setting out some of the middle of the day heat and sunshine there. Seems like we were on our way to Las Vegas. Ain't nothin' between Kingman and Vegas either. Anyway, we were sitting around a picnic table checking a map when this noise came upon us from behind us, from the desert. A tiny spot appeared off in the distance. It eventually became a little, tiny, really noisy 85 cc Suzuki, with an old desert rat riding it. He wore a construction hard hat, jeans, and denim jacket, t-shirt, and boots. The guy had a bedroll tied across his handlebars, a pack with his second pair of socks, and jeans and another shirt. A coffee pot and a frying pan sort of dangled off one side. A short pick axe and a collapsible shovel were tied on the back. He had a five gallon can strapped on each side of the bike. Water in one, gas in the other. He had come in out of the desert for water.

He didn't say a word to us. Didn't even nod when we greeted him. He did show us more contempt than I usually see, and bikers are shown a whole lot of contempt. It was real obvious that, in his eyes, we were sissies, pansies, weenies. All of us riding great big old monster highway machines, piled high with gear and clothes, wearing leathers and helmets, carrying a quart of water each. After he had filled his water can, he started his machine back up. Damn thing sounded like a train wreck. He stopped briefly as he got up to us on his way out. Looked at us hard and announced that he had taken the muffler off because it got clogged with sand, and he got better mileage without it. Glared at us hard, challenging one of us to disagree with his wisdom. One of the guys I was with said it sounded like a good idea to him. The old prospector kept looking at us hard. Then he spit on the ground, muttered something, gave us that defiant look again, like he hoped we would take offense and leap on our bikes to pursue him into the desert, where we would mire our bikes in the sand and then die for lack of water, and then he took off. Back out into the wasteland. Just passing through.

CHAPTER ELEVEN

*********** Heroic, yet Amusing Roadside
Repairs, Gospel Singing, Bar-B-Que,
Killer Tumbleweeds, Local Dialects,
and Signs,
misspelled and otherwise ***********

I mentioned back there somewhere about how you seldom get helped by a guy in a suit driving his Mercedes by you, or by a station wagon on its way to Little League. But sometimes you get to confuse them. Way back when Chuck was still a brand new machine, me and the guy who later killed that Basset hound found ourselves in Florida. We had spent a couple days with a friend down around Tampa, back when Tampa was kind of a sleepy little seaport town. Back when one of the best BMW shops around was in St. Petersburg. Back before you had to go all the way to Sarasota and pay big for parts, and everything else. Back when they were just building the causeway at the north end of Tampa Bay.

We were riding east, from the Gulf side over to the Atlantic shore. We came upon a guy in a suit with one of those giant huge Oldsmobiles they made in the early seventies. It was brand new, didn't have a thousand miles on it. And the guy was walking around it, sort of slapping the windows and occasionally kicking the car. As we pulled up, I noticed the car was running. The guy looked up at us as we stopped and looked at him. He was locked out of his car. Some kind of early idiotic automatic safety device had backfired, and he was locked out of his big assed Oldsmobile with the keys in the ignition. You could tell he wasn't used to talking to guys in denim and leather, but he was pretty desperate and asked if we could help him.

It was like we had been practicing it. I pulled a screwdriver out of my fairing, and the other guy got a length of stout wire from out of his saddlebag, and we approached the car together. The guy in the suit had walked around behind our bikes, to memorize our license plate numbers I think. He noticed that we were from Michigan, because when, about four seconds later, we had his car opened up, he said, eyes wide in astonishment, "Gawd damn! Y'all from Detroit?"

More than once I have stopped to help disabled drivers. It's funny. I don't think anyone has made one of those Sociopaths on Bikes movies in twenty years. I haven't read much about Hells Angels since they all got busted on international drug trafficking charges and Sonny Barger, president emeritus of the San Bernadino chapter, became a media favorite.

You just don't see stories about a gang of deranged, depraved psychosquirrels on bikes trashing remote little towns anymore. Maybe they're still doing it, but there isn't room in the paper to report it around all the urban gunfights, political evildoings, crack crimes, and third world disasters. But people still apparently have fears, trepidations, misgivings, and some hostile prejudices about bikers. Sometimes it's hard to help them.

A few years ago I came upon an old couple with a flat tire. They reminded me of my grandparents standing there beside their car, so I turned it around and went back. I wasn't in a hurry, and the old guy looked to be too damn old to be changing his own tires. I thought they were going to have simultaneous heart attacks when I pulled up and stopped. They sort of huddled together and clung to each other like scared puppies. I stood back and didn't make any menacing moves, and asked if I could help. They were damn near too upset to respond. Finally I told the guy to open his trunk and let me get to the jack and the spare. Told him to put his woman back in the car, and get in himself, and turn the air-conditioning on. It was about ninety-five. I stepped back to let him get to his trunk.

It was one of the fastest roadside tire changes I've ever been around. Pit crews would have been proud. I got him down off the jack, tossed it and his flat tire in the trunk, and was trying to tell them where to go to get the flat fixed when they drove off, damn near over my foot. Just passing through.

Anyway, I don't know why people react like that. I know I ain't the prettiest thing out there on the road, but when was the last time a guy in a suit stopped to help you? Or a van full of kids going to church?

This past summer I had an opportunity to amaze and amuse people with my roadside repair antics on two occasions. Both of them in Georgia, both of them heading back home, about a month apart. I swung onto I-75 around Marietta at about eight o'clock in the morning. It was really stupid. Right up there with believing that story about the goat eggs when I was a little kid. The interstate was wall-to-wall commuter gridlock. As I walked my bike to my place in the mess, I reached up to adjust my right mirror. And broke it off. I stuck it in my pocket and rode on slowly to the next exit, where I luckily found a Kawasaki shop. They weren't open yet, so I began my repair without them. I carved a big hole out of the plastic around the top of the mirror. Used my knife, a Bic lighter and a hot nail. Took the old stem out the hole. When the shop opened, I went in and asked if I could please buy a long ten millimeter bolt, and a nut and two big flat washers. I had the busted mirror in my hand, and the guy at the parts counter felt bad for me.

It was that Pity The Poor Old Burnout look I have come to recognize a lot lately, and he gave me the hardware, wouldn't take money. Then he and everybody else in the shop walked out to watch me. Most of them carried coffee and a donut. I finally got it all but back together; you have to use your imagination. I did. But the damn mirror pointed down, kind of at my knee. My audience, who had been both attentive and admiring so far, all asked how I planned to straighten that out. I got my by now cooled off nail back out, and jammed it under the mirror. The perfect shim. And the perfect pit stop. They gave me coffee and a donut. The traffic had cleared when I left the Kaw shop, an hour after I had pulled in.

The second one was at a rest area along I-75. This time I had truckers and the maintenance crew for an audience. My windshield came apart. It's affixed to the fairing with about four brass rivets at the center. Then it has another couple on each end. And the plastic had broken around the ones in the middle, and the windshield was laying down in my face and headed toward my lap. And, of course, it was raining. I had by now re-placed the broken mirror from the previous ride, so the nail was available for heating and making new holes in the plastic windshield. Then I tied the windshield down with a pair of bootlaces that I usually use to tie up packs. Had to stretch the laces over the fairing, across the headlight, and tie them down to the front fender brace. More imagination.

Speaking of churches, and I was back there somewhere, one time in very rural North Carolina, I got invited to church. Pretty funny, huh? And I accepted the kind invitation. Even funnier, probably. Happened at an African Methodist Episcopal kind of a church, on the banks of the Cape Fear River. Was of a Sunday morning. There was a little picnic pavilion thing beside the road, and I had pulled into it and made some coffee to go with the donuts I had scored down the road. Church was in session across the road. There were ancient pickup trucks, and even older, beat all to hell cars parked beside the building. There was even a big wagon with a team of mules with feed bags tied on them tethered under some trees. I saw a few faces in the windows turn and look across the road to where I was having breakfast. It was about the best singing I ever heard for free, and I was thoroughly enjoying myself there with fresh coffee, donuts, and gospel singing.

Then the church door opened and a little boy walked out. He was dressed up in his Sunday clothes, his white shirt damn near blinded me in the sunlight there. He paused, looked over at me, looked back at the faces in the church window, and then marched across the road and up to me.

"Please, sir, my name is Roosevelt, and I'd like to invite you across the road to attend services with us." I later found out that I was the first white man he had ever talked to. He was seven. Hell, I was the first white man many of those people had ever seen in person.

Roosevelt ate my last donut while I packed my gear away. Then I put him up behind me to ride across the road and park in the shade by the mules. We walked in the church together, Roosevelt holding my hand like I was a trophy. I was glad he was holding my hand. I was as nervous as the proverbial prostitute, and a lot more under-dressed.

They stopped their service to welcome me. I mean the preacher welcomed me from the pulpit, and the congregation came up and each one personally shook my hand, introduced themselves, tried to learn my name, and say how glad they were I could join them. I sat with Roosevelt in the back during the rest of the service. It was short, and I was mostly disappointed I wouldn't get to hear no more gospel singing.

The last prayer concluded, I jumped up to get gone. No, they weren't having any of that. I was invited, attendance mandatory, to the after church bar-b-que out back. The food was as good as the music. There was pork and goat, bar-b-qued by a culinary wizard, and enough other food to make me wish I hadn't eaten those donuts. And there was more gospel singing too. There were four girls and an old woman sang together prettier than the Staple Singers. "Just a Closer Walk With Thee," "Peace in the Valley," and "The Old Rugged Cross." I had a fine, fine time that day. Later, about mid-afternoon, I finally excused myself to be on my way. This was back when I said I could stay in motion for a whole day on twenty dollars. I slipped back into the church, and put a twenty in the collection plate. Figured I'd go home a day early. As I saddled up, little Roosevelt handed me a bag full of bar-b-qued goat to take with me. Just passing through.

Last summer I had another experience with a contemporary black youth. Like Roosevelt, this kid was about seven or so. Little bitty kid. He and some of his friends were standing around my ride when I came out of the Seven-Eleven store. I wasn't introduced, so I don't know for sure, but I bet the kid was named LaVelcro or Rasheed or Loufreakwea. I was at that exit of I-95 on the South Carolina-North Carolina line. The one where Pancho World, or South of the Border, or Overpriced Crap Is Us, or whatever the hell it is spreads out forever. As I opened my saddlebag and stuffed my overpriced, convenience store purchases in it, this little kid asked me what the saddlebag was. So I told him. Then he asked me what it was for. I told him it was for carrying stuff in like he just saw me do. He thought about that briefly, and then he said, "Sure is a ugly old motorcycle."

Well, he kind of had me, so I didn't try to argue or defend the beauty of my ride. I just laughed and got on and started my bike. That's when he went on to explain, "But you a ugly old white dude, too."

That bar-b-que part of that story reminded me of another story. This one happened in the Middle Keys somewhere down between Islamorada and Upper Matecumbe. I was fishing. I'd pulled off the highway and rode down to the base of the bridge, was fishing the pilings one morning. This was back when U.S. 1 was more than a real long, narrow parking lot, and there had been little traffic that morning. That's when I heard the Yamaha coming from the north. It was a brand new 650, and as it went by and then out onto the bridge, I saw the rider looking down at me hard and long. Then I heard him downshift onto the bridge, and he continued to stare at me as he slowed and turned around and rode back.

As he rode up and parked, I set my fishing pole down and moved closer to my bike. There was no need. I have never, ever, before or since, on tv or in real life, seen a bike packed or loaded as badly as that Yamaha. As the rider climbed off and walked up to me, all smiles, his hand out, introducing himself, I took stock of his ride. It was brand damn new. Still shiny and clean and all. So was his helmet. And he had shit piled up above his head behind him on it. He had the heavier stuff up top of his load. There must have been fifty pounds on the tailrack. He had crap dangling and hanging off the bike. Hell, he even had a bedroll tied across his tank in the way of everything.

He was surveying me and my load just every bit as thoroughly as I was checking him and his. I noted his Illinois plate, and he saw I was from Michigan.

"Hi, my name is Kenny, and I don't know what the hell I'm doing, and it looks to me like you do, so would you show me how to pack this damn thing, and how to stay alive?"

I laughed like crazy. He was about forty, some older than me at the time. I learned he had put fifteen years in the navy, most of it as a diver, and then got out to make some of that great money they were paying on the Alaska Pipeline for a couple years. Then he went home, with a pile of money, to Peoria, Illinois. Where he sat through the winter with his mom, talking about what he should do next. His mom told him to get a bike and get out and go see the country. I think she had been watching too many "And Then Came Bronson" tv shows. So he did. Bought a brand new leather and a big Yamaha, and loaded it badly and headed south soon's the snow melted in Peoria. I don't know how he ever got as far as he did.

We spent the next couple days together. I taught him about load distribution and keeping the weight down below and around his butt. He told me stories about diving in the Caribbean. I showed him how to pack his saddlebags. He told me stories about Alaska. I told him stories about rides to the coast. He showed me how to make a fire from coconut husks and grill mangrove snapper on a piece of chicken wire. I lectured on carrying extra clutch and throttle cables, and he dove around the pilings and scavenged enough snagged fishing gear to last me for years. I explained about getting away from your bike if you drop it, and I told him about the High Plains and riding in the rain, and about how you eventually go insane if they shut you down and make you set still. He told me the welds on the pipeline were all fucked up, and that there was going to be a major oil spill at Valdez when the ships started loading there. He also damn near killed me with some roadkill bar-b-que of some kind he concocted. We rode together a couple days, and then he headed out to Texas. He knew a woman in Amarillo. Just passing through.

Between the story about me feeling like a whore in church, and this more recent mention of Amarillo, I recalled the time I rode through there during a hooker convention of some kind. I never did figure it out. But there was a working girl every fifteen feet for six blocks through that town. I still don't know why. In my mind, there was a big rodeo there. That kind of thing happens more than you want it to when you're just passing through.

One time, in either Kansas or Colorado someplace, out there where it's flat enough to play pool, we got into one of these *Twilight Zone* episodes. We'd stopped in Dodge City and played tourist with ten thousand other people, and then got gone. Seems like we were riding old U.S. 50. I got some more U.S. 50 stories too. That's just one hell of a road for the most part. Goes from Washington, D.C. out to San Francisco. Anyway, the bitter northwind was pushing tumbleweeds across the road fast and thick. For the most part, you can pretty much dodge tumbleweeds, or when you can't avoid them you can take an angle and avert total disaster. So there we were, westbound, dodging tumbleweeds. There were three of us. The guy who had done that trick with the mountain and the grapevines back on the Blue Ridge was riding lead, like he should have been. The guy whose clutch was burning up in New York, who had put his woman on my bike the day I killed the woodchuck, was in the middle, in the easy chair, and I was riding drag, like I should have been. We were, all three of us, riding solo. We were going about sixty, maybe sixty-five. Maintaining a safe, tumbleweed dodging distance between the bikes. The tumbleweeds were, for the most part, about three feet across, about the size of really big beachballs. Occasionally a bigger one would blow through. They all came at us from right to left, across the road in the wind from the north.

Then they kind of organized there along the banks of the Arkansas River. I'm not sure how else to explain it. Like they all of a sudden had leadership. The guy in the middle took three direct hits all at once. For an instant I could barely see his bike for the mass of tumbleweeds. I saw him sort of wobble and slow down. So I slowed down and backed off away from it. They were great big tumbleweeds too, taller than a man setting a bike. Then, even though it seemed like the wind stopped entirely, and it got deadly calm and eerily quiet, another dozen of them attacked him from all directions. I mean they came at him from both sides, front, back and overhead. They stuck to him like Velcro. He was surrounded and overwhelmed, a rolling mass of tumbleweed stretching from shoulder to centerline. I saw the whole mess shudder, and was afraid he was going to drop it. I remember wondering if he even could lay it down, or if the damn things were holding him up. He later told me they had held him up.

Then, sort of in slow motion, a couple of the tumbleweeds kind of peeled off and went on their way, then another couple followed their lead, then a few more. A mile down the road, he was clean and clear of most of them. And, I might add, he was pulled over to the side of that road with the most baffled expression you can imagine on his face. He wouldn't take his helmet off. The guy who was riding up front had finally looked in his mirrors, realized he'd lost us and come back. He wouldn't believe us about the Great Organized Tumbleweed Attack of 1977. And as he was laughing derisively at us there on the roadside, three smaller tumbleweeds hit him in his face. Just passing through, probably.

Later that same ride, the prairie dogs tried to do a similar number on us, but we were still scared, and pulled over and let them have it. There was another, comparable, yet more dangerous and deadly situation presented itself to me one time in West Virginia. It was down in one of those nasty little coal towns, down in the valley, where they get about an hour of sunlight every day and most of the people are named Hatfield or Shortridge or Seymore. The roads had been a mess all day that day. There was the usual disasters caused by the high speed trucks dragging dirty, half-slag coal, and losing portions of their load every mile or so. And then there was the added danger of the full moon and dead animals every other mile or so. Mostly hound dogs, deer and coon dogs, but some wildlife too. And I got behind a truck because it was not loaded with coal. I couldn't tell what he was carrying, but it wasn't falling out the back all over me in semi-liquid globs.

This was, typically, a long time ago. And I still don't know what he was hauling, even though I got to inspect it closely. It was either little tiny barrel hoops, or great big headlight rims. About a hundred of them dislodged from the load and came at me at great speed as the truck went around one of those tight curves. The air and the road were suddenly filled with metal circles. I caught one under my eye, and another one bounced off my helmet, and one centerpunched the headlight, and a couple others bounced off the front tire and the fairing and crash bars. I came to an abrupt and bad, skidding stop. Turns out two or three of the damn things were up under my tires too. I felt like the goalie in a really vicious game of Ring O Levio. Never did figure out what the hell those things were. Never trusted a truck that wasn't hauling nasty, half-slag coal to have a better load after that. Never did find a headlight in West Virginia.

Never would have found a decent restaurant in inland Canada if it hadn't been for Lizabeth. You can do OK along the coastlines where there is fresh seafood. But the answer, inland, it turns out, is to find the local Chinese establishment. Canadian food is bland. It's so bland that most of it is either white or clear. Closest they come to spicing food is that trick vinegar on their French fries thing. And the closest they get to adventurous is to once in awhile fry something. I swear they boil hamburgers up there. I learned a lot from Lizabeth, but the thing about the Chinese restaurants looms large as a major lesson. And the way you can tell if it is a good Chinese restaurant is the same way you can tell if it's a good bar-b-que place; you count the black people eating there, or leaving with take-out bags. Brothers might not ride many highway machines, but they sure know their way around good food.

One time up in Orland, California, I had a bar-b-que sandwich save my life. Me and Nancy and Zero had stopped on the way from Reno to the Pacific Coast, the hard way, to get something to eat, and look for a Springer Spaniel kennel there in Orland. Nancy was a professional dog trainer, and, like that time she wanted to see the ponies on Chincoteague, she wanted to visit this famous kennel in California. Well, it turned out that the place had gone out of business. It was of a Sunday, and the place we stopped at to eat should have closed down with the kennel. They had three kids working the off shift there. Average age was about fifteen. Zero had to go back into the kitchen and make his own malted milk because they didn't know how. He and Nancy got hamburgers. I opted for the bar-b-que plate. Bar-b-ques, like breakfasts, are real hard to screw up. And if you get a bad one, you can usually tell it. Hamburgers kind of scare me in unknown, foreign places. Food that you can get by hollering into a clown's face frightens me. Zero got two bites down, and then he looked at Nancy as she spit her first bite back on to her plate. They simultaneously figured out what had happened to that Springer Spaniel facility. The bar-b-que was mediocre, but I wasn't involved in any salmonella incidents.

As we rode away, Nancy reminded me about a Waffle House we had once gotten into which, like this restaurant, was being run by the Sunday replacement children. Seems the Waffle fiasco occurred in northeast Florida, up there by Painters Hill or Hammock someplace. That time, the kids had a flaming waffle in the air like a frisbee, and a pretty deep puddle of orange juice around the counter.

But this was about weird stuff coming down upon me out on the road, not in restaurants. Been got to by mosquitoes a couple memorable times. Once was in someplace like Raton or Taos, someplace in the Sangre De Christos. They came upon us of an evening. We'd found a ridable dirt road off into the distance and set up a camp at a place where a little creek ran through some cottonwoods. Me and another guy were changing our oil, and made a mess of ourselves slapping the damn things. We were about to call it a draw, and pack up and head out. Couldn't find enough firewood to make enough smoke to do any good. That's when the birds came and began eating the mosquitoes. Honest. It was real Biblical, or at least Mormonesque. The birds were bullbats. I'm sure they have a real name, but I never learned what else to call them. Kind of like that eagle-hawk up there on the Million Dollar Highway, I just ain't no damn good at bird identification. They saved us that time.

One other time was in Nevada. Yeah, I get into mosquitoes in weird places. We had gotten east of Tahoe, it was evening again. And we were there where the Walker runs down to the Carson Valley Plain. And it got cold, and we pulled over to get at our jackets. We lost about a pint of blood each right there beside the road while we climbed into our leathers.

The other mosquito story happened down in the Everglades. They got them a little tiny, but really aggressive breed called a salt marsh mosquito down there. As Nancy climbed off the bike, I looked at her and couldn't see her face for the bugs. We rode for an hour at high speed and with great haste before she would even talk about stopping.

Got into a mess of love bugs one time in the middle part of Florida. I mean a mess, too. Me and the bike looked like black Chia Pets. And I was assaulted by killer grasshoppers in Oklahoma one time, but they had an assist from the wind. And we were set upon by butterflies one time down along Big Sur. Fortunately, we were in a scenic view area, looking at seals at the time. It was really pretty neat, butterflies covered the bikes for a little while. And one time down in south Texas, I must have gotten into a tarantula migration. Spent the better part of the day dodging spiders the size of my fist all over the damn road.

But bugs and barrel hoops aren't the only weird things that happen. Alligators ain't either. We got into a nasty crop dusting incident one time in Oklahoma. Nobody was positive what they were spraying exactly, and I guess it was long enough ago that if any of us were going to mutate bad, it would have happened by now. But that retard holding the hand-made sign telling traffic to roll up their "widnows" didn't do any of us a bit of good. Awhile back, mostly in the rest areas on I-75 south of Atlanta, someone went to a great deal of trouble and some expense to make a social comment, a statement of truth. In the bathrooms, at least in the men's rooms, they had put up very professional looking signs on the electric hot air hand dryer machines. Signs said, "For best results, wipe hands on pants."

Used to be that all longriders, and other bikers who had to leave their ride unattended, carried about four feet of heavy link chain and a giant padlock. I don't know if it ever did any good in terms of securing the bike. Only time I was sure I was glad I had it was the time I made a few menacing gestures with the chain and dissuaded a pack of dogs on the Jicarilla Apache Indian Reservation from eating me. That one qualifies as a weird experience all by itself. I had pulled over to mess with my carburetors. Damn float was sticking in one of them, and spilling gas all over my boot. I had a high-speed human torch fear, and had just drifted into a flat, shaded spot. I'd gotten the float loose and blew the jet out and put it all back together and was sitting there drinking a cup of coffee and carefully smoking a cigarette when the dogs appeared.

They didn't come frolicking up to me like a group of Cocker Spaniels. They didn't come up slow and dignified like a bunch of hounds. They appeared. One minute they weren't there, and the next they were. All around me. About six or eight of them. They didn't make a noise. No yapping. No tail wagging. There was no doubt as to their intention. That was when I peeled the chain off my pack and did my gladiator impression. Worked. At least long enough to saddle up and get back in motion. Just passing through, carefully.

Those dogs were a lot more intense and obvious about their goal than the bear we got into up north of Lake Superior that time. We had pulled over because we were cold and had to look for gloves and another shirt. It was August. And the ditches on the north side of the road were still full of snow. As you have by now figured out, I used to ride in Canada a lot. Always in the summer. And I don't recall ever taking my leather off. Anyway this was somewhere up there east of Thunder Bay. And we had found our extra clothes, and were enjoying a hot cup of coffee and some Oreo cookies there at the roadside picnic table in the thin morning sunshine when the bear showed up. He did not appear suddenly. He made enough noise to alert us a long time before we could see him in the dense forest around us. Damn thing made more noise than Cub Scouts. We knew it was a bear right away, so we began picking up our stuff and hastily packing it back on the bikes. When I grabbed the package of Oreo cookies, he growled. I looked over at him. By now he was about twenty yards away, close enough for eye-contact. I reached the same conclusion as my pardner, at about the same time. He said to me as he climbed on his bike, "Tiger, I think he wants the Oreos." I set the cookies back down on the picnic table and backed the few steps to my bike. As we rode off, we could hear the bear munching our cookies.

Oreo cookies got me in trouble on Chincoteague Island too. That's where those wild ponies are. You see them on the tv about once a year when the local firemen round some of them up and swim them to the mainland. I guess they sell them after that. It's a media event. Anyway, it turns out that there is also a kid's book, called *Misty of Chincoteague*. And Nancy had read it as a kid, and damned if we weren't going to stop long enough to see if old Misty was hanging out. And she had, afterall, set with me down at Langtry waiting for the Judge Roy Bean Museum to open. And she had been an understanding companion for a lot of miles.

Well, there's a lady who takes your money at the entrance to the park there. It's a national wildlife reserve and a national seashore and probably a national pony refuge, so the feds charge you money. And the toll taking lady had seen women looking for Misty before. I think this is one of them kid books about horses that appeals to little girls mostly. And she was real nice to us. She had seen bikers before, and she knew we weren't going to park it and abandon everything while we took the nature hike and tour. And she told us that if we were going to see the ponies at all, we would see them in the parking lot. If they weren't there, we were to turn around and come right back, and she wouldn't charge us any money.

Well, they were in the parking lot. Probably twenty or so of them.

Good looking little horses. Which is strange, considering that most of their diet is made up of poison ivy. Many of them were milling around a sign telling the tourists not to feed them, that they were wild animals, big ones, and they could administer a vicious, wicked bite and/or kick. Well, Nancy petted them and played with them, and I got a couple of great pictures of her playing with Misty's offspring. Life was good. The girl was happy. When she got done playing with the ponies, she said she was going to the bathroom in the nearby building to wash the pony off her hands, and I should wait for her. So I did. Got my thermos out and poured me a coffee. Got my package of Oreo cookies out to have me a little snack.

And the goddamn ponies heard the cellophane crinkle on the cookie package. That's what started the stampede. Three of them broke off and attacked a little kid in a stroller whose mother had been feeding him strained carrots. They about licked that baby's face clean off. When his mother began screaming, one of the ponies began licking her face. Several others spotted a car with an open trunk. The guy was looking for more film. I was amazed that the trunk of a mid-sized conventional automobile could hold that many horse heads. They lined up like it was a feed trough. Ate everything in there but the spare tire.

But the main part of the herd had zeroed in on me and my Oreo cookies. I've been around animals, especially horses, a lot. And this was the worst scene I've been in since that inauspicious, freak stampede at the petting zoo in Kansas that time. It was, simply, a feeding frenzy. In retrospect, I don't blame them. I mean if my whole damn diet was made up of poison ivy, I'd kill somebody for an Oreo in a heartbeat. They had me surrounded faster than the police in Uvalde, Texas. They very nearly pushed me and the bike over. I began throwing Oreo cookies in the air, into the distance. It worked, and they dispersed in pursuit of the sweet little morsels. But not before a dozen or more tourists got photographs or videofilm of me being attacked by hoofed beasts. A few of them asked me to do it again.

By now Nancy had returned and was yelling at me for being a terminal idiot. She was right; I knew better. She handed me my helmet, smacked me on my shoulder two or three times, and suggested we get gone before we were held at fault and called upon to account for it. Like that petting zoo incident. As she climbed on the bike, I looked around and found a guy who had just parked his car and gotten out. New York plates. I handed him the Oreo package, crinkling the hell out of the cellophane as I did it. Told him to hold it, and got gone. The little bit I saw in my mirrors wasn't pretty at all. Some of the ponies had the guy down, and another group was chasing several people toward the ocean. The lady at the toll booth asked us what the hell was going on back in the parking lot. I think they had a Code Blue come in over the intercom. We claimed ignorance and innocence, then thanked her kindly when she refused our money. As we exited, Nancy leaned back over the pack and covered up the license plate. She used to do that a lot. But then she would hold me all night long afterward, too.

This is pretty weird. Like I said, the guys I used to ride with are all pretty much gone from my life now. So are the women. And I have no help recalling or reconstructing these stories by myself. Unassisted. And while I was trying to tell about the ponies, I thought about several other stories. A couple of them involve other mis-spelled signs I've run across. One time, in a rainstorm, I pulled up to a place to eat. Seems like it was out in the Sand Hills, in Nebraska. Lights were on. I could see people in there. Couldn't tell what they were doing because the windows (or was that widnows?) were all condensed and fogged over. I rode up under the awning out front and parked. Climbed off and took my rainsuit off. Did it as a courtesy, so I wouldn't drip all over the restaurant. Took me five minutes to get my raingear off, wipe my face and glasses off, and turn to walk into the restaurant. And as I got to the door, I saw a hand through the condensation. It attached a sign to the door just at about my eye level. Sign said "Close."

Yeah, it took me awhile too. I kept wondering Close to what? And How close? Once I figured it out, I knew. Real close to getting their goddamn door kicked in. Don't know why the hell someone couldn't have stepped outside and simply told me that they were no longer open. Close. OK, just passing thru.

Other story came to mind was about the worst restaurant in the world, well, at least the Free World. It was in Texas, down along the borderline. And it was all my fault. Nancy had been in my ear for an hour about stopping to get something to eat. There are some long stretches of nothing out there, and she had already figured out them wide open spaces. And I hadn't taken advantage of the proximity to civilization when she told me to. And there we were. Someplace with no signs of habitation, very few wires in the air along the road. No neighbors. And the sign said it was a restaurant. Did it in good English too.

What it was was a double wide trailer. You walked in the front door and looked around and then looked back out to make sure the sign actually said it was a restaurant. What it was was a house. Roadrunner cartoons on the tv. Kids everywhere. A home. Wasn't a real clean one either. They sat you down at the kitchen table, moved a couple kids to do it. Then they asked you what you wanted to eat. Then they told you they didn't have that. I asked what they had, and after a quick inventory of the refrigerator, they told me we could have bacon and eggs. Tortillas. Good idea. Normally anyway. Worst food I have ever considered eating that I had to pay for. Nancy didn't even try. She did get up to go to the can. Came back almost immediately. I guess she was just passing through.

Now, here we go again. That part of that story about the Roadrunner cartoon on the tv, that reminded me of the Immaculate Coyote. Was three of us running east at night through Nevada. Interstate 80. There ain't much out there between Sparks and Winnemucca, and we were rolling hard, probably doing eighty and ninety. There was so little traffic that the three of us were running abreast of one another across both lanes. It was a real dark night, and riding up together like that lit things up better than riding behind one another.

The coyote broke from the left hand side, from the median. I was way over on the other side, on the far right. The damn thing ran in front of the first bike, the one on the far left. And then it went behind the second bike, the one in the middle. And then it came back up and went in front of me. Did it a whole lot faster than I was able to type it here. It didn't touch any of us, nor any of us it. Hell, it didn't break stride. And we damn near tangled up with one another, and almost had a multiple personal disaster and tragedy at eighty miles an hour in the Nevada night. I mean we came real close. Touched handlegrips. We stopped as soon as we could, and talked about it at some length. Decided sometimes other species are just passing through.

One time up in Montana, I had an eagle come right up beside me as I was riding out along a ridge up high in the mountains there. It was a female eagle. I have no idea how I know that. But I know that. She looked me right in the eye. Apparently I was in her sky.

And here we go again. That story about little Roosevelt and the church services in North Carolina, and the one about the worst restaurant ever, put me in mind of another story. And there are those who think they see signs of early senility. Hah!

That same trip back east through Texas, after I tried to kill Nancy with bad food in that trailer, I managed one of my genuinely classical moves. It's a gift really. Every woman I've ever lived with has commented on it. Not always favorably, but women don't understand such things, not really. I can find the all-night restaurant in any town in America. I can do it in a real short time usually. Depends on the size of the town. Takes longer in Duluth than it did in George, Washington. Took longer in Senneca, South Carolina than any other place on earth. Anyway, I've always been able to do this. It came in more than handy back when I was drinking. Still pays off when you roll into town at midnight, hungry.

However, all-night restaurants tend to be in neighborhoods where they put the Greyhound Bus Station, the Free Clinic, the Salvation Army Men's Shelter, and people named Slick and Toy and Big. Usually pretty good food though. Again, women tend not to fully appreciate this gift.

The other part of this skill, and this is a quote from one of them women, is my ability to "find the Nairobi exit on any expressway in North America." Like I said, it's a gift. The day that I tried to kill Nancy with bad food in a housetrailer almost in Mexico, we rolled into Houston real late, about midnight. From the south. And I got off to get gas. We were out of gas. It was time to look for shelter and food anyway, but I really needed gas.

I am one of the least racist people I know. I have lived around and with black folks, Mexicans, Orientals, Puerto Ricans, Jews, Cowboys, Indians, and Arabs. I was raised to respect everybody until they show me they don't warrant my respect. I remember being left in the care of most of the ethnic groups I just mentioned there when I was a kid. One way or another, I been the Only White Guy lots and lots of times. I've had army bunk mates, and cellmates, and room mates, and office mates, and friends, and pardners, and girlfriends, and wives of various racio-ethnic persuasions. I've been invited to and fed at Pete Isaac's mom's house, and Kenny Brown's mama's house, and Jorge Gonzalez's grandma's, and Jimmy Chow's wife will feed me the best damn egg foo young this side of Lizabeth's any time I show up there.

But the black folks in Houston didn't know any of that. Or the Mexicans in San Antonio that time I got lost when I realized the Alamo was in the middle of downtown, or the Blackfeet Indians that time in Cut Bank, or the Haitians and Jamaicans down in Belle Glade when my front tire went flat there, or them guys in kilts out on the Cape Breton Highlands that time I made the crack about the only thing I knew of that sounded worse than bagpipes was one bagpipe. All they know is what they see. A demented burned out ugly old white dude on a motorcycle.

Or so the women who I take to these places seem to think. But those ethnic and social minorities had me figured out the minute I rode in. Again, women tend not to appreciate this gift properly. Zero appreciated it in Indianola, Mississippi. And again in Kosciusko. It was appreciated and applauded that time in Indiana when I got the Amish or the Menonites or whoever they were to open their restaurant back up for us. And five or six other folks with me damn near formed a religion around me when I found a place that would cook our fish for us at midnight even though none of us could speak Spanish. Or that occasion in New Brunswick when I charmed the French talking children who were closing down the restaurant to trade us some food for some money. And then I had a small group of people proclaim me a genius there in Prince Edward Island when I found the All You Can Eat Supper that the Ladies of the Grange put on. And I drug a friend and two women into a place in South Carolina one time where we had the best flounder I've ever put in my mouth. And the Gullah talking black folks there pretty much stopped everything they were doing to watch us eat it. But women tend to look at the ambience and surroundings closer, or at least different. And not appreciate the gift.

Like that time in Houston. Like I said, it was midnight. And it was an all black neighborhood. A small crowd gathered to look at us. They didn't see many white people. You could tell. So could the girl. I nodded to a couple of the bloods, spoke to an older woman. Nancy stood there beside me. The crowd became medium sized. I filled my tank and then handed Nancy the money. She usually went in and paid for the gas while I was pumping it. And this time she looked at me like I had lost my mind and asked her to take flight and soar with the eagles out among the stars. I just smiled at her and started toward the store myself. She spoke my name softly, through grit teeth. I turned around and she took a step toward me. Told me in a whisper not to leave her out there by the bike alone. So I took her hand and we walked together in to pay for the gas. She asked me if I was afraid to leave the bike out there, unattended. Hell no.

And the reason is, and this is the part women don't get, that those brothers and sisters down in Houston, and the Indians in Montana, and the Iranians at the convenience stores, and the Rastas down in Miami, and most other ethnic minority groups, figure a lone white man amongst them, exposed and vulnerable on a motorcycle, is crazy. Stone mad. And many sub-cultures believe that the insane are holy people. Blood kin to the enchanted wind, heirs apparent to the stars in the sky. And they leave you alone pretty much. I think they even know that you can find the only all night restaurant.

By the time we got back to the bike there at the pumps in south Houston, there was a big crowd around it. I took Nancy's hand again and excused my way through to the bike. As we put our helmets on and saddled up, some of the armed-teenage-thug-gang members, kids who couldn't get a job, but they'd found a gun, got in front of the cycle. I smiled at them and said it was a damn good thing we wasn't going to choose up sides and play rednecks and niggers because I wouldn't know which side to be on. I got more laughs than Bob Hope ever got. The laughing crowd parted, and as we rode off, they all wished us well.

All except for Nancy. She never forgave me for that, not anymore than she did for that mess down above Big Bend, or that unfortunate episode involving the ceramic yard gnomes in Poison Springs, Arkansas. But I do recall she held on to me real tight after that event there at the Nairobi exit in Houston though.

That time we got gridlocked in Yellowstone, it almost resulted in another stampede. There were three of us, and we had somehow broke loose from the Winnebagos long enough to get into third gear. That's when we saw the moose standing in the river. It was real pretty. It was a young male. We pulled over and parked and walked about halfway down to the river to watch him. We were maybe twenty or thirty yards away from him. The moose looked at us like he'd seen it before and went on with his bottom of the river grazing. One of the guys decided he'd run back to the bikes and get a camera and record this scene. It was a spectacular scene, well worth recording. He turned to go and then just stood there. "Uh, guys..."

We turned just in time to avoid being run over by camera laden tourists. And I do mean run over too. Every damn one of them was at a high trot heading toward the river with fifty pounds of photography equipment. I've seldom seen people so intense. Several of them waded out into the river to get close ups of the moose, who was becoming as nervous as we were. They had us and the poor moose surrounded before we knew it. We broke and ran first. But I guess the moose was right behind us. He passed us on the way up the slope to our bikes. Damn moose hit the road at a gallop and kept going. We got as far as the little parking area where we had left out bikes. And the goddamn Winnebagos had us parked in. I mean we couldn't have gotten out of there if we'd been riding Schwinns. It was awful. But, we cleverly decided that we would just sit there awhile and cool off and let the Winnebago people go look for a bear to molest. So we did, for about twenty or thirty minutes. And we ran into all of them again about ten miles down the road. They were riding their brakes going uphill.

But I started out to tell you about how we all used to carry big, heavy chains and massive padlocks. If anyone ever tried to steal my bike, I don't know about it. But I have heard some horror stories. The very worst one happened over in Daytona, at Bike Week. If you've never been to Daytona for Bike Week, well, it's kind of like Sturgis with better weather. In a word, it's a mess. Only time in my life I have had other motorcycles make serious and repeated attempts on my life was in Daytona at Bike Week. Inland from town there is the racetrack. Friends of mine were down from Michigan and had ridden out to the races. They chained their bikes to a huge steel light pole out in the parking lot. Big, heavy chains. Giant, bulletproof locks. Then they went off to watch the races. And the thieves cut through the lamp post with an acetylene torch, lifted all the chains off the stump they left, and loaded the bikes on a truck. Got four bikes.

I knew a guy once who left his bike on the street in New York City, someplace near Central Park. He had a big chain and lock. Chained and locked his ride to a parking meter. Next morning he had a big chain and a big lock and a front wheel. They even took the axle. Another boy I know tells a story about leaving his ride on the street in Boston overnight, chained to the railing on a porch. They took his tank, seat, fairing, and one saddle bag. We wondered about that too.

Over the years and miles I have gotten to listen to a whole lot of different people talk different. Like in New York, for example. Most people in New York sound angry to me. I have a hell of a time understanding New York City dialects. Even real loud, the way they usually talk. Maybe that's why I had such a bad time that one time I tried to make it through The Big Apple on a bike. Couldn't understand a damn thing they yelled at me. Anyway, I have also gotten to listen to some of the prettiest talking people you can imagine.

A bunch of us set and listened to Apache being spoken for about an hour one time in Arizona. As best I was able to understand the answer to my questions, it was the Mescalero dialect. It's one of the prettiest sounding languages I've ever been permitted to listen to. It's real soft and easy, sounds like the wind through the sand and the cactus. I don't think you can holler in Apache. I suspect they would make lousy sports fans. Later that same ride, we were up on the Olympic Peninsula, and we got to listen to a bunch of those fish Indians from up there talking. Real pretty stuff. Sounded like water running over rocks. Sounded like the rush of water on the shore there.

I already told you about that time my friend imposed on me to translate for him after he had dropped his ride off the Peaks of Otter. And Asheville isn't one of those real hard to understand accents. But used to be, back when three or four or five of us rode together, that I had to do most of the talking and all the listening once we got south of the Ohio River.

There has been massive dialect leveling the past twenty-five or thirty years. Actually, I'm sure it's been going on since the Revolution, but I've noticed it a lot in the time I been on the road. Regional and local and social and ethnic dialects used to be much more prevalent and pronounced and obvious.

Like most current problems devastating our culture, tv and the after-industries it spawned are at the root of this one. And there were places in Kentucky and Louisiana and Georgia that, if you wasn't from around there, you might have some trouble understanding them. First time I was to the Outer Banks, I had a hell of a time with that Hoy Toider talk they got out there. First time I got into Boston, it was back in about 1973, I thought I had landed on a different planet. Took me about three days to figure out that when they called "Mack," they were hollering at me. Took me lots longer to figure out that trick thing about a "tonic" being a carbonated soft drink. Had a girl one time on Isle of Palms out beyond the harbor in Charleston, make reference to "all of all of y'all." There wasn't but three of us.

New Englanders really are terse and restrained. You have to ask four questions to find out if there is a place to get gas nearby. And two more to find out where. New England is the only place in the country I ever actually had any real serious trouble understanding people. And they, for the most part, found my speech to be pretty amusing too. Canadians are usually pretty funny too, eh? Had one of them in New Brunswick invited us to "go out cod jigging" with her. Way she said it made it sound dirty.

You get the same kind of local flavor and variety sometimes with signs. Like that ROLL UP YOUR WIDNOWS one. One time out in Montana, amidst the RANGE STOCK AT LARGE signs, we encountered one that said ROUGH BREAK. Yeah, that's what I figured. A social comment. A lamentation. Nope, it was a trick. The pavement dropped a fast foot right there at the county line. None of us was ready. ROUGH BREAK. Kind of like all those signs in Utah telling you that they ENFORCE THE GREEN RIVER ORDINANCE. I think I was told it had something to do with door-to-door soliciting, like specifically the prohibition thereof. But it bothered the hell out of me wondering if I was breaking some local law. WIND GUSTS was another of my favorite western signs. Did too.

Another increasing phenomenon I've noticed and been scared by is a tendency for every place in the whole country to repave roads with huge sections of that nasty damned grooved pavement. First time I ever saw the stuff, I figured the grooves were made by the finger nails of bikers trying to stay upright through it. It's damn near as dumb as those things they got sticking up out of pavement that look like half a helmet. You hit one of those at any kind of speed at all, and you're down and done. That deeply grooved and nasty serpentine pavement is about the worst kind of road surface you can encounter on a bike. Like those grate bridges, it reduces the amount of tire surface you got on the road by about half. You have just about half as much control of the bike too. North Carolina used to have signs with a picture of a guy on a funny looking motorcycle, and under the picture it said RAINGROOVES.

Georgia does it goofier than anyplace else. They have signs that say MOTORCYCLES USE CAUTION RIPPLES. Kind of like that one that told me CLOSE, ain't it? No, hell no, they didn't have any punctuation. I finally figured out that they were calling those nasty, ridiculous, ill-conceived, badly constructed, tortuous, motorcycle-killing, deeply gouged gorges in the pavement "Ripples." They ought to take the guy who came up with those signs out and shoot him. If they lined them up right, they could shoot the idiot in Michigan who decided to put up those preposterous, round, yellow smiley faces and frowny faces to indicate how bad the construction work was going to screw traffic up, with the same bullet. I wouldn't know how to use a caution ripple if I took a lesson and read a book. MOTORCYCLES USE CAUTION RIPPLES. At first, I thought it was the lyrics to a Grateful Dead song.

That ain't as dumb as it sounds. Ain't near as stupid as that sign. One time, someplace up in north Florida, me and Nancy were coming back down home from someplace, and we saw a sign on a kind of a marquee beside the road. Sign said, "Oh, what a long, strange trip it's been." We laughed like hell and sang another verse as we rolled by. And then we realized it was a retirement home. I've been back that way looking for it several times now.

Places in the middle south, in the mountains, you get signs telling you to beware of either FALLING ROCKS or FALLEN ROCKS. Damn near every other sign in New England tells you something is either historic or antique. Gets weird. Historic School Bus Stops. Antique K-Marts. Celebrated, Historic Construction Areas.

The past few years I have noticed an increasing and alarming phenomenon regarding signs. They're neither as plentiful nor as helpful as they used to be. Except on interstate expressways, where they overdo it. I encountered places last summer where someone went to great expense and effort to put up a whole lot of signs telling which civic minded local group was in charge of cleaning up that particular segment of highway. Well, I'm sure that's a noble effort, but I'd sooner know what road I'm on, and how far it is to Spivey's Corner, and what's the speed limit before the cop tells me.

Canadian black people don't sound a bit like black people. Many of the black folks in New England don't sound black either. It's weird. Like that time I ran into a huge group of Orientals at a little nothing truck stop out in Nevada. They were on a tour bus. And I expected them to bow and smile and take pictures and say shit like "flied lice." Wrong. They were from England. All of them named Trevor and Ian and Guy. They did not sound like they were supposed to. They laughed at me. Kind of like reaching on to the tray thinking you're getting a chocolate chip cookie and then you pop a cheese cracker in your mouth.

Me and Nancy ran into another tour group on a bus down in the Glades one time. We were stopped at the Micosooki Reservation, looking for deals on jackets and eating fry bread, when Le Bus arrived. Club Med French people. I've seen Eurotourists before. You get more than three Germans together and they begin marching and screaming at one another's children. Turns out the French aren't militant; they're just really rude and nasty. Don't smell much better than the Germans either. Real French people I mean. Them Cajuns down in Louisiana, and the French Canadians have always been real good to me, and to one another it looks like. But the busload of French in the swamp that time seemed organized and bent on making life miserable for the Indians. They had all learned how to say "too much" in very loud English. All them narrow set beady eyes and Charles DeGaulle noses. And they were way too serious to even think about laughing at me. So me and the girl got gone before hostilities escalated. Them Florida Indians don't push worth a damn. And their language, Lower Creek, is almost as pretty as Apache. Might be some kind of correlation there. Them Apaches didn't push real good either.

Down in New Mexico you get a funny thing goes on, at least linguistically. The folks down there, just like the ones in Texas and Arizona and southern California, refer to the people to their immediate south as Messicans. But they all manage to pronounce New Mexico with a crisp, clear sounding x. Actually, in west Texas they say Messcan rather than the usual Messican. Sort of like in parts of South Carolina they tend to say *neegra* rather than *nigra* the way you hear it in Georgia and Alabama.

Place names are funny too. Sevierville, Tennessee gets said like

Suhvervul, with the accent on the second syllable. New Madrid, Missouri puts the accent on the Mad. And then upriver some, Cairo, Illinois rhymes with the syrup rather than the city in Egypt. New Orleans and around there is full of this kind of thing. Arabi, across The River, has a long i sound. Metaire is said like Met a ree. My own favorite is Tchoupitoulas St. It runs into the Audubon Park and Zoo, and might be a part of the River Road, but I still can't say it. Maxwelton, West Virginia emphasizes the second syllable. Scipio, Nevada has a silent c. Charlotte, in North Carolina accents the first syllable. Charlotte, in Michigan emphasizes the second, heavily. And so does Forsythe, down in Georgia. In Pennsylvania, it's Lan-cast-er, slight emphasis on the middle syllable. Down in the Carolinas, it's Lank-a-ster, with lots of accent on the first syllable.

There are still some southern accents that are so thick it takes me a minute or two to catch on and keep up. But I had more trouble with it in Pox, Minnesota than I did in St. Elmo, Alabama. Garrison Keillor is right about those Minnesotans. But that road that runs from Pox on to Warroad and Baudette and Indus and on into International Falls, I think it's Highway 11, is a monster. Damn near froze to death on it, but it sure was pretty. Runs along the South Branch of the Two River, and then along the Rainy. Those people up there are real nice folks, but they talk like European immigrants, in the nineteen fifties, in black and white movies. And they can't even begin to cook meat rare, or make a dessert without putting miniature marshmallows in it. And, typically, they thought I talked funny. Kept asking me to wait a minute, and then going and getting more people, most of them named Helga and Sven and Arnold, to listen to me, and laugh.

There was a girl at a place in Lake Arthur, Louisiana talked so pretty I proposed to her. She laughed at me, too. Best I can tell you is she sounded like a real sexy version of Pepe LaPue. Girls from New Jersey are incapable of talking pretty. Most girls in Colorado look like they just got off three weeks of K.P. no matter what they sound like. Never did figure that one out. Think it has to do with the flannel shirts and boots. But the people in Colorado hate people from Texas. Texans hate Mexicans. Sort of like people in Michigan hate people from Ohio. People in Oregon hate Californians. People who live in Florida hate just about everybody else. I guess we all need someone to be better than. Or at least to talk better than.

I can't leave this like that. Poor finish. Instead of finishing with territorial hatred, I should have told the story about the Sikh dentist in Baton Rouge who took the stitches out of my friend's wisdom tooth removal after I was unable to do it with a pair of needle nose pliers and a knife. His English was better than either of ours, and he thought that thing with the pliers and knife was pretty funny, and wouldn't take any money for his work. Or I should tell about how a black family who ran a gas station in Rye, New Hampshire gave me a sweet potato pie because I sounded like home to them. Maybe I should have told about how a woman at the store in Edmonds, North Carolina made about six phone calls trying to figure out for me was I the crown prince or something.

A boy I know, an old, about half used-up Harley rider, tells a story about how a gang of wilding urban youth ran him off the road. They did it with a stolen car. They did it three times. The third time they knocked him down. Then they drove by and emptied an Uzi. Fortunately, wilding urban youth gangsters don't shoot much better than they read or write, and he took one in the leg and five in the bike. He was crawling out from under his bike, trying to get away in case it caught fire, when he saw the car turn around. His leg was done, so running wasn't an option. And then an old black woman came running toward him from her house. He was in front of her house. She was screaming at the kids to leave him alone, that he hadn't done anything to them, and to let him be now. The car kept on coming, and when the old woman saw one of the kids lean out the window with the gun, she flung herself across the guy's body on the ground to shield him. Not a shot got fired on the second pass. No matter where you're passing through, seems like somebody there will help you out if you really need help passing through.

Hell, maybe that's what this is all about.

CHAPTER TWELVE

```
*********** Motel Heartbreaks,
         Bad Breaks,
     Heroic Highway Efforts,
 Historic Longriders, Raccoons,
   and Chaingangs ************
```

One of the damndest things ever happened out on the road happened one night in Fort Worth. Two of us were headed west and had to do all of Texas, sideways. Dallas and Fort Worth were, like most urban sprawls, under constant construction. And it was real dark, and real late, and we had hit way too many giant potholes and pavement breaks. Apparently the highway authorities were saving money on signs and lights that year. So we got off and checked into a giant economy highway motel. It was one of those huge ones that are designed by the same folks who make rat mazes and prisons. And these places are usually populated by migrant, itinerant, poor people. We got two breaks right away. Our room's windows faced out toward the swimming pool. It was about midnight, and no one was in the pool. So we took the screen out of our window and went swimming awhile. Felt great.

The second break was that the Chinese restaurant was right across the parking lot, and it was open late. Because of my time with Lizabeth, I am always designated to score the Chinese food. So I did. We moved the coffee table over in front of the tv, and settled down to a Chinese picnic, and a real good movie on the tv. Seems like it was *An Officer and A Gentleman*. For awhile anyway. Suddenly, and I mean suddenly, it became a hard-core porno movie. We looked at one another like slow witted cartoon animals, then laughed and decided that they had just turned on their satellite dish or something. Then we settled back to finish our supper and watch people fuck.

That was when there was a knock at the door. A bold, loud knock. Didn't sound like cops knocking, but it had some authority behind it. Insurance salesman knocking maybe. Or Jehovah's Witness knocking. Anyway, we sprang into action, knocking bits of shrimp fried rice and lo mein about. As I recall, I grabbed my knife and the other guy got his gun out of his pack. But then I have always been prone to bringing a knife to a gunfight.

For those of you who think this may be overparanoid, it probably was. But not a lot. It was one o'clock in the morning. It was Fort Worth. It was at a giant, cheap motel on the interstate. I motioned to my friend that

I would open the door and get out of the way while he covered the doorway. When I jerked the door open, there was no one there. I stepped outside quickly to make sure the bikes were safe. They were. As I turned to go back into the motel room, I stepped on a piece of notebook paper that had been shoved under our door. It was a note. A long, well-written one.

I don't know where that paper is now. I kept it for years. A couple times every year, I would make a copy of it, and send it to the other guy who was there. Usually at Christmas and again at Valentine's Day. Weird note. Even for Ft. Worth in the dark of the night in a cheap highway motel. Basically, in pink ink with hearts instead of dots over the i's, it propositioned us. Both of us. Well, there was really nothing basic about the proposition. It was extended and graphic and very imaginative. The unsigned note said the author had seen us ride in and really liked what was seen. It continued that the author had never done anything like this before, but that the author had never seen anything that looked as good as us. This is hard to write without knowing the sex of the note writer. And we didn't. Still don't, sort of. The handwriting was no help at all. No signature. I read it to my pardner as he stood there in the doorway looking carefully around the parking lot.

When I finished reading, we began laughing. We didn't stop laughing for a long, long time. Weeks. Hell, years. Neither one of us had a clue as to the sex of the author. The note said for us to blink our lights a couple times if we were interested. We mutually agreed that this kind of thing seldom resulted in a night with Julia Roberts or Kim Bassinger. At least not in our lives. Maybe Roseanne, or Oprah. And neither of us was ready for a shrill scene with some motel parking lot faggot. Or a guy named Herb in a wig and heels. Or somebody stupid enough to think we were worth robbing, who was using sex as a clever ruse to get into our room and among our valuables and treasures. So we left the lights on. All night. Took turns sleeping. Got up and looked out on the cycles often. Kept the gun and the knife out.

We left the next morning early. Got packed and saddled up before the traffic got started. On the way out of the motel, a stunningly beautiful woman, who apparently had a room across from ours, smiled and shook her head and waved at us as we left. We damn near tangled bikes in the parking lot. I need to go into some detail here. I don't mean this girl was pretty. Julia Roberts and Kim Bassinger are pretty. This woman looked like Athena rising above the mist, Aphrodite beckoning the tide. Black hair hanging down over one of the cutest butts I've ever seen in a pair of short cutoffs. Big, huge, blue eyes. And a tiny little t-shirt that must have belonged to her little, less amply endowed, sister. Dancer's legs. She looked wistful as she waved us farewell. I guess I probably do too right now.

I just went back over some of this. Going to have to bust it up into sections somehow. Although I don't really see any clear patterns emerging for purposes of classifying and naming. Seems like all I wrote about so far had to do with bad restaurants and bad weather. That ain't been the case at all. If it had been, I might have had enough sense to get off the road a long time ago. Maybe. And I'm still at it.

Now what happened here, is I thought I was out of stories. Run dry. And I was considering making some shit up as I went along, and hoping my memory might kick back in eventually. And then, riding back from work today, I stopped at a stoplight out on the highway, put my foot down, right into a big puddle of oil, and damn near fell over sitting there. I watched a guy do just that one time. I was in Virginia, headed to the Chesapeake Bay Bridge Tunnel thing up to the Eastern Shore. He rolled up to a stoplight going through that megalopolis mess they've made of Norfolk and Portsmouth, on a big Suzuki, and put his foot down in the convenient oil slick, and then put the bike down. Unfortunately the cycle was in gear and he turned it on as he went over with it. It spun and bucked and jumped and sort of screwed itself out into the traffic sideways. It was a terrible mess.

I was behind him at the time. Didn't know the guy, but I had been riding with him through that urban nightmare, purely out of self-defense. Safety in numbers, especially in city traffic. I stopped for the light, carefully avoiding the puddle of oil there, put the stand down on my bike, shut it down, got off and went out to help him get his bike upright. It was still on its side doing donuts, and I had to pull a plug wire to stop it. We managed that in spite of all the help we got from motorists who had stopped to advise and pontificate. Many of them seemed to want to stand in the road and tell one another what had happened.

Well, the guy on the Suzuki got lucky. He had gotten away from the bike before it had a chance to do much damage to him. He was scraped and burned and bruised, but able to stand and walk. That might be another one of them Laws. If you can get up and walk away from it, it was a good wreck. Many of the vehicle drivers who had stopped admonished him not to get up, but to stay on the ground until the paramedics arrived. Yup, some concerned citizen had alerted the authorities. Anyway, the Suzuki rider had also gotten lucky in that his bike hadn't done any damage to anything but itself. And that's where he ran out of luck, but only briefly. His bike was a mess. The technical term for a motorcycle beat and banged and bent this bad is Fucked Up. Front wheel was out of round badly. Forks looked to be several inches shorter than when he had come to a stop there at the oil puddle. We agreed right away that he wasn't riding it anywhere. And he was in a hurry to get gone before the ambulance, police, fire trucks, paramedics, local tv news crews, and a parade of lawyers showed up.

That's when his luck kicked in again. A friend of his drove by in a pickup truck, recognized the guy, and turned around and came back to see could he help. Damn right. We recruited four of the guys who were standing around giving advice to one another and reviewing the wreck, and made them help us lift the bent Suzuki into the truck. I had to tell two or three others to either help or get the hell out of the way. The fallen rider thanked me as he lamely jumped into the truck with his bike and his friend. They sped away as I returned to my own bike and jumped on it and got gone myself. I don't think it took five minutes from the time the guy put his foot down in the oil until he was in the truck and leaving. I never did hear any sirens.

Got one other oil on the road story I ought to write down before I forget. Was in Wyoming. Three of us were eastbound and it had been a long, hot day. When the storm blew up, we were more than glad for the relief and to get off and look for cover. We found a sign saying there was a picnic area at the next exit, so that's where we got off. The guy riding lead got to the end of the exit ramp, got almost to the stop sign there, when he hit the oil. It had already begun raining just a little, and of course that made it worse. And he had both his brakes on when he hit it. That made it worse too. After that, I have no way to explain what happened next. He rolled into the oil slick going about two miles an hour. And he came out the other side of it going about forty. And then his bike leaped in the air a few feet, turned over upside down, and then it came down on him. I mean the damn thing beat him into the pavement. I was riding drag, and got the worst look at it. But from where I was, it looked surreal. Looked like one of those abstract cartoons where they do a lot of stop action and various speeds.

Me and the other guy pulled our bikes over, parked them, and walked out into the road where our friend was still under his bike. It was like we had practiced it. It's funny how you can get real business-like at times like these. It was like we had done it eight hours a day for a long time. We both got hold of the bike and lifted and set it upright. Then, while I pushed the bike off the road, the other guy picked our friend up and set him upright and sort of led and carried him off the road. He had a stunned look. He should have. We managed to get all three of us and all three of the bikes over to the covered picnic table at the rest area where we examined his wounds. Closest thing we had to antiseptic was tequila, so we poured some all over his road rash. He acted like it hurt real bad. His bike was fine. Tore a handlegrip all to hell, and scraped up the top of his windshield in a couple places. Leaked gas out all over his sleeping bag. Bad road rash and bruises, eventually some tequila burns, but no real damage. Except maybe psychically. We discussed it at some length, and no one even had a theory or a guess as to what happened or how. But we managed to pass through.

Sometimes you get real lucky. One morning, coming back east out of San Francisco on the Bay Bridge, I actually thwarted imminent disaster. Probably death. We'd gotten a late start out of The City, and the traffic was packed on the bridge. It's a double-decker. The one you saw so many pictures of when they had their recent earthquake. The eastbound part of the bridge is the underneath lanes. It's as much a tunnel hanging in the air as it is a bridge. About mid-way across, the traffic started slowing down, brake lights all atwinkle in the dim semi-darkness down there. And then individual cars started swapping lanes back and forth like they were jockeying for position at a rolling start. More brake lights. That's when I saw the old, shot to hell pickup truck, overloaded badly and dragging a trailer that was even more overloaded. I mean the rear bumper of the truck was damn near on the ground. So was the front end of the trailer. And the guy was trying to keep it up to speed and run with the local traffic. And he couldn't, and the trailer was swaying and swinging in and out of two lanes. Cars were dodging and stopping and making it a worse mess.

This is the part where I got clever. Read this carefully; it don't happen often. Unlike when the drunk broad ran over me in Michigan, and unlike when the old bitch in Florida decided to move into another time dimension, on this occasion I figured it out in time. I knew that guy was there for the express purpose of killing me, and I downshifted and blew out around him with great haste and at high speed as fast and hard as I could. The only place I wanted that whole mess was in my mirrors. And I put it there in a real hurry. The girl riding behind me said if I hadn't hollered "Shit!" good and loud as I downshifted, she'd have fallen off.

As I swung back into the right hand lane, and shifted up into high gear, I watched the guy lose it. In my mirrors rather than in my face. First he went sideways, then he went the other way sideways. Then he rolled it. I counted three revolutions, and about seven other cars involved with it, and then the trailer came up over the top of the truck and started my way, so I beat it out of there and quit counting. Best part of that one was that the woman with me understood what had happened, and knew that I had saved her life, manfully and cleverly, and thought I was a hero. Well for awhile anyway. All the way back east anyway. Just passing through, sometimes enchanted.

One other time I impressed the hell out of a woman by dodging weather for about three days. There was rain all around us, and I just kept jogging away from it, and back around it, and so forth, occasionally pulling over because I knew we were heading into it, and there was nothing could be done except to hide. We rode on a lot of wet pavement, and saw a lot of clouds and mudpuddles and rainbows that trip. Spent a lot of time setting still under cover too. I had promised her that I wouldn't get her wet. And I didn't. And she was grateful and impressed.

Once in awhile, you run into a sport, encounter a sub-culture that understands that you really are enchanted, a holy man. Once in awhile you get appreciated, you get applauded and rewarded. But most of the damn time, you wind up showing a woman Chincoteague Island, and finding the herd of ponies for her, and instead of being a superstar for that, you wind up being a bastard because of the Oreo-inspired pony stampede. Instead of being hailed as a hero for saving a woman's life on the Oakland Bay Bridge, you wind up being a son of a bitch because of that freak petting zoo incident, even though no one was badly hurt. Most of the time, instead of getting credit for finding Ocus Stanley, who got us up on Fisher's Mountain, so Nancy could hunt quartz crystals, instead of being rewarded for finding the damn post office in Poison Springs so she could mail seventeen pounds of rocks back home, you get blamed for that ill-fated situation with those damned ceramic yard gnomes. Instead of accolades and an ovation because of your standing as an enchanted holy man in certain communities, you get yelled at for finding the Nairobi exit off the interstate. But mostly, you're just passing through.

The same guy who said, "I think the bear wants the Oreo cookies," also once said to me, "Tiger, if the highway don't kill us outright, I don't believe we'll ever die." The occasion was that we were reviewing the scene of his fall from the Blue Ridge there at the Peaks of Otter. We were looking down at the time. The year he dropped it, he had carved his name and the date in a tree on the side of the road there where he had exited it.

And this is also the man who, rolling slow through Pahokee, down by Lake Okeechobee, one day when it was too cold to cut sugar cane, and we had an audience looking at us from every window and doorway and sidewalk in town, said, "Man, these people ain't even brothers. They're Africans."

I hope he's right about that dying thing. But in case he ain't, I want everybody who reads this to occasionally think a good thought about me, spin a prayer wheel, maybe sometimes even mention my name, after I am dead. Hell, maybe that's why I'm writing it. And, yes, it is my intention to die from too much living. What I really want when I die, is I want to haunt a highway. I'd really like to blow off a curve on the highside, going about eighty, and join the other fallen riders that way. And then haunt a highway. That time I set out a rainstorm with the devil, he just about promised me that.

Swamps. I have ridden in the Dismal Swamp, and I rode all through the Everglades. I've been in the Greenswamp and Corkscrew Swamp and Myakka, and I found the road in and out of Okeechobee, and I've ridden the Atchafalya more than once. That bridge out across the Atchafalya is real impressive. Great views. I like swamps. Get to see some tremulous things out there.

I was coming across Florida one time down along the Tamiami Trail. The ditches along the road were filled with egrets. They were massing for migration, or mating, or some other kind of egret thing. There were thousands of them. The mangrove trees along the canal by the road were full of them. The canal was full of them in the shallow places. The ditchbank was filled with egrets. I'm talking chuck damn full.

Those birds won't jump for a car, or even for a semi-truck. But they must not have seen many bikes, because I had them in the air in front of me for miles and miles. It was like an unending, huge, white, feathered wave lifting off along the road to my left, just in front of me as I went. It was beautiful. And I had forgotten all about it until I got to reminiscing about swamps. A bonus. Might be something to this organization thing after all. Watching thousands of egrets take wing along a thirty mile piece of road is a truly beautiful thing to be permitted to see. And an even better thing to be allowed to remember about passing through.

Mountains are, mostly, great places for motorcycles. All that going up and down kind of takes a toll on you and the scooter, but the curves are worth it. We once rode the Ridge of the Rockies for several days. It took us awhile to figure out how to do it, and we rode back and forth across the Continental Divide a number of times in the process. We started south from up around Logan Pass, up in north Montana by St. Mary. Rode U.S. 89 down to U.S. 287 and then down to Helena, and then to Butte, and then down to Idaho Falls and then over to the Hole at Jackson, Wyoming. And then back north to U.S. 287 again and then down to South Pass. That was about as far as it went on the maps we had, so we headed back up to Cody.

The Rockies are pretty scary. I mean they are so damn massive that you get to wondering if maybe the first guy who decided to cross them wasn't crazy. I'm certain the first guy who decided to build a road through them was. It just feels like a place you ought not be. But the Rocky Mountains are a fine ride. Sure get to see some awesome sights.

I got attacked, seriously, by a prairie dog one time in Wyoming. Seems I had parked on top of his hole there in the scenic turn out area. His hole was, cleverly, strategically, right beside the picnic table. So he could beg Oreo cookies and like that from the tourists. Saw marmots do the same thing one time out in California. Anyway, he wanted out of his hole the minute he heard the cellophane crinkle on the cookies. I was afraid he would gnaw through my rear tire trying to escape, so I pushed my bike off it. That's when he went for my foot. That's when I pushed the bike back over his hole.

The Ozarks are real pretty mountains. They aren't really mountains in the same sense the Rockies are. They're smaller and gentler and much more heavily forested. Like most eastern mountains, there is no snowline, no timberline. They're older. You can tell. The Ozarks are real distinctive mountains. The Cathedrals and the Cascades and the Bitterroot Mountains all seem like part of the Rockies to me. I imagine that folks in the west make a distinction, but the Sangre de Christos and the Sierra Nevadas are all just big western mountains in my mind. But that shot across the top of Arkansas along U.S. 62, across the bottom of the Ozark Plateau, is a real good mountain ride. And there are a whole lot of little two lane roads that run north and south off U.S. 62 that are a whole lot of fun. I doubt the highest mountain in the whole state is three thousand feet.

The tallest mountain over along the Blue Ridge there is Mt. Mitchell in North Carolina. It's under seven thousand feet a little. But those Rockies get up into double digits right away and then put you up at twelve and thirteen thousand feet. Big difference. Literally twice as high. Less air, and what there is is lots colder.

And, again, the difference isn't just elevation. Me and another boy come down out of the Berkshires one time way over in western Massachusetts, and we both decided it was twenty degrees warmer down off the mountain and in the town along the Deerfield River. I've had much the same thing happen in the mountains in North and South Carolina. Out west, in the Rockies, it's the same thing, only more. Like you have to stop going up the mountain to put on your leather and gloves. Then on the downside you have to pull over to take them off.

The Blue Ridge is in the Appalachian Mountains. Actually, I guess it is on the Appalachians, along the ridge, as the name implies. Parts of the Appalachian Trail parallel the Ridge. The bottom end of the Allegheny Mountains are some to the west of the top end of the Ridge, which is called the Skyline Drive. Starts up at Front Royal, Virginia. One guy dreamed up the idea of putting a road along the ridge like that. He must have been a hell of a man; it's a hell of a road. It really does run along the skyline. I can't remember the guy's name, but there is a monument to him somewhere along the Parkway. He saw the project through to completion as I recall. It's right up there with that Grand Coulee Dam across the Columbia as an engineering marvel. And a whole lot prettier to ride.

The Smoky Mountains, in Tennessee and North Carolina mostly, are, like the Ozarks, older mountains. They're pretty gentle, and there isn't much of them, again unlike western mountains. The highest mountain in the Smokies is Clingman's Dome, 6643 feet. But there are ways to put a whole bunch of eastern mountains together on a ride. Like across the Smokies to the Blue Ridge, and up the Ridge to some of those northeastern mountains. There are some medium mountains across the top of Georgia and Alabama too. I suspect they are parts of the Appalachian and Smoky Mountain Ranges. And the main problem is that most eastern mountains have some kind of park or something wrapped around them. And they get recreated to death. At least in the summer.

It seems the rest of America takes their vacations in the summer too. Most of them with three or four screaming, nasty, noisy, inconsiderate, whiny damn kids. I once had a ranger in the Smoky Mountain Park tell me that the week after Labor Day was the best, was the most beautiful, most peaceful time of the year on his job. I've heard maintenance workers up on the Blue Ridge say the same thing. And them ferry boat guys, who are all named Midjett, who run the boats out to the Outer Banks. Same thing with the beaches.

Same thing with the corn fields of Iowa and the wheat fields of Kansas. And I have still never been able to take to the road in September, or any other month with an R except April once in awhile. I have always felt sort of cheated by that. I don't know what the hell to do about it, but I sure would like to roll through a National Park, ANY National Park, unmolested by Winnebago traffic. It would be a real thrill to be able to ride along the ocean in Daytona, Panama City, Myrtle, Folly, Atlantic, Ocean City, or any other city with Beach at the end of it without fear of being run over by a convertible full of drunk white kids. And I would give money to be on the Ridge or the Trace by myself. I've managed that for an hour or so at a time both places, but I sure would like a whole day alone. And I would love to be able to see what autumn looks like. Anywhere.

Anyone who rides knows about coldspots. I've heard some riders call them deadspots. For reasons, usually explicable, but often pretty obscure, certain places along the road are real cold. There is one up in Michigan I used to encounter. Was along U.S. 23, along the Lake Huron shore. This is one of those things that Robert Pirsig meant when he wrote about how different driving a car is from riding a cycle. People in cars don't even know about these places. The one in Michigan got the better of us, and we did some research and found out that an underground river ran under the road there on its way to the lake. There is a place in Kentucky where a cave under the road causes the same effect. Had to go to the Department of Natural Resources to figure out that one in Michigan. Got lucky in Kentucky and a guy who worked for the power company and knew about the cave happened to be nearby to tell us about it. But most of the time you have no idea why. You just know that suddenly it's a lot colder, for no apparent reason.

You sometimes hit a spot like that in a swamp. Sometimes, at night, you see some weird lights and like that out in the swamps. Sometimes they turn out to be the eyes of animals reflected in your own lights. Different animals show different colors. One time in between Protection and Meade, Kansas, at the Clark State Fishing Lake, the raccoons came upon us in an organized manner. Three of us had ridden in there late in the afternoon. There was one big, empty picnic pavilion with probably a dozen picnic tables and a big fireplace in it. We rode the scooters right on in and parked. Each of us got our own picnic table to sleep on. We made a fire in the big fireplace and cooked supper. About dusk, three busloads of Baptist Sunday School children, on their annual evening weenie roast we presumed, drove up to the pavilion, took one look at us, and headed for the other end of the park. That's one of the good things about being on a bike. Most of the time the other happy campers are real happy to get away from you.

Anyway, we went to sleep early. It had been a long day, and the next one was going to be even longer. The noise woke us up around midnight. Lots of different noises. Sounded like cats with hormone problems, fighting. And it sounded like a bucket full of women with long fingernails trying to escape, and it sounded like guys fighting with swords and shields. We all woke up at once, and jumped up and bumped into one another in the dark, trying to decide which one was Curly, all of us scrambling around for weapons and flashlights and pants and boots. Finally one of the other guys turned on the headlight of his bike. The far end of the pavilion was suddenly illuminated. It was a weird sight. About a half dozen big, galvanized iron, industrial sized garbage cans were dancing. Don't know quite how else to explain it. Some of them were bouncing up and down. Others were rocking back and forth. Some were kind of slowly spinning. Looked like a damn Disney movie.

Having found weapons and boots, we slowly approached the animated trash containers there in the glow of the bike's headlight in the dark Kansas night. We got about six feet away when the first raccoon popped out. And I mean the rascal popped out. Ejected from the garbage can. That started the exodus. They came toward us. We all managed to yell, but only because men don't scream, and that scared them back the other way. They kept on coming out of the garbage cans for a long time. Lots of them. When we talked about it, shortly afterward, over generous portions of Jim Beam and a little cold coffee, we all agreed that it reminded us of when all the clowns would come out of that little tiny car at the circus when we were kids. Estimates ranged from thirty to seventy raccoons. But we were all pretty well drunk by the time we got around to such speculation.

Next day we rode into the Dalton Brothers Museum in Meade. Hell of a place. Obscure as hell, but typically real authentic. Place was full of old guns and saddles and the like. I think it was a half dollar admission, and then for an extra dime they'd let you go through the tunnel that was dug from the house to the stable so the Dalton Boys could make a fast escape if necessary.

It was a whole lot better and cheaper than the attractions up in Dodge City, where we had been the day before. Dodge was one of those places where you just didn't feel good about leaving your bike and all your gear unattended.

But the Dalton Museum was one of those wonderful places you find sometimes on the back roads. Not many tourists run through Meade apparently. But we did. Longriders visiting the scenes of other longriders.

Then we did it again at the Billy the Kid Museum down in Ft. Sumner, New Mexico a few days later. Again, there didn't seem to be too many people passing through there to visit his grave on their way out to Disneyland. But we did. More homage to another fallen rider. They buried him right there where Pat Garrett shot him. Seems like they took a dollar from each of us at that museum. And it was a good deal too. If you do it right, these are the kinds of things you get to see instead of the Smithsonian, or Gettysburg. Nobody in Meade or Ft. Sumner was going to mess with our motorcycles. Nor did I fear for my possessions down there in Tombstone while I stood among the graves of those old longriders. Hell, they still lynch horse thieves in those places. I expect they'd hang a man for stealing your ride. Ain't many places left that understand longriders. Or just passing through.

So instead of touring around Gettysburg, I got to ride real slow through the Chickamauga and Chatanooga Battlefields. Slow enough to know it was haunted. Some longriders in there too. Instead of the Lincoln Memorial, I got to visit the Patrick Henry National Monument just outside Brookneal, Virginia. Instead of the Empire State Building, I got to ride past the Hearst Castle.

Wasn't ever close enough to Old Faithful or Mount Rushmore to see much really, but I sat out a flash flood in the Roy Rogers Museum in southern California, and between Twenty-Nine Palms and Blythe, California I watched a roadrunner kill a rattlesnake. Never was able to get in to the Alamo, but I sat for a long time at that monument they put up to commemorate Geronimo's surrender. Left a feather there that I had picked up in Georgia. And I did find Chief Joseph's grave, and sat there awhile too. Left a flower there that I had picked down at the Geronimo Memorial. Now there was a couple of longriders. Both them boys knew all about the stories and fables and the true myths about the road. They knew about just passing through.

And I never have been to the Museum of Natural History there in Chicago. But I saw four muledeer come up out of the shallows of the Rio Grande on our left, and run in front of us, and then hit the straight up cliff on our right like velcro, and scale the damn thing before we got up to them. And I got to see a friend of mine come out of curve so hard his knee was nearly on the ground, only to find a real big steer in the road in front of him. He blew around that cow so sweet and clean that the poor animal evacuated right there in the road. I know, because I was behind him and I had to ride through it. Later that day we saw twin baby antelope, about an hour old.

I was afraid to get off my bike and abandon my gear there in Hannibal, Missouri. And I really wanted to see all that Mark Twain lore they got. Same deal with the Jack London home and museum out in Oakland. But I did get to ride through the covered bridge on the way up to Charlemont, Massachusetts before they tore it down. And I followed the trail of Daniel Boone awhile. And I rode the ferry boat at Bull Shoals, and the one at St. Genevieve before they built a bunch of bridges. And me and Zero came upon a ferry boat across the St. Johns River up around Palatka one time.

This is a whole short story. We were out wandering around sort of northward early one morning. And we saw an indication on a map that there was a toll ferry down a dirt road. Decided to find out. Several miles of real loose sand later, having never gotten out of second gear, we came upon a guy sitting parked in the shade on his road grader. Eating what I assume was breakfast, or a real early lunch. I rode up and stopped and shut the bike off and engaged the man in brief conversation. He wasn't real happy about having his authorized break disturbed. He wasn't real happy about anyone being on that road. I suspect he wasn't really doing his job, but I base that only on the fact that the road was like a long, deep sandbox. Was like trying to ride through sugar.

Anyway, I pressed on through his displeasure and asked him how far it was to the river, and he told me it was eight miles. Asked him how far it was back the way I had come from to the hard surface highway. Told me it was eight miles. He was smiling by now. Then I asked him was there a ferry boat down at the river. And he said sometimes. He was chuckling by the time we rolled out of his patch of shade and back into the sandpit roadway. Real glad I was able to bring some joy into an otherwise unhappy life. Then, when he saw us head east toward the river, he laughed like crazy.

Eight miles later, the ferry boat wasn't there. There was a guy in a pickup truck about half drunk. And a sign saying to flash your lights if you wanted the boat to come get you and carry you across. I asked the guy if he had been there long. About an hour. Asked if he had flashed his lights. He had. He said they knew he was over here, and probably as soon as Bubba Joe Junior Bob over there finished his breakfast, they'd come get us. And did we want a beer. Bubba Joe showed up about another hour later. It was obvious why. He was a big eater. The ferry was a fourteen foot jonboat, with an ancient fifteen horse Johnson outboard, strapped to four or five big oil drums with a good, stout piece of plywood on top for the deck. Had just exactly enough room for one pickup truck and one motorcycle. Stand by your bike and hold it up; no chocks, no cleats, no ropes. And no toll either. He wouldn't take our money. Said he had to come get the guy in the pickup truck anyway. He did let us buy him a beer on the other shore when we got there.

We were there awhile. Seems there was a chain gang road crew doing something up the road about a hundred yards from the ferry dock and ramp, which was four pvc pipes driven in the riverbed and another stout piece of plywood set up on concrete blocks. Nice guys, most of the prisoners working the road. We sat and chatted and smoked cigarettes with them for a couple hours before the walkin' boss got tired of his charges fraternizing with scootertrash, and made them clear a narrow strip so we could leave.

We passed through.

CHAPTER THIRTEEN

************* Charles Kuralt
and Personal Alternatives,
The Wall in My Office,
Boiled or Dry Roasted,
and Helpful Hints *************

J ust had another inspirational occurrence, contact from the muse. In this case that means I just remembered some more stories. Had help. Needed help. I have a U.S. map on a wall in my office at work. On it, I have outlined every long ride I've ever taken. That map looks like an eyeball on New Years Eve. Along the top of the map, I have a bunch of motorcycle license plates, a collection of mine going back to 1966. And on both sides of the map there are photographs, probably a hundred or more, of bikes and scenery. Pictures of Charlemagne, and Morgen, and RT. Pictures of other people and their bikes. Bikes named Donner, and Mule, and Gandolph, and Sherman, and Daisy, and Otto, and Reuben, and Casper, and Lefty, and Wally. Pictures from along both shorelines, and both borders too. Pictures in just about every mountain range you can name. Pictures in the desert, and in the snow, and along rivers. Pictures with Lizabeth and Nancy and a couple other girls. There is even an old black and white photo of me and a real pretty little girl whose name I don't recall on one of those old Bultacos. And pictures of guys I used to ride with. Photographs with cactus in the background, and photos with Redwood forests behind the bikes. Pictures, many of them yellowing with age, from just about every year since that first license plate.

Lizabeth or Nancy are in a lot of the pictures. When I reviewed it all, I developed a new sense of appreciation for how tough both of those girls were, for how much they must have thought of me to ride with me where they did. The pictures made me think about how good it felt to take them to new places and show them different things, like the Seven Mile Bridge in the bright sunshine and the desert in the spring. Made me remember how good it felt to have them up behind me, their arms around me, their voices in my helmet, their love on my side. Made me sad.

Down along the bottom border of the map, there are several things. There is a copy of Arlo Guthrie's "The Motorcycle Song." There is a copy of a newspaper article about that tape of epic motorcycle poetry that me and Cousin Doc did. There is a picture of a contemporary longrider on a Harley with a pony express rider sort of vaguely in the background. A velvet painting of Elvis, Jesus, and John Wayne walking into eternity together. Some old cowboy postcards. Some real old, historic BMW ads.

And there is a copy of an article that Charles Kuralt, one of my contemporary heros, wrote years ago. Charles travels a lot, or he used to anyway, and he had written a piece on the Most Beautiful Roads in America, twenty of them. He ought to know. He wrote about a road in Hawaii I'll likely never see and certainly never ride. And it seems like he mentioned the AlCan Highway, or a highway in Alaska. And I will probably never ride either of them. I've talked to a couple longriders who have, and it just don't sound or seem like a real good idea. But me and Mr. Kuralt agreed on a number of our other Top Twenty choices. He mentioned the Blue Ridge of course. It also seems like he included the Natchez Trace and the Outer Banks' Highway 12.

Most of his choices were in the west it seems. For example, he put in The Going To The Sun Highway up there in Glacier Park. I agree it's beautiful, it's majestic, but it sure seemed real short to me. And, because it's in a national park, the feds make you pay for it, and it's usually wall to wall Winnbagoes and other highly serious, professional recreators.

Seems like Kuralt also made mention of Highway 212 from Red Lodge, Montana, up through Beartooth Pass and down to West Yellowstone. He's right. It's beautiful. But Highway 12 out of Helena and then along the Musselshell east all the way to Vananda is lots longer, and just as pretty. Prettier. So is Highway 89 down out of Great Falls through Ringling and down into Yellowstone. I spent most of a day at a bar there in Ringling one time. The wind had been blowing so hard and steady from the west that I had scraped the chrome off the right crashbar leaning into it. That's true. Rode miles and miles at about a forty-five degree angle.

The truckers saved me from it. They were all getting off the road, and two of them guided me into a little bar and grill in Ringling. One of them waved me into a place to put my bike in the lee of the wind by the building. I bought them both a drink. They said if it was too windy to haul freight, it was too windy for a motorcycle. I stayed there until around midnight. The wind went down with the sun, around nine o'clock. Took me another little while to get sober enough to set on a bike. I think Jimmy Buffett wrote a song about this place.

Mr. Kuralt limited his choices to American roads. Very patriotic. I have to, in spite of weather and border hassles, include two Canadian roads on my list here. That ride around Lake Superior is at least half Canadian. Route 17, eh? And over in Nova Scotia, that ride around the Cape Breton Highlands, they call it the Cabot Trail, should be high on anybody's list. And while I'm at it here, the road up the east side of Nova Scotia, from Yarmouth to Wolfville, by way of Culloden and Port Lorne is a real fine ride. Not the new expressway, but the old road that goes right down along the water. You get to race the tide as it runs up the Bay of Fundy.

And it also seems like to me that Mr. Kuralt and I concurred about

West Coast Highways, too. I believe we both think Highway 1 from Monterey south down the coast to Morro Bay is a magnificent ride. So is the northern end of that road, from Bolinas on up to the Oregon line. I don't recall Charles' opinion on this one, but I would include the whole entire coast of Oregon, Highway 101, in my own little best roads list. Not much in the way of awesome cliffs above the ocean like there is in California, but it sure is pretty. And coastal Washington, especially the Olympic Peninsula, is spectacular. I'm sure Kuralt has that one penciled in on his list. And if he didn't, he ought to also include that Washington road east out Mount Vernon and Sedro Woolley, Highway 20. Goes through places like Twisp and Okanogan before it drops down to Grand Coulee, some of it of along the Skagit River, some of it along the Omak. And I still think just about all those roads down along the Rio Grande, down in Big Bend, and the roads that run north out of there, from Highway 170 up to Highway 90, especially the one that runs you by Elephant Mountain, are worth doing again.

California is full of roads that ought to be on a top road list. Any of the rides through and around Yosemite are worthy of the honor. Same thing with Sequoia and Kings Canyon Parks. Lassen too, and the ride around Joshua Tree National Monument ought to be on a list. And I still think Death Valley ought to be seen. I mean how often do you get to be at two hundred eighty-two feet below sea level and real dry? I made another couple guys ride through there one time. See, I don't limit these things to women I'm living with.

We rode it different from what Nancy and I did. We turned west at Parump, Nevada and rode into the Valley from the south on Highway 127. Stopped at Furnace Creek. This one is a more spectacular ride, much more awesome scenery, than the one across the north end. And we stopped because our feet were about to burn up. BMWs are boxer twin engines; the cylinders are right over your feet. And it was about a hundred and seventeen that day. The road must have been closer to a hundred and fifty. There is, oddly, a pretty little creek there at Furnace Creek. Trees and shade. And a real ritzy hotel/spa/inn. So we parked in the shade and got in the water while the ritzy hotel/spa/inn people frowned at us. And this is where we discovered that boiled is hotter than baked, or maybe dry-roasted.

Some of us took our boots off, got our feet wet, got our socks wet, and then put our boots back on. And some of us just stood in the shallow water with our boots on, cooling down our feet. A half hour later, we were all in the shade of that tree there at Stovepipe Wells, ripping our boots off and fanning our feet. Those of us who had gotten the insides of our boots wet were much worse burned than those who only got the outside wet. No, I ain't goin' to tell you which group I was in. Figure it out. Highway 395 up the Owens Valley in California is a truly scenic road.

And you get a look at Mt. Whitney. And California Highway 49, from Sonora on up to Vinton, is on Mr. Kuralt's list. I think from Santa Maria back around to I-5 is a better ride. But I guess it's three roads, 166 and 33 and 126. And I think the ride from Mt. Shasta south and east to Susanville ought to be on somebody's list. And that ride along the Trinity River, Highway 299, is a hundred and fifty or so of the very prettiest miles in all of California. And California probably has more roads that should be on this list than anywhere else.

This piece Charles Kuralt wrote is from 1979. He puts the road down into Jackson, Wyoming on his list. I rode through there long before he wrote this article, and I know why they call Jackson a Hole. Kuralt writes about U.S. 89 down the east side of the Grand Tetons. Must be he was out there when there were no Winnebagos. Or he was one. I'm sure that what is a good road for a bike isn't necessarily for a vehicle. Although he and I do tend to agree on most of these choices.

And then there is Colorado. Seems that me and Charles Kuralt agreed on that road through the Rocky Mountain Park and on into the Canyon of the Big Thompson. I do wonder if he was On The Road in his Winnebago when he made this list. I rode through Big Thompson Canyon in the summer after The Killer Flash Flood. There were vehicles still stuck up in the sheer rock cliffs above the road. Some of them were a real long way above the road. The road is U.S. Highway 40 out by Steamboat Springs. Then it's Highway 34 on the west end of The Park, and then it's Highway 36 on the east side. No one knows why. Another mystery. That might be the prettiest, most dramatic road in all of Colorado, but there are many, many others.

And it also seems to me that Kuralt listed The Million Dollar Highway. I probably ought to disqualify myself on that road. It disqualified me pretty good. By the way, it's called the Million Dollar Highway for one of two reasons. Depends on who tells you the story. One version is that it cost that much to build it. Other way they tell it is that there is a million dollars worth of gold and gold dust in it. And then that ride down along the Gunnison on Highway 50 is real cold, but real pretty.

Same deal with New Mexico. Top west side of the state is full of scenic places. In fact, most of that Four Corners area is real pretty, so there are abundant roads to be ridden in northwest New Mexico, southwest Colorado, northeast Arizona, and southeast Utah. And Highway 180 down in southwest New Mexico is a fine road too. Runs from Luna down to Deming. And then there is that south Arizona road that takes you from Tucson up to Low Show. And most of Highway 50 over in western Utah is worth riding. So is most of Idaho.

Charles Kuralt also listed Highway 100 in Vermont on his top twenty. So I rode it one time when I was up that way. Because he had it on his list. And, once again, I didn't get it. It was OK. But it was full of intense vacationing yuppies in Saabs and Volvos they couldn't drive, making traffic a mess, and it was also pretty much covered up by the little, historic, antique bed and breakfast commercial endeavors. When I got home, I reread the Kuralt article. He said to ride that road in the fall, so you can see the pretty leaves. Actually, he said to DRIVE that road in the fall. He also mentions U.S. 1 along the Maine coast. I rode that road. It was cold and crowded. Kuralt says in the wintertime you can have it all to yourself. I bet. Similarly, he writes about Massachusetts Routes 2A and 119. Hell, Paul Revere didn't even finish that ride.

And then there is the Great Void, you know, the one where the fold is on the double-page map of the U.S. The Dakotas. Actually the Black Hills of South Dakota used to be one of the finest places on earth to run with a scooter. Again, it's a comparatively small area. And now it's all pretty well clogged up and overrun with gambling tourists. The Badlands up there are a hell of a ride too. Highway 44. But it's only about an hour's worth no matter how you do it. Nebraska. Highway 26 along the Platte River, out in the west end, through the Sandhills is a real pretty ride.

Kuralt mentions Nebraska Route 2. Kansas. Highway 56, from around McPherson down to the Oklahoma line in the southwest corner, is another real pretty ride. Oklahoma. Oklahoma is OK. And the forty or so miles of Highway 56 that cut across the Panhandle are OK too.

Missouri. Some of the roads along the Mississippi and Missouri Rivers are pretty. And if you run north out of Poplar Bluff up toward Rolla and Sedalia on the back roads, you get into some real pretty stuff there. That strip across the bottom end of the state of Missouri has some great roads. Mostly short ones. Same deal with Arkansas. That strip across the top end is beautiful. And Kuralt's article also mentions U.S. 61 down through Vicksburg and Natchez to New Orleans. And he also puts Highway 17 from Savannah to Brunswick, Georgia on his list.

Iowa. Illinois. Indiana. Ohio. Wisconsin. Minnesota. Michigan. Pennsylvania. Oddly, Kuralt writes about Pennsylvania Route 34. I have no idea why. But then he also lists a ride around Minnesota from Duluth to Ely, to Silver Bay and then back down the Superior shoreline. And he also sort of cheats by putting together a ride across Indiana and Ohio on Highways 56 and 156 into Cincinnati, and then beside the river awhile into West Virginia. Well, some of these rides have shorelines. And some of them have beautiful rivers to ride along. And then Delaware and New Jersey and most of Maryland. And they all have to be passed through.

That tale of burning our feet to death in Death Valley got me to thinking about clothing. I've talked to lots and lots of people about this over the years. The consensus is that you can't beat a leather jacket. I've known some guys who have tried all the new miracle fabrics, you know the ones with bizarre names like Macho-tex, and Rhino-fab, and Eterno-substance. Weird stuff, most of it. Sometimes, it's just too damn hot for a leather.

My tendency is to go right for the denim jacket. I've been down a couple times with a denim jacket on. They provide no protection at all. Not much does except leather.

And sometimes it's cold. Back in the middle seventies, it must have been because I was with Lizabeth, and that girl found more practical things like this than I ever knew about, they invented and she found one of those scary sounding fabrics that worked: Damart long underwear. The ads tell you the Olympic Ski Team and the League of International Polar Expeditions all wear it, or something like that. They ought to. It's real light, and it rolls up into tiny bundles, so it doesn't take up a lot of room in a pack or a saddlebag. They make socks and hoods and gloves too. Hard to find a warm glove. About the worst weather I ever get into anymore requires a basic pair of thin leather gloves.

After that, like the next coldest glove, is the combination wool/leather shells the army issued us. And when it gets down into temperatures ending with -teen, a pair of those Damart gloves, inside a pair of mittens, almost does it. There is no way to keep your feet warm enough if it is real cold. There is no way to keep your feet cool if you are in Death Valley. But, that badly packed brand new Yamaha rider I met down in the Keys that time taught me something about that. He said to me that the reason your feet get cold is because your knees do. Said he had learned that diving down to serious depths. Next time I had to ride in winter weather, I tried an experiment involving a pair of those basketball playing knee pads that I took away from a little kid for a while.

That boy on the Yamaha wasn't much good at packing and balancing his load, but he was right about this cold knees and feet thing. I'm not sure bright orange basketball playing knee pads are the answer though. More of that getting laughed at. Although I didn't cause near as much merriment as that time Charlie Simms got the electric socks in the mail. They plugged into the cigarette lighter in his fairing. He claimed they worked better than having a woman in bed with you, but he kept trying to sell them, too.

That silk scarf wrapped around your face fashion statement I invented in the early sixties is still a good way to keep your face warm. And beards. Unless you want to stick your head in one of those massive full-face helmets that are much like sticking your head into a bucket with a viewport. I had one on once. Couldn't hear a damn thing. It was like that time I put the ski mask on under my helmet; I couldn't even hear the bike. And I couldn't see as well as I wanted to in that full-face helmet either.

Back when I started riding, I mostly wore goggles. Now that I've thought about it, I guess I did that because they held the top of the silk scarf up and kept it from sliding down my face, and resulting in a frost bit nose. Faceshields were a new invention, and they were mostly for racing anyway. This is funny, I just remembered something else, something I haven't thought about in years and years. On real cold days, and nights especially, I would buy a newspaper and stuff it in my jacket over my chest to keep warm. Worked pretty good as I recall. There wasn't any such thing as helmet laws back then. I always wore one. Figured it was a good idea, but I never figured it was any of the government's business, no more than whether my socks matched.

But then there wasn't any such a thing as no smoking laws, or seat belt laws, or censorship laws, or constant personal and public surveillance, or nutrition laws, or fashion police in the damn plazamalls, special accommodations for the intelligence impaired, or pissing in the bottle, or mock cultural diversity, or taking lie detector tests, or corporate cowardice, or political correctness laws either. All of which are real good reasons for and examples of why I am so much more comfortable in the past than the present. Back to the past, when there really was not only cultural diversity, but mutual respect as well, and real differences, and giants walked the land, and longriders rode it. Back to when you could ride thousand mile days, when there was still cheap gas and good two-lane highways. Back to when plastic was a new substance and a rain suit would last about a month.

I bet, over the years, I have used up two dozen rainsuits. They freeze and explode, or they get hot and cold and hot and cold and sort of fall apart, or they just eventually get beat to death. Fabric fatigue. I bought a Dririder rainsuit several years ago. I'm still in it. And I'm still dry. I knew they were serious about it when I saw it had no pockets. It cost more than I like to spend on such things, but I still have it. And I finally found a pair of light rubber pull-over boots. The Dririder pants come down over the little rubber boots and have elastic stirrup straps to keep them there, and I wind up with dry feet. And the collar turns up and velcros shut like a turtle neck.

Because it is protected by your body, the stuff piled on behind you gets wet last. If you stay out in the weather in motion, it gets soaked. So does the stuff in your saddlebags, no matter how well they're sealed. It took me awhile, but I finally beat both those. Most of what goes in my saddlebags is either in sealable baggies, or double wrapped in those nasty plastic bags they insist on giving you at the grocery store and all stores with Mart in their name. Same thing with most of the gear I pile up behind me. For years I carried a shower curtain with me to use as a groundcloth. Finally I figured out I could wrap and cover the load behind me in it when it rained. I learned that one about the sealable baggies from the guy who pointed out that the bear wanted the Oreo cookies. Figured the other one out unassisted.

The other thing that I have gotten into some is heat. I'm able to handle heat better than I can cold. My belief is that man evolved skin with pores in it so we could sweat through them, not so we could form goosebumps around them. I'm no scientist, but I have been told the human body is something like eighty-five percent water. And water freezes at thirty-two degrees. Anyway, about the worst heat I ever got into was down in the southwest. The only thing I know for sure is that you ought not go west of about Clovis without you have a tarp or something with you to make shade.

That reminded me of a funny thing. That year I broke my shoulder on the way west, I rode home alone. Stayed in San Francisco, convalescing until the folks out there made me leave. If you remember the story about the Downfall North of Durango, you will recall I ripped the centerstand off the bike there on Red Mountain. Which was kind of OK, because I couldn't heave the bike up on it with only one arm anyway. Well, it was OK until I busted my side stand in Colter Bay, Wyoming on the way back home. A Volkswagon bus full of hippies stopped and helped me pick the bike up when the sidestand broke. And then, there I was, crossing Wyoming, to the other side, where I had friends with a welding torch in Douglas. That's the punchline. Turns out there are just exactly nine trees between the Wind River Canyon and Nebraska. And none of them was along the road. I had to look for real big boulders to lean the bike on if I wanted to stop.

And that touched off another funny story. Used to be a boy named Miles Edwards, who lived in Casper. And apparently me and him looked enough alike to confuse the hell out of people. And, at least twenty-five years ago, we rode the same ride. He had a BMW just like Chuck. On more than a few occasions, I had people come up to me on the street, in places like Ann Arbor and Independence and Tampa, start talking to me about antelope horn knife handles and snakeskin belt buckles. Miles Edwards, it turns out, was a craftsman. Anyway, a woman I knew lived in Casper, and knew both of us. She wrote to me a time or two and told me that the same kind of things happened to him, that people mistook him for me and engaged him in conversations about poetry, teaching, and writing. So I stopped in Casper to see if I could find the guy. Asked around where I figured he'd hang out. That's the punchline. Most of the folks at the bars and scootershops and places that sold antelope horn crafts thought I was him, and that I was fucking with them. And I was just passing through. Looking for a welding torch. Or a big boulder.

The other kind of heat you get into is the kind you get in the southeast in the summer. The break in this area is that by the time it gets real killer hot, it usually rains and cuts you a break. But not always. I've seen the heat and sun do some real ugly things to longriders. You can get real hot inside a helmet, sitting astride an internal combustion engine. I watched a boy go into heat stroke one time in Georgia. Didn't look like no fun at all. And I have seen people get sun poisoning from being overexposed on a bike. It don't look like a lot of fun either. Sunburns are damn near unavoidable. Most bad sunburns on a bike are more windburn than sun. And

I think that might be worse. My best move in such conditions anymore, is to ride it at night. Less traffic anyway.

An old boy I used to ride with bought his first BMW, this was back in 1973 or '74. There were a bunch of us, five or six of us who had BMWs and rode together back then. And this guy joined us one day with his new ride. I rolled up a steep driveway, and then rolled down and in a half circle backward and back up so I was facing back down out of the driveway. The guy with the new bike tried it and fell over. He picked his new ride up and frowned at me and asked how the hell a skinny little bastard could move all that heavy iron around like that. A discussion ensued. Turns out the answer is balance. And either timing or rhythm. Or maybe both. The guy who fell over to start the discussion was about my height and weighed a couple hundred pounds. I used to ride some with a guy who was so damn big, I once watched him pick his ride up and shake it when it wouldn't start. Worked good.

Years ago, at a new job, I was backing my scooter down off a hill. There was a slab of cement with a cover over it at the top and I had parked there in the rain. As I backed down off it, I heard applause. When I got it down on level ground, I saw the guy who had been clapping. It was an old guy who also worked there. I had been introduced to him, but didn't really know him at all. And I knew by the way he was smiling that he knew exactly how hard it was to do what I was doing. So I asked him. He rode Harleys and Indians back when he was young, up in North Dakota. Leather helmets and dirt roads. Before he went in the air force in World War II and became a hero. We wound up being good friends. And you know, both those boys I just wrote about are dead now. Done passed through.

But this wasn't about fallen riders, this was about weather. Well, it might be about what a good woman Nancy was, too. Intense heat is another thing. Once upon a time in the west, in Arizona it was, we almost dehydrated to death. It was way up over a hundred as it tends to get out there in the summer. But the bad thing was the humidity. Or the lack of it. We felt like we were gasping for water. And the humidity was up in double digits, which seemed to bother the locals almost as much as that ten day dose of sunshine got to the people in Seattle that time. Folks in Fort Thomas and Pima were bitching to one another about the terrible humidity, and apologizing to us about it. And we were about to die from the terrible dry. I mean it was a lot drier than it was hot. And about once an hour, we would pull into a convenience store, and the girl would go in and get two or three cans or some kind of drink. While she did that, I took the hose that they all had hooked up out front, and filled my canteen, and soaked myself down to the skin. How convenient. I suspect they put the hoses out there so the Indians won't try to come in the stores. Anyway, I filled our helmets with water, and then when Nancy came out of the store, I soaked her down too. We even tried tying water soaked bandannas around our faces.

Then, before we got into high gear, we were dry again. It was like an evil miracle. No steam rose from us. The air sucked the water off and out of us. And we would have two cans of grapefruit juice gone at the end of a mile and be thirsty again before the next mile was done. We almost evaporated to death. And I got the answer to this one too. Ride at night. Watch out for enchanted coyotes.

Riding in the southeast is muggier, but, like I said, it usually rains once it gets up hot enough. And then there is that scamper for cover maneuver. And then it's cool enough to ride comfortably. But then it's raining. Guess that about sums it up.

CHAPTER FOURTEEN

```
************* Shucking, Jiving, Magic
              Tricks,
The Rich and Secure, Tropical Islands,
    and Endings *************
```

Might wind this up, too. I just read through these last couple pages, and it becomes obvious, even to me, that I'm shucking and stalling. Maybe even jiving. I might be done. Lots of women have told me that. But what I mean is all done except for the proofreading and editing and rewriting. Done with the easy part. Funny. Seemed like when I started this, I was afraid it wouldn't amount to much. And then, after I got going good with it, it seemed like it would go on forever. And I know better. It ain't nothin' lasts forever, not even the rocks or the wind. But this seems real anticlimactic. But then a big part of just about everything is knowing when to quit.

Nope. Was another trick. And that's what vicariously inspired this continuation. Today, earlier, I was talking to one of the girls I've written about in here. You're surprised any of those women still speak to me, ain't you? Me too sometimes. Anyway, I told her I was writing this, and she asked me had I mentioned my fire starting magic trick. And I didn't know what the hell she was talking about.

So she told me a story about a ride we took one weekend, real early on when I had come courting. It was brutal cold. November in Michigan. But I wanted her to know. And she wanted to. Love is blind. And often shows signs of severe retardation. Anyway, somewhere along the line that first day out, she got to shivering real bad up behind me. So I found a place to get out of the weather some, and made a fire for her. Hypothermia is every bit as nasty as heat stroke. The magic trick was when I opened my gas tank, stuck a couple paper towels in it, and used them to start the fire. She said she thought that was about the neatest thing she'd ever seen. Except for striking a wooden match on my helmet and lighting my cigarette, at eighty or so.

I'd about halfway forgot about that ride. Still can't remember stopping and making a fire for her, but she did. And I been making fires with gas out of my tank my whole life, so that really didn't seem much of a trick to me. Not near as tricky as getting her back on the bike after that miserable weekend in Michigan weather.

Mostly what talking to her tonight reminded me about was some women who never did get back up for another ride. Back to that thing about when your best line is, "Get up behind me," you only attract certain kinds of women, in limited numbers. Makeup, stiffly styled hair, and fashion have been at the crux of the problem most of the time. Women who are hard into things like mascara, lipstick, hairspray, mousse, seriously manicured nails, pantyhose, shoulder pads, contact lenses of various shades, or anything that's fake or false (eyelashes, hairpieces, finger nails) usually don't do well on a scooter.

I flat ruined a set of mufflers one time when a girl I was trying real hard to impress got on behind me wearing a pair of those silly platform heeled shoes. Damn things were plastic and melted down over the mufflers. Girl had to get out of her shoes to get off the cycle. Then we had to chip the shoes off after the mufflers cooled down. And she was real upset about it. I tried to tell her that those shoes weren't any better for riding than they were for walking, but she was also real upset about the effect the helmet had on her big hairdo that wasn't supposed to move, and wouldn't listen. Had helmet problems with another lady whose name I disremember, but she got her goddamn ear ring caught up inside the helmet, and I thought we were going to have to get a drill or an axe to get her out.

For awhile one time, I tried real hard to hang out with a girl who owned more clothes than you can find in a Sears and Roebuck Catalogue. That woman had three closets, and two dressers, and another extra room full of clothes. She had clothes she hadn't worn in years. She had clothes she had only worn once. She had clothes she had never worn. She had clothes she was never going to wear. Hell, she had clothes no one was ever going to wear. But she did not have a pair of blue jeans. And you just can't get into riding much while you're concerned about your white silk pantsuit.

That woman I was talking to also mentioned my propensity to send the women in first. Not just me. All of us. She mentioned a couple different situations where she and the other ladies had been required to go into the restaurant first, just to see if it was the kind of place we wanted to be in. Scouts. The girl said she felt more like the canary being sent into the coal mine. But I mean you can't always take a woman to the all night restaurant by the bus station, or make them eat at the kitchen in a double wide trailer on the border, or surrounded by sissies in San Francisco. Sometimes, you try to be a sport, to do good by them, and find a "nice" restaurant for them. But, you don't want to wander into a Bill Knapp's with your helmet in your hand. Or stumble into the Sunday, post-church brunch at the designated local fine eatery. Or into a place that's going to want you to put on a tie and a coat. Or get into the middle of the weekly Rotary meeting. Or a place that doesn't have the prices on the menus.

The story that I was reminded of during the gasoline fire-starter conversation happened down in either Arkansas or Missouri. There were four or five bikes, and I had the only woman along with me. The place we stopped at had a parking lot suspiciously full of year old Buicks and Lincolns. As the story was retold to me this evening, we opened the door, and then did a serious multiple shuffle, and shoved her in ahead of all of us. She's right. We did. We talked about it over hot dogs up the road. It was either the organ music, or the smell. They had a guy playing Lawrence Welk music, and it smelled like your grandmother's house of a Sunday afternoon. The girl took one step in and one look around, and then she about faced and pushed us all back out into the lot to our cycles. She said there was a young waitress in there who looked at us and almost laughed as she shook her head in a negative gesture. Didn't get to see her myself, so I don't know her name.

Talking with that woman tonight put me in mind of a couple other stories that ought to go in here. She was involved in one anyway. We were southbound down the Blue Ridge one summer. Turns out we were close to her aunt and uncle's place there in Virginia. And it was near her birthday, and she wanted to stop and visit. And I wanted her to be happy. And we were invited.

I should digress here for a brief rant. Remember that part back down the line where I went on about how I was the least racist person I knew, and that other part about me not being homophobic. Well, lest you get to thinking I am an all-around gentle soul, without prejudice, and probably a great humanitarian, you should know I hate rich people. Actually, that ain't right. Turns out I just liked the hell out of this girl's aunt and uncle. But they ain't real, born with the money, rich people. This boy started out an orphan child, and made every damn dime he's got with his inventions and hard work. And he's got a lot of dimes.

Anyway, my prejudice against the rich is that I don't think they should ever be put in charge of other people. It's like those third-worlder cab-drivers in New York City. And for the same reasons. They just don't know what the hell they're doing. It's a foreign language and an alien culture. Most rich people couldn't identify a job, much less do one. They are like Haitians in that respect. Reality has very little to do with most rich people's lives. It isn't that most of them have not ever been hungry; it's like they don't even know where the hell groceries come from or what to do with them. And when the rich are put in charge of others, they make a mess of those people's lives. If it wasn't for rich people, there wouldn't be no homeless.

Anyway, I am wary of the rich. Many of them think their surplus of money makes them royalty, somehow inherently better than regular wage slaves with less money. I don't begrudge them their money. I just distrust them as a group. I think we should make a deal with the rich. We won't go anywhere near their polo matches and sailboat regattas, and they ought not come anywhere near a job.

And I didn't even know the girl had rich relatives. Not until we made the turn into the rich people's area. You know the area. Had a really silly name that ended with Estates. Real seriously manicured lawns, edged driveways and sidewalks, trees that look like they'd been hit with a cookie cutter, really retentive flowerbeds, covered pool, huge houses that all look like they got painted last week, three car garages with electric door openers, not a vehicle in sight over two years old, no pickup trucks, tight, even little fences, lots and lots of recently washed windows gleaming in the light, lots of yard lights and sidewalk lights and street lights and porch lights, security devices everywhere.

As we rode by, rich folks stopped their various wealthy activities, like tennis, and clipping coupons, and playing with their pedigree dogs, and counting their money, and hanging out around their pools, and reading the stock page, and watching the chauffeur wash the Rolls, and figuring dividends, and belting down overpriced Vodka, and conniving ways to make more money, to stare at us. The black guys mowing the lawns and washing the cars stopped to look at us too. And laugh. The guy riding with me and the girl turned and looked at me like I had lost my mind and I was going to get us all killed. Rich people are the worst bosses I have ever had, and they are as serious about their security as they are about using up and making a mess out of the people working for them. I turned around and looked at the girl with the same expression. She laughed. We rode on. The rich and their hired servants continued to stare. We finally got there, and her uncle was the kind of guy who insisted we leave the bikes out in the driveway to fuck with his rich neighbors.

About the same thing happened up in Connecticut one time. A boy I went to school with, lived with for awhile, is up there, and said to come by. So we did. I knew he had a good job, and that he made a lot of money. But I really didn't know how much. Same damn neighborhood as in Virginia, only more money. Same looks from the indigenous locals and their hired Latino help. Same look from the same guy I was riding with down in Virginia. We pressed on and got to my friend's house, only to find him gone. He had left a note telling us to ride back out to a telephone and call him at work and he would come home. It took us lots less time to find his secret, hidden, emergency housekey and get indoors than it took me and that other guy to break into that Oldsmobile that was locked up and running that time. Called him from the phone in his kitchen.

Last summer I stopped in Atlanta to see my niece. I knew she had married a guy with some money, but once again, I didn't really expect to be rolling through a neighborhood nicer than I envision Heaven. This one was so damn high class that they had third-worlder surgeons and like that living there. Was strange watching the Iranians pause from their croquette game, and their hired help white boys pause from cleaning the pool, to watch me ride by. I'm pretty sure some of them called the Private Estate Security Police on their little portable telephones.

I have a fantasy. Might be the only one I have left. Used to be, I'd ride from Michigan on down to Florida, to Coconut Grove, and then catch the $24 round trip seaplane out of Miami to Bimini. Where Julian Brown would let me stay at his hotel for very little money if I would promise to pay my bar bill before I left. Some of the best times I ever had, not in motion on a bike, were in Bimini. It's a Bahama. Adam Clayton Powell used to hang out there. So did Hemingway. I was there for the Bahamas' first Independence Day. Seems like it was in the mid-seventies sometime. I've been there for New Years, and Junkanoo, and Christmas, and Easter, and Boxing Day, and my birthday more than once. Some real fine people out there.

Before you get too excited, and book passage, it ain't there no more. It's like I told you all about the Florida Keys, and the Outer Banks, and a whole bunch of other places. It's gone. The wooden docks got replaced with concrete and steel that doesn't sway in the tide in the moonlight. The Red Lion and a couple other restaurants, where you could get conch and Bahamian lobster and fish so fresh you had to go across the street and help carry it from the boat sometimes, are gone. I suspect the Denny-Jerry-Etc. folks have taken over. Same deal with the hotels. I imagine HoJo-Holiday-Marriot ruin. One day, I walked the beach all day, and didn't see another human being. Doubt you could do such a thing today.

Anyway, Bimini is two islands, north and south Bimini. The north island is where damn near all the population used to be. The south island was infested with Chickcharneys. I don't know how it is anymore. But back when I used to go out there, there was one road on the north island. It ran from the town, Alicetown, up the island to the end. About a mile and a half. It was about a narrow lane across. It was badly paved, and even worse repaired. Huge potholes and cracks and piles of sand and coconut husks everywhere. Foot traffic mostly, but lots and lots of little bikes, like Honda 50s and like that. And they had them one official car, but it never ran seemed like. But mostly that road was full of little bitty fifty and sixty cc bikes sort of zipping up and down. Full. This road was called The Queen's Highway.

My fantasy is that I would like to take a boat full of giant huge, all chrome and noise, chopped Harleys, about a dozen would do it, out there. Along with twelve guys with beards and hair to their butts and tattoos and so forth. And then pull the boat up to the dock there, like mid-day of a Saturday, drop the gangplank, and just roll off it like one of those old Hells Angels movies, exhaust smoke and noise in the air, and the natives blinded by the sunlight on the chrome. Run them bikes real slow down the dock and onto the Queen's Highway all the way to the end, through around and over the little 50s and 60s, and then back, and then back down the dock and onto the boat. And then leave. Passin' through.

Had a sort of a fantasy come true one time out in Reno. Me and Nancy and Zero showed up out there at some friends' place. The guy, Jim the Bear, played the trombone at the MGM Grand, and I told him we wanted to go to one of their big review shows. So he spoke to his friend, the boss waiter. And when we showed up, we were ushered past the crowd of people in their furs and suits and evening gowns, all bunched up waiting in line, and shown to our table. We looked like we had just ridden cross country on a motorcycle. The whole way past this line of rich people, they kept trying to identify us, asking one another who we were, were we rock stars, or movie people, or what, to get such special treatment. Nope. Just regular scootertrash. Just passing through.

And, this is the good part, it happened again. Inspired. A young man was in my office today, looking at that wall I told you about, while I finished a phone call. When I got off the phone, he asked me didn't I ever get scared, and if I had ever been lost. Contemporary young people get a lot of bad press, but some of them are pretty perceptive and cut right to the heart of things.

Told him yes and no. I been scared lots of times. The few seconds just before dropping it every time I ever went down were absolute terror. So are the few seconds in between making eye contact with the bad driver and being hit. Cars with heavily tinted windows kind of frighten me. I got no idea if they are paying attention in there. I think the thing that scared me most was watching another rider drop it. That Evel Knievel biography movie had some footage from that Caesar's Palace fiasco. First time I saw the movie, I was home alone. Pretty embarrassing to discover that you are screaming all by yourself in the dark. I really do think every kid that has aspirations of riding should have to watch that scene several times. I've had more than one woman flat refuse to have anything to do with me because I ride. Many of them were nurses. One was a doctor.

And the only thing that really scares me is the thought of not being able to ride at all.

Now about that being lost thing. Well, not lost exactly, but kind of seriously misplaced a time or two. Genuinely baffled occasionally. Most of it was the fault of bad signs, but I managed to wander around disoriented unassisted a few times. Always briefly. Hard to stay lost in contemporary America with all the signs and interstates and cities and crowds and traffic.

Anyway, I got to talking to this kid with the scared and lost questions. He asked about fear of the local law enforcement groups, bounty hunters, the state highway heat, and other authorities. And it put me in mind of a time I was down in Coconut Grove. Coconut Grove is part of Miami. I think it was the first part to be settled in fact. Black folks from the Bahamas if I remember correctly. Anyway, it used to be paradise. There used to actually be coconut trees, and there wasn't a building over a couple stories tall, and you could eat breakfast at The Tom Thumb for about a buck. Waitress there was named April June Audrey Lee. And you could drink at Bubba's all day for another five. Set and fish all night off the dock there in front of Monte's Conch. And you used to could park your ride at any of those places and wander off knowing it would remain unmolested.

One day I was in Bubba's, I think I was doing research for a paper. There was a pretty good afternoon crowd. Whole lot of authorities. Sheriffs deputies, and Grove cops, and a whole lot of federal types, swamp rangers and poacher cops and fish cops and citrus cops and like that. And suddenly a guy burst through the door and screamed, "The Glades are on fire!" That place emptied faster than if the guy had hollered that it was on fire. I mean it was about the fastest fire drill I ever saw. Ten seconds after the guy had yelled, there was me and the bartender sitting there alone in the dust they'd raised on the way out. I made a comment about the intense dedication and civic spirit and commitment to the environment. The bartender chuckled, as he picked up everybody's change, and explained that all those boys had marijuana plots out in the swamp and they had gone to protect their crops.

One time I was lost was in northwest Massachusetts. I'd ridden up there to visit an old friend, Ed Calver, who had retired to a hermit's life on a mountain there. Oh, not a real hermit exactly. He taught the local kids Latin and Greek, and how to play the harpsichord, and he got involved in local politics to get them straightened out the way he thought it ought to be. But most of the time he hung out on his mountain, alone. Reading and writing and thinking, when he wasn't cutting firewood or pulling water up out of a hole with a bucket and a rope. No electricity, no running water, no amenities. Hell, he didn't even have a door on his outhouse. When I asked, he explained there was no one around for miles, and it was too beautiful a view to obstruct with a door. And he had built it so that the wind was at the back of the building most of the time.

One night, by the fire's light, after several gin drinks with no ice, he engaged me in a conversation about riding. Asked me why I did it. Told him I couldn't help it. Said it was a kick to be one of maybe a hundred guys who have done what I've done. Quoted from a poem of mine and told him that without a machine and a road to ride, I'd be like eagles condemned to the ground. Explained to him about watching the sun come up different. Told him I did it so I'd know where the road went. Said it wasn't one of those things I had to decide; it was just what I was.

And he told me bullshit. He said I did it because it was dangerous. Claimed it was a risk, that I do it because I could die of it. I don't think so. Didn't then, still don't. Might be why I go to work or got married, but not why I ride. However, a long discussion ensued. Ed Calver is one of the very smartest people I have ever been allowed to hang out with. And my life has been rich in smart people. And the man taught me more about teaching and learning than almost anyone else I can name except maybe my Grammaw. But I disagreed with him then, and I still do. Ain't got a damn thing to do with dying. Got to do with living. Ain't got a thing to do with being someplace. Has to do with being someplace else. Has to do with the getting there.

And I believe I am. There, that is. At an end. Hope you liked it. I had fun with it. And if I'm half the man I pretend to be, I'll come up with one more good story to finish it with. I guess I could go ahead on and explain about and defend that freak stampede there at the petting zoo. But if I did that, and certain lawyers in Kansas ever happened to read this, I'd be admitting fault or culpability or something, and there is still that class action suit pending. Or I could confess to that incident with the ceramic yard gnomes. But if I did that, I'd never be able to ride through portions of Arkansas ever again. Or I might could tell you about that time I set out a rainstorm with the devil. He told me I was an old unreconstructed rebel irregular. I explained to him about how I hope I get to die out on the highway.

But something else comes to mind instead. When my brother's kids were little, I was sort of an event in their lives. Old Uncle Weirdo comes to visit. And of course they all wanted a ride on my cycle. The look on my brother's face was a lot like the look on Charlie Wasson's when he let me ride that new BSA Victor of his. Terror. But it was nothing compared to the look on my sister-in-law's face. But those kids all got their rides.

And now they're grown. And come Thanksgiving, they are all gathering at my niece's place up in Atlanta. And they invited their old demented burned out Uncle Weirdo. They had to. And they've got kids of their own now. And I'm taking an extra helmet.

Later, that same week. Been sitting here going over some of this, and one more story I ought to get on paper came to me. The year those people moved out to Paonia, Colorado so that years later they could save us from the Flood at the McClure Pass Detour, they did it in a big Ford truck. Think it was a thirty-four foot box. Anyway, they had to get the truck back to Virginia, and asked me would I come out to Colorado, load my scooter on the truck and drive it back east, unload my ride there, and then ride it on home. Said they'd buy the gas and motels and meals eastbound for me. So I headed off to Paonia. It was a very good ride west. I sort of wandered west and north until I got to Colorado. That was the trip I discovered the prettiest view of Mobile Bay I know of. I rode a lot of Highway 50. Real fine road. Runs through Rocky Ford and Pueblo and Canon City. Runs to Gunnison. Runs along the Tomichi and Gunnison Rivers. Pretty road. Pretty rivers. I crossed the Gunnison and rode Highway 92 up to Hotchkiss and on to Paonia. Another fine road.

I spent a week or so in Paonia, taking short rides around the area, being taken on tours by my friends, seeing major portions of the prettiest country I know of. I was given an arrowhead by a guy I met up on top of a mountain. He was hang gliding. I noticed his arms were all scarred up and asked him about the dangers of hang gliding. He laughed and told me he got chopped up on a bike, not a hang glider. Told me he had since quit riding, and limited himself to safer pursuits. Then he stepped off the cliff and began soaring down toward Grand Junction. It was a couple miles down and fourteen miles away.

Then I loaded my cycle on the big Ford truck and headed back to Virginia. Took as many expressways as can be taken between Paonia and Grundy. Stopped in Golden to visit with a nephew there. Stopped and got a pair of throttle cables at a BMW shop I just happened to encounter along the way. My throttle had been turning hard climbing those mountains, and I suspected the cable was fraying.

Somewhere in Kansas, Hays I think it was, I was at a truck stop getting gas and something to eat. I opened the back of the truck up and climbed in to make sure the scooter was still tied down tight. A driver on his way in to the restaurant looked in my truck and noticed the BMW. He had one too, and we got to talking and had lunch together. As we walked back to our trucks after lunch he handed me three or four of those big black beauty speed capsules. Told me they'd get me to Virginia.

Somewhere between Abilene and Junction City, I dropped one. It was dark by the time I cleared Topeka, and I was flying high, figuring to drive all the way to Virginia before stopping. Times like that I wish they'd build a bridge to Europe. Anyway, I got up around Kansas City, and come up over a hill and suddenly, there in front of me, was a giant flying saucer. For a brief moment I thought the aliens were among us. Never saw anything that big that bright or that awesome before. Or after. Turned out to be the giant professional football/baseball stadium thing out there. Home game. Scared the hell out of me.

I somehow got into Grundy, where I was well received and treated like kin, and got the truck returned and my bike unloaded, and I headed out south. Got on the Blue Ridge as soon as I could. And around Asheville, on a downhill hard curve to the right, a throttle cable snapped, and stuck, and the bike revved up to about seven grand, and tried to get out from underneath me almost before I had the presence of mind to turn it off. And then I coasted down into a little scenic turnout and changed cables without further incident.

When I got off the Ridge, I rode out into the apple orchards and got a couple apples. Found a river with a short waterfall to sit beside while I ate them. The sun got into the water and made rainbows in the mist and the spray. It was as fine a ride home as it had been westbound. And I was just passing through.

No, that ain't right. I can do a better ending than that. Wish I could write that I had a ride planned for next summer. Or a new lady to tell these old stories and show the highway and my magic to. But I ain't. I expect I'll go somewhere. Me and Zero been talking about another Perfect Ride. Maybe I'll head west and ride out across the Llano Estacado one more time before I'm done. Might ride out toward Organ Pipe and find a place to watch the desert sky at night. Sure was worth watching that last time. Maybe keep on to the Joshua Trees. And once you get that far, well hell, Death Valley's right there, almost. And there's a boy in L.A. who's got one of my puppies. And once you get that far, you're kind of committed to riding the coast road some. And that goes right up to San Francisco. Hell, I might get to see the Olympic Peninsula again.

And I'd hate like hell to think that young girl was right, and that the best part of me really is my memories.

CHAPTER FIFTEEN

* * * * * * * * * * * * * * Aftermath * * * * * * * * * * * * * *

It is now months later. I have been to Atlanta for Thanksgiving with my nieces and nephew and their various and assorted spouses and kids. And I had a fine, fine time. Laughed so much my face hurt for days afterward. At one point, I had one woman getting me more coffee, another one getting me a piece of pie, and two small children looking for my cigarettes for me. Sometimes I think a man ought to be allowed to live like that.

But that wasn't the point of this. The point of this is that if it weren't for irony, there would be no humor at all in my life. It was fifty-nine degrees at my house at eight o'clock in the morning when I started out northbound. And when I pulled into my niece's driveway, up there above Marietta, four hundred and eighty- seven miles and eight hours later, it was forty-seven degrees. In between, I fucking near froze.

And then, the weather deteriorated. No small children used the extra helmet. And therein lies the irony. Some of it, anyway. I don't know who was more disappointed, them or me. I do know there were several relieved parents smiling at the rain through the windows. And three days later when I saddled up southbound, it was forty-two degrees and raining. As I left, my prettiest niece, the one I love the most, said "You might be old and burned out, but you're still a tough son of a bitch."

It rained from there all the way to south of Valdosta some. It rained hard, very hard. And it was very, very cold. The road was reasonably clear, and I made pretty good time in spite of having to stop several times to dry off and warm up and put on more clothes. It didn't get much warmer at all.

Not until I rode out from under the front somewhere around Ocala. It went from fifty to eighty degrees in between expressway exits. I had to pull over and tear several layers of clothing off before heat prostration set in. So, I got to ride the last hundred of almost a thousand miles in the bright sunshine. More irony. More passing through.

CHAPTER SIXTEEN

****************Last Summer****************

There I was with some saved up money and time off all at once. Not enough of either one to go ride the Four Corners, so I saddled up and rode west. I didn't have much in mind except going west as far as the Mississippi River and checking it out again. Left out of here one morning in August. As you've by now noticed, most of what you've been reading is stray memories of former rides sort of randomly strung together. Well, this is memories of the ride from last summer. Probably randomly.

There was very little of a memorable nature the first day out. I got on several roads, going mostly north and some west, including a couple busy interstates, and made it up to Phenix City, Alabama. I managed to ride all day without getting wet, and that in itself is pretty memorable in the South in the summer. More about weather shortly.

The next day I rode from there over to Tupelo. There are some real pretty places across Alabama and Mississippi, especially the northern parts, and I managed to ride through several of them. There are some gentle mountains, and lots of those greens that Captain Zero noticed fifteen years ago. I rode by The King's old house there in Tupelo. And I stopped at the Welcome Center there on the Natchez Trace long enough to use the facilities and fill my canteen. Then I rode a piece of the Trace, just for nostalgia's sake, and then I headed to Memphis, where I rode past Elvis' other house there.

Then I spent the next couple hours in a traffic jam trying to get across The River. What a fiasco! The folks in charge of making a construction mess had outdone themselves. The road went from six lanes to a single rut faster than it took me to write about it here. If it hadn't been for a couple boys driving semi-trucks, I think I might still be there. I thought about swimming across, but probably only because the temperature was in the mid-nineties.

Eventually I got across The River, and headed north up the west side of it. Like I said, I had at best vague notions of where I was headed when I started this ride. The first thing was I needed to see that river again. Just to make sure it was still running south I guess. It was. So I rode beside it upriver to Sikeston, Missouri, there in my ancestral homeland. That was sort of another one of my vague ideas, to make a pilgrimage to southeast Missouri. I rode the last hour or so in a steady drizzle, and the kind lady at the motel gave me a room on the ground floor where I could get my bike up under the steps to the second floor. I walked across the street and got a Genuine Dexter Bar-B-Que for supper. It was good.

When I took my room key back to the office in the pre-dawn darkness the next morning there was another kind lady at the desk. She asked where I was heading, and I told her west, to Poplar Bluff and then probably north. And she told me how to get out of town, and where to expect the local cop.

The fog was really heavy all the way to Poplar Bluff. It was the kind of heavy fog that necessitates going slowly. I mean it was the kind of fog that piles up on your windshield so you can't see through it, and occasionally you hit a bump and about a quart of water bounces back over the windshield and into your face.

So I turned north there at Poplar Bluff and headed on up out of the fog and into the hickory hills toward Jefferson City, and Rolla, and Sedalia. Put me in mind of a fog me and an old highway bloodbrother got into up at the top end of the Blue Ridge, on the Skyline Drive, ten or more years ago. The ranger lady at the entrance damn near begged us not to go up into that fog. She said we should either wait or ride over east and find a less foggy road. She was right, but we pressed on. That fog was so thick I thought we'd drown. I had to stay about a foot off his rear fender in order to be able to see his tail light. It was lots worse than riding in a hard rain.

This Missouri fog wasn't quite that bad, but I wanted to get out of it anyway. That's a real pretty ride north out of Poplar Bluff. It put me through portions of the Mark Twain National Forest and the Ozark National Scenic Riverways. Very scenic. Pretty good road surfaces for two lanes too.

Probably because Jefferson City is the state capital, I kept running into high ranking cops in undercover cars. Apparently they weren't so high ranking that they wouldn't stop scootertrash for a ticket, or so a real pretty woman who was working the stop sign for the construction crew told me. Besides encountering these cop cars, the other thing that happened is that I ran into about eight construction zones, all of which had really pretty women operating the stop signs. Good idea.

I kept on working my way north and west until the storms began rolling down from the north. I zigged and zagged, and got near lost a couple times on unnumbered, unlettered two lanes. The storm clouds got closer, and I could hear thunder getting closer, and I began looking for picnic areas or rest areas on my map. The two that I found didn't have any kind of covers over anything, just picnic tables out in the open. By now the storms were upon me, and I was riding in and out of squall lines trying and failing to stay dry.

That's when I rode into Port Waverly on the banks of the Missouri River. There was a former liquor store there that had a convenient awning overhang. I rode up under it. There was just about enough room for me and the bike up under cover. Just before the serious storms got under way, the local cop came by to check me out. He smiled and shook his head knowingly and drove on by. About a block over I heard him singing "Happy Birthday" to someone over his public address system. The last lyric went something like, "Happy birthday to you. You belong in a zoo."

It rained on and off for the next three hours. The lightning kept up even when it wasn't raining, and the thunder sounded like a damn war as it rolled down the Missouri River. The rain came down at various angles, and I had to move the bike around every time the wind shifted. During a lull in it all, I rode about a mile to a store and got some milk and a candy bar and an apple. I got as far as the bridge north out of town, but it was a hard sheet of rain and a flooded road on the other side. So I beat it back to my abandoned liquor store refuge and made some coffee and studied my map.

The rain quit in time for me to get back on the road mostly north and some west on up into Lamoni, Iowa. Ran a couple of real nice roads there in the north of Missouri on my way to Iowa. I know a woman who lives up there in Lamoni. Hell of a place, Lamoni. I was there a couple weeks, so I know. Nice people.

My gracious hostess even consented to getting on behind me and riding around southern Iowa and northern Missouri some. We found some real scenic rides out there in the gentle hills of the Heartland. Turned some heads out there with that girl up behind me, too. I love it when the good citizens damn near drive off the road trying to figure out why the pretty woman is with the old geek.

Besides the usual riding around exploring the local area, I fished. Caught fish, too. Yeah, who knew? I didn't even know that they had water in Iowa. Corn. Anyway, they not only have water, but they have some real big bass in some of it, and some huge catfish in some of it. And they have guys who own the water who will let you fish it.

And, while I was having a real good time, I eventually had to head back home before the Fun Police found me. I live in constant fear of being found out by the amusement authorities and being taken off my scooter and off the road. You never want to let on like you're having a good time.

And the ride back home east was much more memorable than the ride out there had been. I left Lamoni early, so early that I had to pull over about an hour down the road and put more clothes on in the early morning fog and chill. Found a fine place for such an activity. Somewhere east of Lamoni on Highway 2 there is a tiny little roadside chapel. There is some literature there telling you what it's about, and copies of a couple newspaper articles about it. There was no one else around, so I went in and checked it out. It was about as big as the back of a van. I put on another couple layers of clothes, and used the convenient and clean port-o-john. Then I left a contribution in the collection box, and offered a sacrifice of blood and smoke to the gods of longriders. Then I got outbound east toward Keokuk.

I came south out of Keokuk on Highway 61 to Hannibal. Then I found Highway 79. What a fine ride. It runs down along beside The River. It's full of gentle hooks and hills and curves, and some magnificent views of the high bluffs across The River in Illinois. I stopped at a couple different places, walked down to The River, watched it roll on south to the Gulf, washed my hands and face in the water. Then I found a sign that said something about a ferry boat, and I headed down to The River. It was a trick. There was a recreational boat ramp, but no ferry. And by now I wanted to ride on a ferry boat.

And I also knew I didn't want to get anywhere near St. Louis, and there were no bridges up where I was, so I got my map out and found an indication of a toll ferry at a place called Winfield. Most of the old ferry boats have been replaced by interstate bridges that lack the charm and the chance to get right down on the water. By the time I found the Winfield ferry dock, it was threatening to rain.

There was a guy with Illinois plates sitting in a pickup waiting for the ferry boat, so I engaged him in brief conversation, and he assured me there was, indeed, a hard surfaced highway on the other side of The River. Seems like the trip cost a dollar and a half. I gave the guy two bucks. I'm a hell of a sport sometimes. Stand by your ride and hold on to it for the five minutes it took to get across to Illinois on the other side. The pre-storm wind was by now blowing whitecaps across the Mississippi, and about three inches of water sort of sloshed up over the deck and into my boots.

Within those five minutes the threat of rain had turned into a reality. It was coming down hard enough to make me want me to put on my rain gear, but I couldn't find a place to stop. I mean there was nothing, and noplace to hide from it over there in Illinois. There was a paved road like the guy in the pickup had promised. And there was rain. But that was all there was.

You should probably consult your map here. I was on a very long, very skinny peninsula that was formed by the Illinois and the Mississippi Rivers. Very long, very skinny. One main road running north and south, up and down it. And stone empty. Oh, there was some real pretty farmland, but there was nothing in the way of an abandoned liquor store to hide from the weather in. There was nothing like a restaurant to stop at. Nothing like a picnic area. Just barely paved roads. No local traffic. And nothing in the way of signs telling me where I was, or which way out.

So I just sort of kept trying to go east, mostly making decisions based on which road had the best surface. That was a hard decision most of time. I did that for what seemed like a long time, and a longer distance, especially considering that I was trying to cross a long, skinny peninsula. The whole time I was in and out of several rain storms. And eventually I came to another ferry boat that took me across the Illinois River. Stand by and hold on to your bike again; and no charge for it at all.

Then, as luck would finally have it, there was an abandoned Dairy Queen of some kind there in Grafton, Illinois with a nice awning and a better view of The River across the road. I jumped under that overhang like the proverbial duck on the proverbial Junebug. And I hadn't hardly been there long enough to wipe my glasses off when the local cop showed up. He smiled and told me I was trespassing. By now the rain had gotten intense, and I couldn't even see across the road to The River. I politely asked the local authority if I might be permitted to set out the storm there if I promised to be good and not even spit on his ground or throw a ciga-rette butt down in his jurisdiction. Nope. Bastard wouldn't even let me get my rainsuit out and get into it. Nope. Just keep on passing through. No pausing. No drying off.

Well, as you know by now, I learned about trying to argue with guns and badges years ago, so I just saddled up and got back to it southbound along with The River, just rollin' with the flow. I never have been real fond of riding in the rain, but it beats going to jail. I enjoy the bein' free way too much for that.

That's a hell of a road there. I think it's Illinois 3. I bet it is real pretty when it's dry and you can see beyond your windshield. But I couldn't. There is The River running along on the west side of that road, and the high bluffs of Illinois on the other side. It runs down to East St. Louis through what used to be an industrial-manufacturing corridor, but what now looks like lots of recent flood damage and a whole lot of people out of work. The rain finally let up, and I pressed on south.

Until I got somewhere around Alton. The sky to the south looked like it was bruised, only darker. Lightning ripped ragged holes in the clouds down that way, and I could feel the thunder before I could hear it. As I pulled up to a stop light which was swinging around in the wind like a wounded butterfly, I glanced over to my right and saw the perfect place to set out a rainstorm. It looked like a giant 7-11 store under construction. There was a huge awning overhanging the whole front of the building and a real nice slab concrete porch under it.

The lights were on in the building and I could see that it was empty except for a couple guys doing drywall work. There was one other guy with a dumptruck spreading gravel in the parking lot off to the side of the building.

So I whipped in and rode right up under cover on the nice new porch. Parked the bike up close to the building. The guys doing drywall, one of who turned out to be a woman, looked up and checked me out and then went back to work. The guy with the dump truck waved and went back to what he was doing. I dried myself off some and lit a cigarette and poured a cup of coffee. By the time I had finished them both, the storm was just about on me.

The guy who had been working with the dump truck walked over. He looked out at the weather coming in on us, smiled and said he hoped I wasn't headed south. I explained that I was, but unless he was going to throw me out, I was going to set right there until I could see the sky again. And he laughed like hell, and explained that the building was the future site of his son's motorcycle shop, and that I was invited to stay right there until their grand opening in two weeks.

Then he hollered at the woman who was putting up drywall to come look at the storm coming in. She turned out to be his wife, and when she noticed my Florida license plate, she started talking to me about Florida, where they spent their winters. We had a fine time there in the shelter as the storm descended upon us. We talked about a couple places in Mexico that we had all been to. I got a tour of the unfinished cycle shop. It's going to be a real good one. An hour or so later, the weather had slacked off and my hosts excused themselves to go home, and told me to stay right there all night if I needed to.

The storm and the traffic let up finally, and I was able to leave before dark. I rode beside The River some, crossed back into Missouri at the Jefferson Barracks Bridge, just like the nice people back at the unfinished scooter shop told me to. The rain never did actually stop, and I rode in and out sort of a soft mist all the way downriver to Sikeston, where the nice lady at the same motel apologized for not having my former room available. I had to take a room on the second floor. But I did get me another one of those Genuine Dexter Bar-B-Ques.

The next morning was still and hot. There wasn't a breath of air, and there was kind of a nasty, ominous, oppressive, almost anticipatory feel to it all. I crossed back east across The River one last time at Caruthersville after getting breakfast and gas in Hayti.

There is a waitress there, girl was named Cindy Ann Clara Jo. I asked. As I was paying my bill, a wasted trucker stumbled in, and looked around with bleary, road weary eyes, and asked where the hell was he. The waitress told him, in the prettiest downriver voice you can imagine, that he was in Hayti, and then she spelled it for him. He blinked a couple times, looked at me for some sort of confirmation, and then when I nodded, he turned around and walked back out shaking his head.

When I asked Cindy Ann Clara Jo if it would be OK with her if I just sat back down and listened to her talk pretty for the rest of the day, she explained about her husband, Marvin Kenneth Edgar Bob. Then she began telling me that her mom was available and would be coming in to work the afternoon shift in a couple hours. That had me leaving shaking my head too.

By mid-morning it was a hundred, and the sky was a hot white glare. There wasn't a bit of wind, and the humidity was up around aquarium level. It was one of those days when the dust won't even rise. There were no animals crossing the road, no dogs trying to commit suicide, even the cattle in the fields were lying down in whatever shade they could find. There were no birds in the air at all. Didn't even see a vulture. You know something is wrong when the birds won't trust the air.

But I still managed to ride east across Tennessee on some real pretty two lane roads. I stopped often for shade and beverages. It was dehydration hot. It got hotter. By mid-day the highway looked like liquid in the distance. You could feel the barometer dropping, the air was almost mashing me down on the road.

I dropped down into Alabama and rode that pretty ride south and east through the Talladaga Mountains. I found some fine two lane roads and spent most of that ride alone out there. And that was where I encountered one of the mysterious highway witches. She rode an all black cycle, a 650 Honda, with New York plates. She had on boots and jeans and a leather, and you could tell she knew how to ride. I came up behind her somewhere around the Georgia line. Noticed it was a woman right away by the way she set her ride. I got up behind her and settled into her mirrors, some off to her right side, and just let her set the pace.

I rode with her like that for awhile, until she got behind a log truck and didn't go around him. I figured she didn't want my company and swung into the passing lane out around her and the truck. She looked me over closely and smiled at me as I went past her. I couldn't tell much about the way she looked, but I could see that she was a little woman. Then she pulled out and followed me around the log truck and stayed in my mirrors.

Awhile down the line, I had to get off to get gas and get on a different road. She followed me to a nearby gas station, pulled up to the pump with me, introduced herself, and asked me where I was going. I told her I wasn't. Said I was going back. She had just rode down the Blue Ridge, then through the Smokies, and had started to New Orleans by way of the Natchez Trace when she saw the weather report about Hurricane Erin.

Yup, turns out that a misdirected hurricane was headed up the Gulf set to centerpunch Pensacola and then come inland toward us. There I was in the midst of named weather once again. And my new companion had decided to alter her plans, and she was now headed to Palm Beach to her granddaughter's birthday party. We filled up on gas, and I invited her to ride the road to Florida with me. She said she was hoping I would ask, that it looked like to her that I knew what I was doing, and that she was kind of new at it, and had noticed my Florida plates, and would appreciate the opportunity and the experience. Said she would follow me.

The next couple hours were an on and off high speed horror show. The hurricane's feeder bands, the pinwheeling squalls that are thrown off the main storm, slammed at us every half hour or so. Some of the real old Crackers in Florida still refer to these as Hurrakan clouds, after Hurrakan, the Arawak god of storms. A few of these tempests were brief enough to ride through. Others required that we seek cover. We got to be pretty good friends that way.

By late afternoon we were up under cover at a remote rural rest area while Hurricane Erin raised hell all around us. It was pretty spectacular. The first wave of the storm was an icy cold blast that damn near had our bikes sideways in the wicked wind. I hollered at her that I had a fear of becoming roadkill, and we beat it for refuge. I made some coffee, and the lady had some cookies, and we sat and talked and watched the weather for some time together.

Neat lady. She was a lawyer. And I would bet money that she's a good one. Before that, she worked for NASA, something about a Ph.D. in physics. Told me she got bored with it. She used to fly airplanes. Then she sailed boats. And, having mastered, and apparently gotten bored with both of those things, she had recently turned to motorcycles. I asked her about traveling alone. Asked her if she had a gun. She laughed and said no she had a cellular telephone. Times change as you're passing through.

We talked about marriages gone all to hell, and she told me about raising kids by herself. We talked about Ann Arbor in the Good Old Days, back when we were both grad students there. I explained about being the Omega Man, and she laughed like hell. She told me stories about going to big deal lawyer conventions and meetings on her cycle. The wind blew the rain at us sideways in sheets.

I told her about ridin' the Rockies and about how the desert blooms in the spring. She wanted to know about the west coast road, and Big Sur, and about the way the sun goes down in Monterey. So I told her. She asked about the desert sky at night and about Organ Pipe and had I ever seen the Northern Lights. She told me some about being a lawyer, and about how she was able to do some good sometimes. She told me sailboat stories.

She inquired about riding The River. And I told her I had also ridden beside the Walker, the Red, the Gila and the Snake. I explained that I had ridden out along Okeechobee, and all around the Great Lakes. The storm intensified, and some of the lightning was too bright to look at.

She had never been down, so she asked me about the Highside and about the Lost Highway. And I told her all about the quarter ton of high speed iron and the quarter mile of cold concrete. And about how today was a good day to die. I even told her about the Grand Tetons, and the goddamn Winnebagos. She asked about other places I had been. And I told her about where the Feather River ran and about the Outer Banks sand, and about the road out around the Olympic Peninsula, and about the one out along the Gaspe'. The hurricane bore down on us so hard my arthritis damn near had me whimpering.

She asked me about packing and balancing her load. When I examined her gear, I told her she had it together just about perfect. I guess a Ph.D. in physics is worth something. I told her about the Natchez Trace, and she said she would get back to it sometime when the weather was better. She told me airplane stories, and we compared notes on the Blue Ridge. She had lots of questions, and was a real attentive and appreciative audience. I told her about setting just inside the centerline, and then letting it out slowly, and listening to the exhaust pipes rumble, and to the engine stretch and whine. I tried to tell her about the distance and about the bein' free. Told her all about being bound for Glory. And I believe she understood me. The eye of the hurricane passed nearby, and then the storm apparently turned east.

She asked me how long I had been at it out there, and I told her all my life. She wanted to know, so I told her about riding The McClure Pass Detour, and about Big Thompson Canyon in the summer after the killer flash flood. And I told her about runnin' through Wyoming in the dust and the sand and through Kansas in the mud. And then I told her about a wreck I had seen one time out on Interstate 5, when the highway ran red with blood. The aftermath of the storm came through, and it rained harder than it had on the leading edge.

I got a map out and showed her how to get over to Palm Beach when she split up from me on down the line. She asked about riding across the borderline, and about places to hide from the rain. She inquired about different kinds of tires and cold weather riding and about city traffic. So I told her.

Eventually the storm used itself up, just about the time a full moon came up, and we saddled up and got gone. She rode with me most of the way home, and then I waved her good-bye as she headed on over to Palm Beach. I only had about fifty miles to ride alone, but I missed her just the same.

An hour later I was back home. I had come to the end of my journey, but my soul still longed to fly. And as I unloaded my ride in the soft moonlight, I was real glad I was by myself so no one else could see me cry.

Some of us belong to be nomads, allowed to run wild and free.

GLOSSARY

Accessories: Big bikes, especially those ridden long distances, usually have a fairing, crash bars, saddle bags, a tail or luggage rack, maybe a tank bag. See specific entries for specifics.

Bitch Bar: Also called a Sissy Bar. It refers to a backrest, usually made of chromed metal, that sticks up behind the seat and permits the passenger on the back of the bike to lean back.

Crash Bars: As the name implies, these are tubular appendages, usually chromed, that stick out from the sides of the motorcycle. If the bike goes down, they protect the rider's lower legs from the pavement as well as keeping the engine up off the concrete.

Fairing: Fairings are the big, plastic aerodynamic pieces that are on the front on many contemporary road bikes. The windshield is mounted on the top of the fairing itself. They serve to protect the rider from the elements, and good ones make the bike more stable at high speeds. Most frame mount fairing have a small storage compartment on each side.

Highside: Stretched out on a curve as far, hard, and fast as the machine, the road, and your own riding ability will permit. The highside is where riders lose it. Most riders who have been there don't live to tell about it. Hunter Thompson, in his classic *Hells Angels Chronicles* discusses and explains this concept better than anyone else.

Highway Heat: State Police

Hog: Harley Davidson Motorcycle

Leather: Most longriders own a leather jacket. Those who have been beat half to death by the highway often wear their leather even in hot weather. Many riders also have a pair of leather pants. The jacket by itself is your leather. The jacket and pants together make up one's leathers.

Longrider: Anyone with out-of-state plates and most of what he owns tied on behind him.

The Lost Highway: In scootertrash mythology, The Lost Highway is the last one any of us will ever ride. Some believe it leads to a place called Hole in the Wall.

Luggage Rack: Also called a tail rack. These are tubular metal appendages that hang from the back of the seat, over the rear fender. Because of their position, you can't put much weight on them without tipping the front of the bike up in the air.

Motorcycle: The last syllables rhyme with *pickle.* Also called a bike, a ride, a scooter, a cycle, a machine.

Rice Rocket: Any Japanese motorcycle, also called Rice Burners, Ninja Rockets, and Chinese Chain Saws, all of which are demeaning, disparaging terms usually used by Harley riders.

Saddle: Motorcycle seat. Also used as in *Back in the saddle*, and *Saddle up*.

Saddle Bags: Like many motorcycle related things, these are pretty much the same as you see on horses. They used to be made of heavy leather, and were flexible and damn near indestructible. Now they are mostly made of plastic, and are neither of those things.

Scootertrash: Any kind of serious rider (as opposed to those who put a thousand miles a year on their bikes), sub-cultural term by which we recognize one another, along with renegades and rounders and misfits and old outward bounders, and unreconstructed rebel irregulars.

Shut It Down: Stopping at some length, at least long enough for the cycle to cool off.

Tank Bag: These are usually made of soft plastic, and affix with bunji-like tiedowns. Many of them have a clear pocket on the top into which you can shove a map so you can refer to it without pulling over. I had a tank bag on during my Downfall in Durango, and it got in my way when I tried to get off and away from the scooter. I left it there on Red Mountain.

Tricked Out: A bike gaudily over-dressed in all sorts of aftermarket, decorative, cosmetic accessories, such as extra lights, extra chrome, custom paint jobs, electric fringe, etc.

About the Author

Mark Edmonds–Tiger–rides a BMW motorcycle as often as he can. When he isn't riding it, he's hunting with his dogs atop his horse Nokomis. *Gather 'Round Me, Riders*, his tape of epic motorcyle poetry, is available from White Horse Press. Tiger teaches at St. Leo College in Florida.